PATRIOTS

not

WELCOME

THE AUTHOR

Brittany Sellner is a Catholic American political activist and author. Her passion for politics, which began at a young age, compelled her to enter the political scene in 2016. Since then, she has produced numerous videos, from interviewing notable public figures to reporting on-the-ground across America and Europe. She is the author of *What Makes Us Girls*, a self-help guide for girls, and the co-author of *Hatred Day*, an award-winning science-fiction novel. *Patriots Not Welcome* is her third book. She lives in Vienna with her husband, Austrian political activist Martin Sellner.

PATRIOTS NOT WELCOME

BRITTANY SELLNER

Edited by Nicole Pettibone
Copyedited by Justin Reamer
Cover photo and author photo by Lucy Brown
Cover design by Martin Sellner
Formatting by Polgarus Studio

ISBN eBook: 978-0-9972029-8-4
ISBN Paperback: 978-0-9972029-9-1

First Edition

CONTENTS

AUTHOR'S NOTE

My intention in writing *Patriots Not Welcome* was to offer an honest and accurate account of my life since 2016. I do not wish for any of the people mentioned in this book—public officials, journalists, leftist activists or otherwise—to become a target as a result of its publication. Therefore, I respectfully ask all readers to please refrain from contacting those mentioned.

Secondly, due to a despotic new Austrian law, I am prohibited from promoting the names and logos of the political movements Identitäre Bewegung (Generation Identity) and Die Österreicher (The Austrians). Consequently, I decided not to include personal photos in this book, as many of my most relevant personal photos contain the Generation Identity logo. Furthermore, I was forced to delete all of my YouTube videos that featured these names and symbols, meaning that I am unable to use these videos as sources.

Lastly, while this book chronicles the most significant details of my story, I have excluded a handful of my experiences in order to protect the privacy of my peers.

For Martin

Away from this sinking ship,
beyond the mighty burden of duty,
there lies a shore.
One day, I'll meet you there.

PREFACE

VIENNA, AUSTRIA
JULY 2020

'It's easy to be a criminal in the future; all you have to do is tell the truth.'

This is the tagline of a science-fiction novel I was writing shortly before I entered the political scene in 2016. What has occurred to me over the course of my four years as a political activist is that these words aren't fiction, nor are they true of the future.

They are true of today.

From the booming metropolises of America to the historic cities of Europe, patriots across the West are facing repression: censorship by big tech corporations; defamation by the mainstream media; assaults on their livelihoods, including revoked access to private banking; violent assaults by establishment-backed movements such as Antifa; house raids by law enforcement; trials for artificial crimes such as hate speech; and some are even being imprisoned by their governments. The price for opposing the leftist cultural hegemony is becoming greater by the day. In 2021, if you truly want to be a patriotic dissident voice, you have to accept that persecution will inevitably follow. Even if you ultimately win the political game, it will be after a series of debilitating losses. I suppose I always knew the West was headed toward totalitarianism, but the process is unfolding more rapidly than I anticipated.

I struggled with the decision of whether or not to write this book. My first concern was that, in telling certain parts of my story, I would be confronted with revealing private information about other political figures whose stories are interconnected with my own. The goal of this book, however, is *not* to divulge the personal beliefs, choices and actions of others. Therefore, I have chosen to omit a handful of my experiences—ones that can fortunately be left untold without affecting the most significant parts of my story.

My second concern was that I would be leaving myself vulnerable and exposed. What changed my mind was a brief Google search. I discovered that the majority of the third-party information about me, particularly from the mainstream media and from strangers who have assumptions about me, is false. Ultimately, I came to the realization that my story would be written one way or the other—either by me, or by people who despise me.

My story is as long as it is large, spanning four years and two continents, and serves as a web connecting courageous patriots all across the West; patriots who, like me, made the conscious choice to risk everything for love of God, family, and homeland.

1

The most terrifying words in the English language are:
I'm from the government, and I'm here to help.
  —Ronald Reagan

IDAHO, UNITED STATES
MAY 2019

The two men standing on my doorstep didn't look like FBI agents. With their unshaven chins and plaid shirts, they could have passed for average street civilians. Their FBI badges alone, imprinted with a wing-spread American eagle, were what gave them distinction.

"Good morning, Miss Pettibone," one of the agents said as I opened the door.

"Good morning, sir."

"Thanks in advance for your cooperation. We just have a few questions about your political activism here in the States and in Europe."

"We're also aware your fiancé was banned from entering the United States," the second agent added. "Maybe we can help you two out."

I thanked the agents, despite my reservations. They had tried to convince my mother of similar goodwill after showing up unannounced at my house two days earlier. Since I hadn't been at home, arrangements had been made for them to return today.

"Do either of you want coffee?" I offered.

The agents politely declined before making themselves comfortable on the great, burgundy couch in our living room.

As I also took a seat, I caught a glance at myself in the antique oval mirror that hung in the entryway. I had made an effort to dress well in a classic dress patterned with red and yellow flowers. But beneath the hot-ironed curls, the freshly applied make-up, and the polite smile, my eyes betrayed my exhaustion. The nightmarish events of the last few months had taken a toll that, try as I might, had become impossible to conceal.

Before the interview started, I passed an assuring glance to my parents, who watched from the adjoining dining room. My father, with his neat haircut and starched button-down, sat as erect and alert as a guard dog. My mother, on the other hand, regarded the agents with a warm smile. If she was concerned, she concealed it well enough that even I couldn't tell. At this point, few things managed to shock my parents. They were used to the fact that my political work brought trouble. Thankfully, neither were about to leave me alone with the FBI. Perhaps because, like me, they suspected the agents hadn't come in good faith.

The agents took turns asking questions. They covered a wide range of topics, from why I had decided to become politically active to if I was a member of any political movements in the United States or Europe. They even asked me how I had met my fiancé.

I responded honestly, but briefly. I told the agents that if they wished to learn about me in more detail, they could simply watch my YouTube videos, for I was always open with my audience. As surreal as a meeting with the FBI was, I later came to discover that my door wasn't the first the agents had knocked on. Figures all across the political right had received visits.

Ten minutes ticked by. Then twenty. By the time thirty minutes had passed, it suddenly occurred to me that my calm disposition might be misplaced. It was my first (and only) interrogation with the FBI, but for some reason I had reacted to it without stress or concern. I couldn't explain why. I only knew that, on the scale of thorny situations I had found myself in over the past three years, this one placed on the lower end.

The agents continued the interrogation. Due to the nature of their questions, I had started to pick up on their true motive: determining whether or not I was a threat. I told myself there was no point in getting defensive. They were just doing their job.

By the end of the interview, I had two questions: Why had the FBI been ordered to question me, and by whom? If I was truly 'a threat,' if I was truly someone who 'needed to be watched,' it certainly wasn't in in the traditional sense. I wasn't hateful. I wasn't violent. I had never committed a crime. I simply opposed policies that any patriot should oppose—policies that would have been accepted as normal just five to ten years ago: illegal immigration, mass migration, the eradication of borders, and so on. But in a country that had largely come to be run by self-interested criminals with no loyalties and no flag, I figured I shouldn't be surprised that such beliefs had put me on their radar.

How did I get here? I wondered.

Three years earlier, my life had been the portrait of normalcy. Like so many others, I had simply wanted to make my way in the world. I had no international infamy. No slander by the media. No bans from countries or threats of imprisonment. No investigations for terrorism. The decision that had spun the wheel, shifting my course toward the eye of the storm, was my public declaration of support for Republican presidential candidate Donald Trump in 2016. While, naturally, this decision wasn't what started the story of my life, it's what started this particular story.

2

All the forces in the world are not so
powerful as an idea whose time has come.
　　　　　　—Victor Hugo

CALIFORNIA, UNITED STATES
OCTOBER 2016

My hand hovered over the computer mouse, slightly trembling. *Publish.* All I had to do was click the button and the YouTube video in which my twin sister, Nicole, and I announced our support for Republican presidential candidate, Donald Trump, would go public.

"Are you sure you're ready to do this?" I asked Nicole.

She stood nearby, tugging on the end of her blonde braid. Eyes fixed on the computer screen, she pursed her mouth in a hesitant line. I didn't blame her for having second thoughts. Publishing a video in support of Donald Trump wasn't exactly a strategic decision for our career. Ten years earlier, when we had first begun writing science-fiction books, holding a neutral political stance was harmless. But due to the recent escalation of American politics, our silence now felt cowardly. We wanted to do more than shrink into the background, whispering privately about our opinions, as the battle for our country's soul played out on a global stage.

"Yes," Nicole finally answered. "Publish it."

Click.

The video was live.

"I need to grab some air," I said, toeing on my shoes.

"I'll go with you," Nicole said.

Although we believed strongly in our political stances, we weren't yet accustomed to receiving online criticism. Plus, our video wasn't what one would call a masterpiece. Neither of us had a natural talent for public speaking. Fidgety and shy, our camera presence lacked the easy confidence that comes from experience.

Our professional peers were the first to react. From agents to book reviewers to fellow authors, all of them made it clear they no longer wanted any association with us. Some of them quietly unfollowed us on Twitter, while others took a more direct approach. 'I thought you two were Hillary Clinton supporters, not racists,' one author tweeted. 'Good luck trying to get a traditional publishing deal now,' tweeted another. It was then that we realized our decision to reveal ourselves as Trump supporters wasn't simply controversial, it was career-destroying. Within a single day, the goodwill we had worked so hard to cultivate within the writing industry was shattered.

"How are you doing?" I asked Nicole, in the midst of the fallout.

"I knew we would get backlash for speaking out," she answered. "But not to this extent. It seems like all of our work over the past ten years has been for nothing."

"I'm sorry if you regret it," I told her.

"I don't," she assured. "I don't want to fit in with those people."

Neither did I. While it was heartbreaking to watch our dreams be crushed under the boot of literary gatekeepers, at least we were free of existing within the repressive confines of the writing industry's ever-changing rules. The years of biting our tongues, of tiptoeing around ideas that we fiercely disagreed with, were over. For the first time in our lives, we had complete autonomy. We were free to act and speak as we wanted, starting with our public support for Donald Trump.

His critics rightly pointed out his flaws. Trump was guilty of inappropriate comments in the past; he was also embroiled in multiple scandals. But, unlike the Democratic presidential candidate, Hillary

Clinton, he seemed to be a genuine outsider, one who was courageously challenging the power of the political establishment. 'Make America Great Again' was his campaign slogan. We trusted in the sincerity of this America-first pledge, and we believed that, along with fulfilling his Populist campaign promises, he would attempt to rid Washington, D.C., of the corruption that was rotting at its core.

As our video gained traction on YouTube, Trump supporters reached out to us. Messages trickled into our inboxes, welcoming us to the 'Trump train' and encouraging us to make more videos. A few of them even added us to their Twitter direct message groups, inviting us to join them in campaigning for Trump. Nicole and I, wanting to contribute more than a single video, seized the opportunity.

The online Trump movement was unlike any community we had ever been a part of. Dedicated and passionate, full of laughter, jokes, and positivity, it generated a hypnotic energy that usually produced one of two reactions in people—love or hatred; people rarely felt indifferent towards it. The most popular Twitter accounts, some of which boasted hundreds of thousands of followers, spearheaded meticulously coordinated pro-Trump campaigns; meanwhile, anonymous users on sites like 4chan and Reddit pumped the internet full of clever and humorous pro-Trump videos, comments, and memes that left Hillary Clinton supporters spiraling, at a loss to combat or duplicate their tactics.

Social media was like the Wild West back then. Few rules, little censorship. Just a wide and open terrain, upon which countless battles of intellectual quickdraw were played out. It was a chaotic but inexhaustible kind of freedom that allowed for conversation, debate, and trolling to be taken to its fullest capacity, which was something that most conservatives, libertarians, and centrists loved, but that most progressives and socialists hated.

Nicole and I had little trouble fitting in. Within days, we were officially participating in the pro-Trump campaigns and making dozens of new friends. The only downside was that we didn't know most of their real names; we knew them by online monikers. Anonymity was common amongst online friendships. Rarely did one learn the true identity of the person they were speaking to, and even more rarely did one ever meet the person in real life. But oddly enough, it was common to feel closer to online friends than to those in the real world.

Nicole and I spent all of our time together. Not only when it came to supporting Trump on social media, but also when it came to viewing election-related events.

The second presidential debate, held at Washington University on October 10, 2016, was one of our favorite moments. Nicole and I chatted with a few of our internet friends over Skype as we watched it via a YouTube livestream. Two podiums were positioned on a blue-carpeted stage which was overseen by the debate moderators. Overhead hung an emblem of an eagle and an American flag, proudly bearing the phrase: 'The Union and the Constitution Forever.'

"Here he comes!" we cheered, as Trump arrived.

Donald J. Trump, with his trademark orange suntan and sleek platinum overcomb, had a face and voice that every American had come to know. Dressed in a navy suit with a red silk tie, his body language was bold and sweeping, as if he had little doubt in his ability to win. Hillary Clinton, however, seemed to possess a similar resolve. Standing primly in her blue-and-white pantsuit, her tone self-assured, she immediately launched into attacking Trump over a scandal involving 'locker room talk.'

In 2005, Trump had made a series of lewd sexual comments in a recorded conversation with *Access Hollywood* host, Billy Bush. Among these comments, Trump had said:

> Donald Trump: "Yeah, that's her. With the gold. I better use some Tic-Tacs just in case I start kissing her. You know, I'm automatically attracted to beautiful—I just start kissing them. It's like a magnet. Just kiss. I don't even wait. And when you're a star, they let you do it. You can do anything."

Billy Bush: "Whatever you want."

Donald Trump: "Grab 'em by the pussy. You can do anything."[1]

I agreed that Trump's comments, which had been leaked to the press in the form of an audio clip prior to the debate, were offensive. I wasn't going to defend them. On the other hand, I questioned why Hillary and her supporters were acting as if she had the moral high ground. Hillary's own husband, former president Bill Clinton, had been accused of sexual harassment and assault by four different women.[2] And Hillary herself had been accused by one of Bill's alleged victims, Juanita Broaddrick, of attempting to intimidate her into silence.[3]

"This was locker room talk," Trump explained during the debate. "I'm not proud of it. I apologize to my family. I apologize to the American people. If you look at Bill Clinton, far worse. Mine are words, and his was action. Hillary Clinton attacked those same women…and attacked them viciously."

"He has said the video doesn't represent who he is," Hillary replied, referring to Trump. "But I think it's clear to anyone who heard it that it represents exactly who he is."[4]

As the debate progressed, Donald Trump and Hillary Clinton shifted into discussing their policy positions, circling each other on the stage in verbal combat. Most of the moderators' questions focused on topics such as Russia and Syria, although Trump and Hillary often found ways of inserting personal jabs into their rebuttals.

"Fight, fight, fight," we chanted.

"You know, it is uh…it's just awfully good that someone with the temperament of Donald Trump is not in charge of the law in our country," Hillary Clinton quipped.

"Because you'd be in jail," Donald Trump replied.[5]

The audience went wild. Social media erupted.

"Daaamn," everyone whooped. "That's a knockout."

I laughed until my cheeks were sore. Aside from being hilarious, Trump's comment hadn't come out of nowhere. At the moment,

Hillary was in the spotlight over what many Americans believed was the worst scandal for a presidential candidate since Watergate. Instead of using an email server managed by the U.S. government, Hillary had set up a private email server for herself shortly before being sworn in as the U.S. Secretary of State in 2009. Despite the fact that her private server had an open webmail portal, making it vulnerable to being hacked, the private server contained dozens of emails filled with classified information. Hillary had also deleted thousands of the emails from her private server using a software program called BleachBit. In response, the FBI had launched an investigation to determine if Hillary Clinton had violated the Espionage Act of 1913 by allowing national defense information to be 'lost, stolen, abstracted, or destroyed' through 'gross negligence.'[6]

In the end, FBI Director James Comey concluded that Hillary Clinton should not face criminal charges,[7] a decision that millions of Americans contested. We believed Hillary was one of the most corrupt politicians ever to have set foot in the White House. Our votes were not merely a sign we supported Trump; they were a sign we opposed Hillary. We were hopeful that, if elected, Trump would further investigate her. In fact, he even promised to do so during the debate.

"If I win, I am going to instruct my attorney general to get a special prosecutor to look into your situation," he told Hillary. "Because there has never been so many lies, so much deception. There has never been anything like it."[8]

Even after the debate ended, the eyes of the American people remained on Donald Trump and Hillary Clinton. For countless people, this election was more significant than ones that came before. Many believed the United States was in such a delicate state that the outcome would determine its survival as a whole. The Democrats had their reasons for rejecting Trump, but we also had our own for rejecting Hillary. With Hillary as president, we believed our country would be overrun with destructive policies from which there could be no recovery: unchecked mass immigration, attacks on freedom of speech and the right to bear arms, and possibly even a war with Russia, which is why Nicole and I wanted to do more than sit idly by and observe. We wanted to help in a tangible way.

While we hadn't yet realized it, our opportunity to help had come just three days ago, on October 7, 2016, in the form of a man named Julian Assange.

Quiet, pale-haired, and unassuming, Julian Assange was the founder of a multi-national non-profit media organization called WikiLeaks, which prided itself on publishing news leaks from anonymous sources. Few can deny that any man had more influence on the outcome of 2016 presidential election. WikiLeaks had come into possession of thousands of emails and other documents from the Democratic National Committee (DNC) and from Hillary Clinton's campaign manager, John Podesta, which they published during the weeks leading up to election day. The result was like tossing a lump of raw meat into a kennel of starving dogs. Hundreds of thousands of people spent their days circling the official WikiLeaks Twitter account, watching and waiting for the moment they could tear into a new batch of emails.

CNN anchor, Chris Cuomo, claimed it was illegal for the American public to read or to possess the Wikileaks emails, but that this rule didn't apply to the media.[9] In the same way one ignores a fallen leaf blowing across their path, the majority of the American public ignored Cuomo's warning.

Nicole and I were among this majority. As soon as we caught wind of the bombshells being exposed, we volunteered our efforts and combed through the various email dumps. The number of emails was countless, but the internet worked quickly, often discovering relevant information within minutes of each release. One of these internet researchers went by the online moniker: *Baldwin IV*.

Curious how Baldwin sorted through the emails so quickly, I did something that, at the time, I was far too naïve to understand the potential negative ramifications of: I messaged him my phone number and asked him to call me. I didn't consider the fact that the internet is chock-full of cat-fishers, infiltrators, and predators. I believed in the goodness of every person who called themselves a Trump supporter. And I trusted them, too. While I've had my fair share of disastrous internet encounters since then, Baldwin fortunately turned out to be genuine. Despite only being in his late teens, he had a thorough knowledge of history and politics, and he was a devout Christian. Within minutes of starting our call, we were already chatting like old friends.

"I think we'll get a lot more done if we search through the emails as a team," Baldwin suggested.

"True, but we might have to spend hours together on the phone," I pointed out.

"I've got time," he assured.

Baldwin, Nicole and I got to work straightaway. Among the many emails we stumbled across was an email in which the DNC appeared to be compiling specific questions for *CNN* anchor, Wolf Blitzer, to ask Trump when he interviewed him.[10] Other searchers came across a WikiLeaks email revealing that in a private speech Hillary Clinton had stated her dream was a hemispheric common market with open trade and open borders.[11] And still more searchers came across a WikiLeaks email revealing that former *CNN* contributor, Donna Brazile, had supplied Hillary Clinton with a debate question ahead of time.[12]

The sheer number of *CNN* anchors, journalists, and contributors who seemed to be in league with the DNC was alarming to say the least. The façade of *CNN* being a bipartisan media outlet started to crack before our eyes, exposing them as something more akin to a mouthpiece for the DNC.

"You're not gonna believe this," Baldwin said one night, when he was helping Nicole and me dig through WikiLeaks emails. His voice quivered, as if he was stifling a laugh. "The DNC staffers think Megyn Kelly is a *bimbo*."

"Are you serious? Send us the link."

Nicole and I both echoed Baldwin's laughter as we scrolled through the email. The blonde and brazen Megyn Kelly, who had worked as a Fox News anchor at the time, had never been shy about her hatred of Donald Trump. She often seemed to enjoy provoking him. In response, Trump had called her a bimbo, and it appeared as if staffers from the Democratic National Committee (DNC) agreed. The beginning of the email read:

> Yes, Trumpet was right Megyn Kelly is a Bimbo.
> According to an online definition a Bimbo is an attractive but empty-headed young woman, especially one perceived as a willing sex object in other words a slut. If you need help with that definition, you need to stop reading and go back to school.[13]

I couldn't resist publishing a tweet about the email, which instantly created a stir, racking up hundreds of retweets within minutes. While I admit I felt bad for Megyn Kelly, even if I didn't hold her in high regard, I figured the email was reflective of how most people in politics spoke about one another—if not in public, then certainly in private.

Baldwin whistled. "Wow, your Megyn Kelly tweet is really taking off. I wonder if she'll respond."

"I doubt it," I answered, a bit distracted. I had taken to reading through the newest messages in one of the Twitter direct message groups I was a member of. The discussion, which concerned Julian Assange, was brimming with hope that he would one day walk the streets as a free man.

In 2012, the United Kingdom's Supreme Court ruled that Assange should be extradited to Sweden to be questioned over four sexual offense allegations. Assange, who denied the allegations, applied for diplomatic asylum at the Ecuadorian Embassy in London. Concerned that Assange's human rights might be violated if he was extradited, Ecuador agreed to grant him asylum.[14]

Given that I didn't know much about the sexual offense allegations,

I didn't add a message of my own to the conversation. All I knew was that, in publishing the DNC emails, Assange had performed an inestimable service for our country. He had given Americans a glimpse behind the political curtain, confirming the corruption that we had long suspected but had been unable to verify. Consequently, even if the sexual offense allegations against him turned out to be false, even if he was completely innocent, I doubted his enemies would ever allow him to return to living a normal life.

The hours turned into days. During our downtime, when Nicole and I weren't searching through WikiLeaks emails, we filmed YouTube videos, accepted interview requests, participated in Twitter hashtag campaigns, and tried to keep up with responding to the messages that continued to flood our inboxes.

Our social media followings had grown quickly over a short period of time, and the realization put us on edge. It was bizarre—not to mention, overwhelming—to imagine that thousands of people were reading and listening to what we had to say. But the fact that all of these people were online put us at ease. It wasn't as if we had to take the stage and deliver a speech before thousands of human faces. Instead, we simply saw numbers: five thousand likes here, a thousand retweets there.

Our long work nights generally ended around 6:00 a.m., when the first light of morning trickled through our bright red curtains. Collapsing into bed, we tried our best to grab a few hours of rest. It was in these moments, halfway between awareness and sleep, that our conversations slipped into the past. How different our lives had been only a month earlier! No one had known our names then, but still, we had been happy. We had almost always been drawn to solitude, to peaceful and private spaces of our own where we were free to explore creativity. Not just when it came to writing, but also to singing, painting, and drawing. Being in the public eye, visible for all the world to see, was the most difficult part about being politically active.

Another difficult aspect was the hostility. I never could have predicted the cutthroat behavior I would witness and oftentimes experience in the political sphere. I wasn't accustomed to people severing relationships, attacking, slandering, and even wishing death upon each other over a difference of opinion. I had only ever known a civilized world of civilized people. It was during this time I came to understand the great gift my parents had given my siblings and me by sheltering us. We had grown up in a parallel society of sorts—a small but healthy Catholic community that deliberately maintained its distance from the greater society for the protection of its parishioners. In some ways, until October 2016, Nicole and I had never seen the world as it *truly* was.

But we didn't regret the choice we made. We had faith in Trump and in the patriotic movement that we had come to be a part of. At the time, we didn't have a long string of goals we wanted to accomplish, nor did we necessarily want our accomplishments to be large. Just noticeable. A ripple in the endless tide of human contribution. A small footnote in the archives of history, documenting that we were among the thousands who had taken a stand when it mattered most.

THE RABBIT HOLE

In November of 2016, a week or so before election day, Wikileaks published a fresh batch of emails. Baldwin, Nicole, and I got to work searching through them right away. While we had expected to unearth another bombshell or two, none of us could've predicted the nature of what we were about to uncover.

In one email, Tony Podesta, the brother of Hillary Clinton's campaign manager, John Podesta, was invited to a 'Spirit Cooking' dinner by a Serbian performance artist named Marina Abramović. Dated June 28, 2015, the email read:

Dear Tony,
I am so looking forward to the Spirit Cooking dinner at my

place. Do you think you will be able to let me know if your brother is joining?

All my love, Marina

Tony forwarded the email to his brother, John, asking:

Are you in NYC Thursday July 9

Marina wants you to come to dinner

Mary?[15]

We were confused. Several remarks followed.

"Spirit Cooking dinner? What the hell is that?" Baldwin asked.

"Whatever it is, I doubt it has anything to do with food," I replied.

"Let's see if we can find more information about it online," Nicole suggested.

The three of us began a search. We soon discovered a video on YouTube entitled: Zerynthia—Association for Contemporary Art in collaboration with Studio Stefania Miscetti Presents: Marina Abramović 'Spirit Cooking' (1997).

In the video, Marina Abramović used a paint brush and pigs' blood to inscribe three phrases on a filthy-looking tan wall. The first phrase: 'Mix fresh breast milk with fresh sperm milk. Drink on earthquake nights.' The second phrase: 'With a sharp knife, cut deeply into the middle finger of your left hand. Eat the pain.' And the third phrase: 'Fresh morning urine sprinkle over nightmare dreams.' Toward the end of the video, Marina Abramović tossed a bucket of pig blood over a wax sculpture with the likeness of a child.[16]

When the video ended, Nicole and I sat in silence, exchanging puzzled glances. Neither of us knew what we had just watched, much less what to conclude from it. I was about to ask Baldwin for his opinion, when, through the phone, I heard him burst into laughter.

"So you mean to tell me that the Podesta brothers might be...like...holed up in a mansion somewhere eating fresh semen and breast milk, and then sprinkling their nightmares with urine?"

The thought of such a possibility was bizarre, too freakish to be real; on the other hand, the message wasn't something we were imagining. The words 'Spirit Cooking' were there, clear as day, in John Podesta's own leaked emails.

"What should we do with the video?" Nicole wondered.

"Put it on Twitter," Baldwin voted.

"We could, but I mean…what are we supposed to say?" I asked. "Hey Democrats, by the way, the politicians you're supporting are being invited to weird spirit dinners that involve fresh semen milk and pig blood…"

Baldwin laughed even harder. "That's exactly what you should say."

In the end, we decided to post the information on Twitter. Spirit Cooking didn't seem to involve any acts of criminality, but still, we felt the video raised legitimate questions about the nature of Hillary Clinton's campaign associates. As it turned out, so did the rest of the world. The reaction was immediate: a nationwide eruption of confusion, disgust, and most commonly, mockery. Thousands of tweets flooded Twitter, making jokes at John Podesta's expense and surmising about the ritualistic undertones of Spirit Cooking. For nearly two days, Spirit Cooking remained the top trend on the platform. The discussion spread so widely that Marina Abramović eventually issued a statement.

"I'm outraged, because this is taken completely out of my context," she claimed, in an interview with *ArtNews*. "It was just a normal dinner. It was actually just a normal menu, which I call spirit cooking. There was no blood, no anything else. We just call things funny names, that's all."[17]

Some on the internet accepted her statement, while many others rejected it, labeling it damage control. They were angry the mainstream media didn't see fit to investigate the matter for themselves, instead opting for softball questions and puff pieces, which mainstream journalists only seemed to offer those who they aligned with ideologically. The result was an irreversible corrosion of trust. In my opinion, the mainstream media's failure to objectively report about the Wikileaks emails, as well as their maliciously biased coverage of Donald Trump, were the origin for the large-scale disdain Americans currently have for the mainstream media. A *Gallup* poll from 2019 revealed that Americans' trust in the mass media sat at a paltry 41%.[18]

Baldwin, Nicole, and I watched the online reaction to the Spirit Cooking email and video closely. While some people simply believed that Marina Abramović and the Podesta brothers were bizarre individuals with bizarre pastimes, others suspected that, in reality, Marina Abramović and the Podesta brothers were involved in some kind of cult. This suspicion only grew stronger when Wikileaks published a series of emails that appeared to contain strange code words.

One e-mail in particular was from Susan Sandler, the daughter of the late Herbert Sandler, a billionaire philanthropist who was the co-CEO of Golden West Financial Corporation and the World Savings Bank. In the email, dated September 2, 2014, Susan Sandler wrote to John Podesta:

> Hi John,
> The realtor found a handkerchief. (I think it has a map that seems pizza-related. Is it yorus [sic]? They can send it if you want. I know you're busy, so feel free not to respond if it's not yours or you don't want it.
> Susaner

John Podesta replied to the email, writing:

> It's mine, but not worth worrying about.[19]

At first, Baldwin, Nicole, and I didn't know what to think of the exchange. All we knew was that words like 'pizza,' which were present in multiple WikiLeaks emails, didn't make much sense in the context provided.

"I'm not trying to jump to any conclusions here," Baldwin began. "But I should point out that 'map' is a commonly used acronym for 'minor attracted person', or, in layman's terms...people who are sexually attracted to minors."

"I mean...I guess so, but it's a bit of a leap, don't you think?" I asked.

"Hey, I'm not just pulling this out of thin air," he defended. "There's also a weird Breitbart tweet that's been making the rounds on Twitter..."

Baldwin was referring to a 2010 tweet by the late Andrew Breitbart. The founder of Breitbart News and a highly-respected conservative journalist, Andrew Breitbart had died of a heart attack in early 2012. The tweet read:

> How prog-guru John Podesta isn't [a] household name as [a] world class underage sex slave op cover-upperer defending unspeakable dregs escapes me.[20]

We thought about it more.

"You're telling me you don't think that's suspicious?" Baldwin asked.

"Of course, it's suspicious," Nicole and I agreed.

But suspicions aren't evidence.

The three of us decided it was foolish to speculate, especially publicly. While there have been reports of pedophiles using cheese and pizza emojis as code on platforms like Twitter and Instagram,[21] there is no solid evidence that 'pizza' is a standard code word or symbol for pedophilia. As far as we knew, in the context of the WikiLeaks emails, 'pizza' could have been code for any number of things. And given the severe nature of the crime of pedophilia, we didn't want to be responsible for associating it with innocent people.

Many on the internet, however, felt differently. They continued their investigative efforts, and, somewhere along the way, inadvertently opened up a rabbit hole that was destined to swallow us all. The internet investigation, largely spear-headed by average concerned citizens with no background in professional journalism, officially began when a 2008 WikiLeaks email surfaced in which John Podesta was invited to give a speech at a Barack Obama fundraiser that was being hosted by a man named James Alefantis.[22]

At first glance, there was nothing particularly notable about James Alefantis. He was a homosexual man who owned a pizza restaurant in Washington, D.C., called Comet Ping-Pong. But at second glance, people found it strange that he socialized in the same circles as influential elites like John Podesta, and even stranger, that GQ had listed him as one of the fifty most powerful people in Washington D.C.[23] Curious to learn more, researchers tracked down James Alefantis' Instagram account—created under the username 'jimmycomet'—where they stumbled across a series of alarming photos. One photo showed a young child sitting at a table, her palms upturned, her wrists taped onto the table with multiple pieces of thick white tape.[24] Another photo showed a German baby doll that had a price tag of $1200; beside the photo, Alefantis had commented 'way overpriced.'[25] Another photo showed a grown man holding a young child, a single yellow-bead necklace connecting them together at the neck; beside the photo, Alefantis had commented, '#chickenlovers.'[26]

"*Now*, this is getting creepy," Baldwin exclaimed. "What kind of person posts such demented shit?"

I was asking myself the same question. A single glance at the photos and comments was enough to leave a cold pit in my stomach. While we were unable to verify what Alefantis had meant by commenting 'chicken lovers', we discovered that the term 'chicken' had been defined by author, Bruce Rodgers, in his book *Gay Talk: A (Sometimes Outrageous) Dictionary of Gay Slang* as gay slang for 1. any boy under the age of consent, heterosexual, fair of face, and unfamiliar with homosexuality 2. juvenile, youthful, young-looking.[27]

Baldwin, Nicole, and I decided to post Alefantis's Instagram photos and comments on Twitter, but we took care not to make direct accusations. In truth, we had no way of definitively interpreting Alefantis's intent. We couldn't claim to know for certain what he had been thinking when he had posted them. The most we could say was that we found the photos and comments disturbing. And we also found it strange that, like John and Tony Podesta, James Alefantis appeared to know Marina Abramović—if not in person, at least by reputation. On his Instagram account, there was a photo of Marina Abramović holding a bundle of sticks; beside it, Alefantis had commented, 'Marina and Faggot.'[28]

We decided to dig deeper. Our efforts led us to a 2015 *Washington Life Magazine* article in which Tony Podesta proudly revealed that he owned artwork from Serbian painter, Biljana Đurđević.[29] A standard Google search revealed the alarming nature of Đurđević's artwork. One image was of a row of six young girls, stripped to their underwear, pressing their hands against their buttocks. Another image was of a young boy, also stripped to his underwear; he was hanging from the ceiling, arms crossed over his head, his wrists bound tightly in cords of black rope.[30]

Later in the *Washington Life Magazine* article, Tony Podesta mentioned that Marina Abramović was among his top five favorite artists. He also said that he regularly opened his house to casual pizza parties co-hosted by his friend James Alefantis, the owner of Comet Ping Pong.[31]

"One thing is for certain," Nicole said. "These people...James Alefantis, the Podesta brothers and Marina Abramović...all of them seem to know each other."

"All of them seem to have an obsession with disturbing artwork, too," I added.

As time passed, and as various researchers uncovered more information, we held out hope that the mainstream media would report on the investigation. Eventually, they did, but the majority of them labeled it a conspiracy theory. The only mainstream journalist who saw fit to deviate from this conclusion was Ben Swann. At the time, he hosted a news segment called *Reality Check,* which was an associate of CBS46 in Atlanta.

In December 2016, Swann summarized the investigation in a six-minute video report. On top of referencing some of the information we had found, he went a step further, saying that in John Podesta's emails, leaked by WikiLeaks, it had been revealed that Tony Podesta was friends with Dennis Hastert, the former Speaker of the House,[32] who had recently been sentenced to fifteen months in prison for abusing boys. The federal judge who presided over the case had labeled Hastert a 'serial child molester.'[33]

Ben Swann went on to note that, according to *The Washington Post,* visitors to Tony Podesta's home had 'gotten an eyeful when they walked into a bedroom at the Podesta residence hung with multiple color pictures by Katy Grannan, a photographer known for documentary-style pictures of naked teenagers in their parents' suburban homes.'[34]

Immediately, Ben Swann's video report created waves—perhaps too many and too big—because oddly enough, a few days after its release, CBS removed Ben Swann's video report from their website. From there, it was virtually scrubbed from the internet. These days, copies can only be found on shady-looking blogs in all but abandoned corners of the internet.[35] And this begs the question: *Why?*

In his video report, Ben Swann explicitly stated that the investigation was unproven. That no solid evidence had been presented, and that it was merely a compilation of suspicious emails, photos and connections that were worthy of exploring. But this didn't stop other mainstream media outlets from going on the offensive. Former *Daily Beast* editor, Ben Collins, penned an article in which he accused Ben Swann of perpetuating 'pseudo-investigative reports of elaborate conspiracies.'[36]

AMERICA'S 45TH PRESIDENT

Baldwin, Nicole, and I took a break on Election Day. Having divided our time between the investigation, searching WikiLeaks emails, and campaigning for Trump, the work-filled days and sleepless nights finally felt like they had paid off. The highly anticipated climax had arrived.

I remember November 8, 2016 like it was yesterday. The excitement exploding from millions of social media accounts; the tension erupting between various media outlets as they cast their predictions; the arrogance puffing up the smile of every Democrat, so blinded by a false sense of superiority that they didn't take a moment to consider Donald Trump might pose a threat. *CNN* went so far as to claim Hillary Clinton had a 91% chance of winning the election.[37]

Nicole and I spent Election Night glued to our computers, with half a dozen internet tabs pulled up on our screens: one for tweeting, one for monitoring the electoral votes, one for chatting with Baldwin on Skype.

Our family viewed the election on the living room TV. Every so often, their excited shouts sounded through the open door of my bedroom.

"Texas! Trump won Texas!"

I scrolled through Twitter, my hope climbing, yet unable to relieve my nervous tension. *Mystery.* Often it can be a wonderful thing, but on this particular night, when so much hung in the balance, the suspense was almost too much too bear.

"Now he's got Florida!" my dad called.

I bowed over in my chair, forehead sunk against my hand, bubbling with nervous laughter. I couldn't do it anymore. I couldn't watch. I remained in this position for minutes that dragged by like hours, silent and waiting, until I heard my dad shout, "Pennsylvania is Trump's!"

And a few short minutes later. "That's it! Trump's won! Trump's won the election!"

Lunging out of our chairs, Nicole and I raced into the living room. Our family was huddled around the television, laughing, cheering, and punching the air with their fists. I stared at the television in disbelief, which read that Trump had won with 304 electoral votes. Shock pulsed through my body. The victory seemed too good to be true, too remarkable to be real.

But somehow, it was.

Donald J. Trump was the 45th president of the United States.

Nicole and I passed the night intoxicated with a new, hopeful conviction. It had been a risky gamble to support Trump, an unpredictable toss of the dice. If Hillary had won, sacrificing our literary careers would have been all for naught, and worse, our new president would be one working in stark opposition to our values. But here we were, somehow victorious. And in the midst of this victory, we found ourselves fiercely excited for the future. Along with thousands of others, we had found purpose in campaigning for Trump—one that we knew would go on to have profound meaning if Trump fulfilled his campaign promises: weeding out political corruption, deporting illegals, combating mass immigration, securing our southern border, bringing American jobs back from foreign countries, and withdrawing our troops from the Middle East. We would have a chance at a future without the threat of war or tyranny.

America was finally going to come first.

THE RABBIT HOLE DEEPENS

The day after the election, Baldwin, Nicole, and I got back to work. While we hoped Trump would launch a formal investigation once he was inaugurated, we were curious if we could root out any more information on our own. We made for a great team; however, it was often difficult to stomach the subject matter of our research. Never in a million years could I have imagined that I would end up stumbling into such a rabbit hole. Not just me, but Nicole, Baldwin, and thousands of others as well. I won't deny that it disturbed me deeply; half the time, I wasn't able to sleep, and the other half, I had recurring nightmares. But neither Baldwin, Nicole, nor I wanted to walk away just yet. Not until we were certain there wasn't any relevant information we had missed.

Unfortunately, in the weeks that followed, we noticed an alarming shift in the investigation. Armies of disinformation accounts were popping up across the internet, promoting unsubstantiated claims about James Alefantis and the Podesta brothers, even going so far as to directly accuse them of being pedophiles. There were also calls to dox, harass, and physically threaten them.

This, of course, we condemned, as did thousands of others. Many of the people involved in the investigation were talented researchers, taking care to check and recheck their facts while actively discouraging the promotion of false information. Yet the false information persisted nonetheless, growing more and more rampant with each passing day. It got to the point where, in some instances, we weren't entirely certain how to separate fact from fiction. Eventually, Baldwin, Nicole, and I decided to break off from the wider investigation.

Over the next few weeks, we expanded our research to include convicted sex-offender, Jeffrey Epstein. Tall, with white-shot hair and a Gatsby-like air of sophistication, Epstein was a wealthy American financier who boasted connections to a slew of powerful global elites. At the time, much of the general public wasn't aware of Epstein. Despite having confessed to two felony prostitution charges, he was offered a 'non-prosecution agreement' by the Justice Department in 2007, under which he served a mere thirteen months in jail.[38] The man responsible for cutting this deal, Alexander Acosta, later admitted he had done so because he had been told to back off; that Jeffrey Epstein was above his pay grade. "I was told Epstein 'belonged to intelligence' and to leave it alone."[39]

Baldwin, Nicole, and I couldn't believe Jeffrey Epstein, a convicted sex-offender, had managed to emerge from prison with his reputation intact. Now a free man, he had returned to openly brushing shoulders with powerful global elites: former United States President Bill Clinton, Prince Andrew of the British Royal Family, American business magnate Bill Gates, and even Donald Trump.

According to a *Fox News* article published in May of 2016,[40] Bill Clinton flew on Jeffrey Epstein's infamous jet much more frequently than previously reported, with flight logs revealing he had taken at least 26 trips aboard the 'Lolita Express.' While Bill Clinton denied ever visiting Epstein's private Caribbean island, Little St. James—where it was alleged that Jeffrey Epstein engaged in sex-trafficking—a longtime tech worker on Little St. James named Steve Scully claimed he once saw Bill Clinton at Jeffrey Epstein's villa home.[41]

A few of the other public figures listed in Jeffrey Epstein's flight logs were lawyer Alan Dershowitz, supermodel Naomi Campbell, and even the Hollywood actor Kevin Spacey,[42] who was accused of sexual misconduct by fifteen different people.[43] As of December of 2019, three of Kevin Spacey's accusers have died—one reportedly from cancer, another from suicide and the third from being hit by a car.[44]

We wondered if Epstein's position among the elites was destined to last. Of all the people we had researched, he by far presented the largest red flag. One of his most prominent accusers, Virginia Giuffre, had filed an affidavit only a year earlier, alleging that she was a survivor of a child sex trafficking ring that Jeffrey Epstein had operated.[45]

"We need to keep our Epstein investigation separate from Alefantis and the Podesta brothers," I told Baldwin one day. "The information we have about Alefantis and the Podesta brothers is creepy, sure, but it's all speculation. As for Epstein, he's a convicted sex-offender, and he has credible accusers."

"You're right," Baldwin agreed. "To be fair, though, this investigation stopped only being about Alefantis and the Podesta brothers weeks ago. Some people are looking into the sexual assault allegations against Prince Andrew and Bill Clinton."

"I wonder if any of this will ever be formally investigated," Nicole put in. "I definitely think digging up all of this information is helpful, but it won't amount to much unless law enforcement gets involved."

"It's hard to say." Baldwin sounded thoughtful. "I guess there's a chance Trump will launch an investigation once he's inaugurated. What worries me, though, are the internet fanatics. I'm starting to see Twitter comments where people are talking about driving to Comet Ping-Pong to investigate for themselves."

I shook my head. "What are they hoping to find at the restaurant?"

"Well, there's a rumor that's recently been gaining steam...I have no idea who started it...but at this point, it's unsubstantiated, and it claims that Alefantis is running a sex-trafficking ring in the basement of Comet Ping-Pong."

"Oh, crap." Now I understood his concern. If someone showed up at Comet Ping-Pong, not simply for a harmless look around, but in a threatening manner, it risked delegitimizing all of the information that internet researchers had found. Most of the researchers wished no harm to come to James Alefantis and the Podesta brothers, regardless of what we thought about them personally. Our goal was to persuade law enforcement to open a formal investigation, not for people to start taking the law into their own hands.

"Like I said, I hope I'm wrong," Baldwin added, "but given the unrest I'm seeing online, I'd give it another week or so before we hear about some nutter showing up at the place."

He wasn't wrong.

On December 4, 2016, a man named Edgar Maddison Welch entered the Comet Ping-Pong restaurant and fired an AR-15 rifle into a door. While no one was injured, Welch revealed to police that he had intended to investigate the rumor that the restaurant was the site of a child sex-abuse ring.[46] He eventually pleaded guilty to federal charges of assault with a dangerous weapon and transporting a firearm over state lines, and was sentenced to four years in prison.[47]

The reaction to the Comet Ping-Pong attack was nationwide. Mainstream media outlets labeled us conspiracy theorists, while big tech platforms like Twitter, Reddit, and YouTube banned all promotion of the investigation from their platforms. Many of the researchers, however, weren't ready to give up. After transporting all of the information they had collected to alternative platforms, the researchers resumed their investigation. In 2017, the majority of these researchers ended up joining forces with an even larger movement called QAnon. While I am unaffiliated with the QAnon movement, from what I can tell, the movement appears to believe that President Donald Trump is waging a secret war against 'the deep state,' a ring of elite Satan-worshiping pedophiles in government, media, business, and Hollywood.

At the moment, the investigation remains up in the air. Most of it is still unproven and lacks concrete evidence. The only confirmed suspicions are those involving Jeffrey Epstein. In 2019, he was arrested in New Jersey on charges related to federal sex-trafficking.[48] Amidst the fallout, it was alleged that he was sitting on enough criminal evidence to implicate dozens of powerful elites. Which is why few were surprised when, just months after his arrest, news broke that Jeffrey Epstein had been found dead in his prison cell. The official cause of his death was ruled a suicide. But given evidence to the contrary—such as a forensic pathologist claiming that Epstein had unusual fractures in his neck,[49] or that two cameras outside his jail cell malfunctioned at the time of his death and failed to record[50]—it's a widely accepted theory that he was murdered.

As for other figures at the heart of the investigation, such as James Alefantis and the Podesta brothers, none have ever been formally investigated by law enforcement, at least not publicly. But thousands of people across America continue to believe that they should be, including Baldwin, Nicole, and me. While our suspicions don't hold proof, nor would we ever make direct accusations, we still believe the questions we asked were legitimate; questions the mainstream media would have relentlessly asked had they in any way involved Donald Trump.

In my view, the mainstream media had a right to react to our investigation with disbelief. They also had a right to call out people who were making direct accusations. What they had no right to do was disparage the general public from asking questions. The mainstream media is not the global arbiter of what people can and cannot research, nor are they some kind of all-knowing institution. In fact, when it comes to reporting on pedophilia, the mainstream media doesn't have the most reputable track record.

Firstly, in the case of *BBC* television and radio personality, Jimmy Savile, who was revealed to have been a prolific sex-offender after his death in 2011. Investigators believed that Savile had preyed on approximately five-hundred victims as young as two years old.[51]

According to former *BBC Radio 1* DJ Andy Kershaw, who worked with Savile at *Radio 1*, it was impossible for him to believe that complaints about Jimmy Savile had never reached *BBC* senior management. Kershaw also said that he believed the *BBC* senior management were 'still trying to cover their tracks' over Jimmy Savile's sex abuse as late as 2012 due to the fact that a *BBC Newsnight* investigation into Jimmy Savile's sex abuse had been tossed out.[52]

In another case, *ABC News* anchor, Amy Robach, was caught on a hot mic in 2019, admitting that her network had scrapped a story about Jeffrey Epstein. The scrapped story was an interview with Virginia Giuffre, one of Epstein's most prominent accusers, who alleged that she had been recruited to be his sex slave.

In an excerpt from the leaked footage, published by the investigative journalism enterprise, *Project Veritas,* Amy Robach can be heard saying:

"It was unbelievable what we had, Clinton (Bill), we had everything. I tried for three years to get it on to no avail. And now it's all coming out....and it's like these new revelations, and I freaking had all of it. I...I'm so pissed right now. Like everyday, I get more and more pissed cause I'm just like, Oh my God, we...it was what...what we had was unreal. Other women backing it up. Hey. Yep. Brad Edwards (Giuffre's lawyer), the attorney, three years ago saying like…like we…there will come a day, when we will realize Jeffrey Epstein was the most prolific pedophile this country has ever known. And I had it all three years ago."[53]

In highlighting these mainstream media blunders, my intention isn't to accuse the mainstream media of having nefarious motives for disregarding the suspicions surrounding James Alefantis and the Podesta brothers. I'm merely pointing out that the mainstream media isn't infallible. It's also worth noting that the mainstream media is a business, one that seems to be far more interested in its bottom line than it is in the truth. Nowadays, reporting risks are rarely taken by the mainstream media; instead, they are taken by independent journalists and citizen investigators. As much as the mainstream media despises such competition, it became inevitable the moment mainstream media journalists decided to prioritize activism over journalism. The public has a right to ask questions, even to request formal investigations, without seeking permission from the mainstream media beforehand. Which is exactly what Baldwin, Nicole, and I—and thousands of others—did.

THE WHISTLEBLOWER'S FATE

"Attention, passengers: We will be arriving in Washington, D.C., in ten minutes," a voice sounded from the train's PA system. "We have a full train today, so please be patient while collecting your luggage. Next stop, Union Station."

"I can't believe we're really here," I told Nicole, giving her an excited smile. "That we're actually going to see Trump's inauguration in person."

"It beats watching it on a YouTube livestream," Nicole agreed. She was sitting in the train alongside me, a pair of headphones in her ears.

Her blonde hair, pinned into a tidy updo, gleamed brightly against the dark wool of her peacoat. As always, she looked well put together. The only thing out of place was her demeanor. In contrast to my excitement, her mood was quiet and pensive, as if she had other things on her mind besides the inauguration.

"Is everything okay?" I asked her.

"Yes," she assured. She pulled the headphones from her ears. "It's just that…I've been asking myself a lot of questions lately."

"What kind of questions?"

"What I want to do after the inauguration. I've accomplished what I set out to accomplish. We both have. We wanted Trump to get elected, and he was. I'm grateful and happy to be here in Washington, D.C., to see him be inaugurated, but once it's over, and we go home, I've been thinking it might be better if…"

Her voice trailed off, but she didn't have to finish.

I sat back in my chair with a frown. In truth, I was shocked Nicole felt this way. Perhaps I had been naïve. Or perhaps I simply hadn't been paying attention to her feelings. But I had expected us to go on working together as political activists for many years to come.

"Why do you want to leave politics?" I asked her. "Don't you like working with me?"

"Working with you isn't the issue. The issue is that I think you're better cut out for politics than I am. I don't have the temperament for it that you have. When I look into the future, I see myself writing books, not doing political activism. I realize that I don't have a chance in the mainstream publishing industry anymore, but I might still be able to self-publish. I hope you're not upset."

"No, I'm not upset," I promised. "Just disappointed."

As disappointed as I was, though, I had to admit that I completely understood why she felt the way she felt. The past three months had shown us that, aside from being detrimental to our careers, political activism was also detrimental to our reputations, and even to our physical well-being. Since first coming out in support of Trump, we had amassed a total of somewhere around seventy-five thousand followers. As a result, the attacks against us were becoming more and more frequent. Leftists harassed us online, spread vicious rumors about us, doxxed our personal information, and even threatened to show up at our house to harm us and our family. On top of these attacks, we were also defamed by the mainstream media. Despite us making it clear that we were American nationalists, the mainstream media falsely labeled us alt-right. Moreover, they didn't even bother to use 'alleged' in their articles. Instead, they outright accused us, leading countless people to believe their lies as facts.

There was a time when, like many, Nicole and I had trusted the mainstream media. In our teenage years, we never imagined their reporting was anything other than the truth. In fact, one of our goals was to be featured in a mainstream media article for our work as authors. Little did we realize that you can only expect to be portrayed fairly by the mainstream media if you have progressive beliefs. These days, most journalists have sacrificed their integrity in order to be activists. Although they would never publicly admit this, the evidence lies in their work—puffed-up articles about their ideological allies and hit pieces about their ideological opponents.

Despite the numerous attacks, Nicole had rarely expressed difficulty in overcoming them. She had already lost her writing dreams, and therefore had little left to lose. Fear wasn't the issue. The issue was that she didn't have a political calling.

"Have you thought about leaving politics, too?" Nicole asked. "It won't get easier from here, even though Trump won the election. The Democrats want revenge, and it won't be long before they start coming after Trump supporters, and when they do, the mainstream Republican establishment won't protect you. Just look at Julian Assange…I realize he isn't right-wing, but Trump won the election because of him. And yet many people are already starting to abandon him. It's as if they only cared about him when he was valuable."

Nicole was definitely right about Assange. What began as a large movement in his favor was now a fraction of his former support. Fewer people spoke his name, and still fewer bothered to protest the fact that he was only free so long as he remained inside the walls of the Ecuadorian embassy in London. One of the most popular public figures to maintain their support of Assange over the years was a journalist friend of mine named Cassandra Fairbanks. Day after day, month after month, Cassandra reminded the world about the injustices being committed against Assange. On top of meeting with Assange twice, she also protested in his defense outside the Ecuadorian embassy. In 2019, she was one of the first to report that Swedish authorities had discontinued their investigation into a rape allegation against Assange after a review of the evidence.[54] But still, Assange wasn't allowed to walk free. On the contrary, on April 11, 2019, he was evicted by the Ecuadorian embassy, and shortly thereafter, arrested by Metropolitan Police. To this day, he remains locked inside a cell at HM Prison Belmarsh, his health on the decline as he awaits the United Kingdom's decision of whether he will be extradited to the United States. If extradited, he will be tried for allegations by the Department for Justice that he conspired with former U.S. intelligence analyst Chelsea Manning to download classified databases.[55] In hindsight, this shocking outcome was perhaps one of the largest disappointments of Trump's presidency. At the end of his presidential term in 2021, Trump had the opportunity to pardon Assange, and in doing so, to openly defy the Democrat and Republican establishments. But sadly, in a decision that upset a large portion of his support base, Trump chose not to pardon Assange.[56] Instead, he abandoned Assange to a cruel fate, one that will likely end up with Assange dying in prison.

Back then, I could never have predicted what would become of Assange. I was far too idealistic, perhaps to the point that I allowed myself to become blinded. However, in some respects, I'm thankful for this starry-eyed naïveté. Had I truly understood the vicious nature of the political arena, had I truly understood that the war for America's soul had only just begun and that it was on the brink of becoming increasingly more dangerous, perhaps my strength would've faltered. Perhaps it would've even given way.

"No, I can't leave politics," I told Nicole. "I feel like I've seen too much. It's gotten to the point where it's all I can think about. I'm not sure where I'll fit into the picture going forward; all I know is that I want to contribute in some way."

"I knew you'd say that." Nicole smiled. "And I think it's because, unlike me, political activism is a life that you've been called to. You're meant for it. Even if it takes a while, as long as you stay true to what you believe, I'm sure you'll find your place in it."

I squeezed her hand, hesitant to let it go. If I did, I felt like the conversation would be over. The decision final. I needed Nicole, perhaps more than I was willing to admit. She wasn't just my twin sister; she was my best friend. I had no idea how to navigate life without her. I wasn't even sure if I was capable of it. But I had to respect her wishes. Just as she supported my political ambitions, I also had to support her writing ambitions. As for the rest, we didn't have to think about any of it now. All that mattered was that we were together. And that after all of our hard work campaigning for Trump, we were a mere day away from witnessing it come to fruition.

"Attention passengers, we have arrived at Union Station," a voice sounded over the train's PA system. "Please stand clear of the opening doors."

"I'll get us a taxi," I told Nicole, letting go of her hand.

INAUGURATION DAY

The crisp, tree-lined streets of Washington, D.C., teemed with thousands of National Guard troops. Stationed at the Capitol Visitor Center, its white pillared dome rising out of the fog, the troops had been ordered to fulfill a critical task: protect Donald Trump as he was sworn into the office of 45th President of the United States.

The day was January 20, 2017 and the hour was shortly before 6:00

p.m. Raising the collar of my coat, fingers numb from the cold, I followed Nicole through a security checkpoint and on toward the capitol. The sun burned low, and its pale, yellow light slanted through the rainclouds that hung heavy in the sky, touching the happy faces in the crowd around us. We had never witnessed such a sight. It was one thing to experience the excitement of thousands of Trump supporters online, but quite another to experience it in real life. These Americans, like Nicole and me, had traveled from every corner of the United States to witness the inauguration. All of us came from different walks of life, but hope united us—hope that Donald Trump would fulfill his promises, easing our desperation and lifting our country from its knees.

"This is incredible," Nicole gasped.

I laughed. "It's like Twitter come to life."

As we moved through the crowd, I used my iPhone to keep tabs on the news. Violent riots, helmed by a movement of black bloc protestors in full-face masks, had erupted in downtown Washington, D.C. Bricks and trashcans were hurled, shop windows were smashed, fires were started. In the midst of the turmoil, around ninety-five people were arrested.[57]

At the time, I didn't know much about the protestors. I had been targeted by a few of them online, but I had yet to encounter them in real life. All I knew was that they called themselves 'Antifa,' an abbreviation for anti-fascists, and that their roots could be traced back to the organization 'Antifaschistische Aktion,' originally the paramilitary arm of the Pro-USSR German Communist Party (KPD). The modern day Antifa, despite having no formal link to the first Antifa, stood for a mix of anarchism and communism.[58] In some ways, they were a tolerated terrorist group that was allowed to take to the streets because they were a useful tool, willing to enforce the soft totalitarianism that the leftist establishment required. Just a few of the tactics they employed to neutralize right-wingers were physical violence, property damage, doxxing, defamation, and de-platforming.

In the minds of Antifa, Trump had resurrected the decades-old war between communists and fascists, which, given that Trump wasn't a fascist, abolished all justification for their existence. Granted, a few people on the fringes of the right-wing supported fascism, but for the most part, you were hard-pressed to find a true fascist, particularly one who espoused their beliefs under their real face and name.

"We need to be careful when we leave the capitol," I told Nicole, showing her video footage from the riots.

"We'll be fine if we stay close to the military and police," Nicole said.

Cold rain was misting from the sky when we arrived at the capitol. Gratefully, we accepted a pair of blue plastic smocks from a man freely handing them out. By the time we put them on, we had forgotten the rain, for Donald Trump had taken the stage. Dressed in an immaculate black suit and classic red tie, he seemed to tower above everyone else.

"Chief Justice Roberts, President Carter, President Clinton, President Bush, President Obama, fellow Americans, and people of the world: thank you," Trump began, his voice projecting earnestly across the crowd.

The media captured every moment, broadcasting his speech to millions of televisions across the world.

> "To all Americans, in every city near and far, small and large, from mountain to mountain, and from ocean to ocean, hear these words.
>
> You will never be ignored again.
>
> Your voice, your hopes, and your dreams, will define our American destiny. And your courage and goodness and love, will forever guide us along the way.
>
> Together, we will make America strong again. We will make America wealthy again. We will make America proud again. We will make America safe again.
>
> And, yes, together, we will make America great again. Thank you, God bless you, and God bless America."[59]

Passionate cheers rolled through the crowd. "Make America great again. Make America great again," people chanted. Eventually, I joined in, my heart swelling with hope. The speech felt like the end of an era. And in a way, it was. One chapter had closed, and as the next one opened, the Trump movement was already making plans for the future. I had first gotten a sense of this new chapter the night before, when Nicole and I had attended a party with over a thousand other Trump supporters. The party, entitled the 'Deploraball,' was a throwback to the campaign speech in which Hillary Clinton had proclaimed that she would place half of Donald Trump's supporters in a basket of deplorables.[60] Held at the National Press Club, the atmosphere was one of glitz and glamour: dim lights and perfumed air, well-groomed men in dashing suits and women in chiffon gowns, crystal flutes of champagne and rowdy, celebratory speeches.

In contrast, the street outside the National Press Club was in chaos. Mobs of Antifa and leftist protesters surrounded the National Press Club's entrance, jeering at and insulting the Deploraball attendees as they arrived and attempted to enter the building.

"Nazis! Fascists!" the protesters screamed.

I wasn't worried, despite the commotion. The police, who had positioned themselves between the protestors and attendees, appeared to have the situation under control. Plus, I didn't think any of the protesters were actually planning to resort to violence. I thought they were simply using intimidation tactics. A few hours later, however, I learned that a protestor had allegedly struck a Trump supporter, James Allsup, on the head with a flag pole. Photos following the attack show James Allsup crouched on the street, his hand drenched in his own blood.[61] Equally horrifying, a man named Scott R. Charney had allegedly been planning to spread butyric acid through the National Press Club's ventilation system. The plot had been exposed by James O'Keefe, the founder of the journalism enterprise, *Project Veritas*. James O'Keefe had secretly recorded Scott R. Charney and two others discussing the plot over beer at a pizza restaurant, which resulted in

Scott R. Charney being arrested a few hours before the Deploraball was scheduled to take place.[62]

I realized then how dangerous it was to be a Trump supporter, at least in certain American cities. The political divide was driving people mad, causing them to go to barbaric lengths. Even if Scott R. Charney had never truly planned to follow through with the attack, the situation opened my eyes to the malevolent nature of many leftists.

Given James O'Keefe's role in exposing the alleged plot, I was happy for the opportunity to meet him during the party. I also met a few of my online friends, Mike Cernovich and Jack Posobiec, two activists who had gained substantial online followings while campaigning for Trump. I met Owen Shroyer, a reporter for *Infowars*. And lastly, Lauren Southern and Faith Goldy; at the time, both worked as reporters for *Rebel Media*, but would later go on to become independent journalists. Somewhere in the midst of my various conversations, I came to notice a common thread. All of these people seemed to understand their place in the political landscape. I, on the other hand, didn't even understand the political landscape, much less my place in it. I knew little about the innerworkings of D.C., I had no contact to any politicians, I had no journalistic experience, and I had never been to a protest. But these people appeared to be professionals. Confident in themselves and their goals, they moved about with a sense of purpose that I could only hope for. In the moment, I didn't yet know where my place was among them. But, just as Nicole had said, as long as I stayed true to my convictions, I was sure that I would soon find out.

3

In the beginning of a change the patriot is a scarce man,
and brave, and hated and scorned. When his cause succeeds,
the timid join him, for then it costs nothing to be a patriot.
　　　—Mark Twain

CALIFORNIA, UNITED STATES
FEBRUARY 2017

In the aftermath of President Trump's inauguration, the politically-charged tensions continued to escalate, widening the divide between Americans more than I had witnessed in my lifetime. Rather than accept President Trump's victory, Democrats transformed our country into an all-out battleground. Enraged at their loss, they sought revenge with unrelenting aggression, beginning with the unsubstantiated allegation that Trump and his campaign had colluded with the Russians to win the presidential election.

As I watched the charade unfold, I realized that Nicole had been accurate in her prediction: even with Donald Trump as President, things weren't about to get any easier. Trump needed support from his voter base, perhaps now more than ever. In the midst of offering such support, however, I found myself wanting to accomplish something more than political cheerleading. I wanted to contribute something of my own.

It took several months to find my footing. As much as I felt confident in my beliefs, I needed a broader education. I needed to understand the various political players and the ever-changing, oftentimes unspoken rules of the political arena. I had to learn the different political theories, ideologies, movements, and jargon.

Thinking it was wisest to keep an open mind, I spent time investigating and interrogating new ideas. Little did I know, the mainstream media was marking my every move, listening to my every word. As one of their ideological opponents, I wasn't permitted to be inquisitive or to have a period of growth or maturity. In their eyes, I simply had to know everything all at once. A single carelessly-spoken phrase or poorly-worded tweet had the ability to cost me greatly—both of which I ended up being guilty of.

In the meantime, Silicon Valley was beginning to weaponize political censorship. While the right didn't agree with the left on much, it was mutually understood that social media had been instrumental in the outcome of the election. The big tech companies, largely controlled by the left, seemed to unanimously agree that freedom of political speech was a liability, one that couldn't be permitted to continue. As a result, they launched an aggressive crackdown on Trump supporters and right-wing dissidents, justifying their censorship tactics by accusing us of spreading 'fake news' and committing 'hate speech.' Few were surprised when the mainstream media, who often published dishonest stories themselves, failed to call out the bias of Big Tech. Instead, the mainstream media reacted by celebrating the censorship, continuing to slander us with false labels such as alt-right, fascist, white supremacist, and Nazi.

For the most part, I laughed off the attacks against my reputation. Most of the mainstream journalists weren't to be taken seriously because they weren't journalists at all. They were leftist activists. Rather than expect fair representation from them, it was a far better use of my time to make fun of them on Twitter.

Sometime in early February, I debated the idea of launching a full-time YouTube channel. Aware that I could be banned from Twitter at any time, I wanted to extend my reach across a variety of platforms.

The only problem was that I was reluctant to film videos on my own. Not only was I still camera-shy, I didn't know much about filming equipment or editing software.

"We can co-host a political podcast together if you want," one of my online friends, a British girl named Tara McCarthy, offered. With her velvet-dark hair and husky voice, she was blessed with a natural air of tenacity and grace. "I've been on YouTube for a few years now, so I'd be happy to show you the ropes."

"I'd love that," I told her. "What kind of topics are you interested in focusing on?"

"I think it'd be fun to interview other right-wing political figures," she replied. "We could focus on topics like censorship and immigration."

While I liked Tara's suggestions, I suggested we also focus on cultural topics such as feminism, dating, the nuclear family, and traditional gender roles. As strange as my values might have seemed to others, their values were equally strange to me. I was surprised to discover that not just leftists, but even many right-wingers supported abortion and divorce, which once again highlighted the uniqueness of my upbringing. Raised on a farm on the outskirts of a small town in Kansas, my siblings and I had learned the value of hard work and responsibility from a young age: caring for horses and sheep, mowing ten acres of lawn weekly, and tending to four flower gardens and two vegetable gardens. My mother, who spoke three languages and had achieved an MBA in International Business and Foreign Language, had chosen to be a stay-at-home mother. Day in and day out, she dedicated her time to our formation and upbringing, while my dad worked grueling jobs that he didn't particularly like in order to support us. Cable television was off-limits in our home, as was internet usage until we reached our mid-teens. Instead, we were encouraged to play outdoors, read, harvest the garden, tend to the animals, and do arts and crafts. In hindsight, I am more thankful now for my childhood than I was at the time. I never could have predicted what a rare and precious gift it was to grow up with such selfless, loving parents.

In Kansas, I attended a private Catholic girls' school. The beautiful stone building was originally constructed by the Jesuits, and during my time there, it stood beside the haunting, overgrown ruins of a burned down church. Religion classes were taught by a traditional order of nuns, who had taken vows of poverty, chastity, and obedience, and wore the black habit. The school was challenging, with a code of conduct, modest uniforms, and a rigorous curriculum. Despite the strict rules, however, I eventually grew to appreciate the discipline. Given that I hadn't experienced any other educational setting, the level of orthodoxy was natural.

Large families were common in our Catholic parish. My parents had eight children, although I knew other families with as many as sixteen. Divorce was extremely rare; abortion was unthinkable, even if a child was prenatally diagnosed with a disability, defect, or a genetic disorder. Most spouses abided by traditional gender roles, with the husbands providing for their families and the wives staying at home in order to keep house and care for the children. Of course, in situations of financial struggle, wives also worked. But men and women didn't view each other as competitors; they acknowledged the value in one another and respected the other's distinct role. Parents in my area encouraged masculinity in boys and nurtured femininity in girls as their children matured. Most important of all was faith and family. We were a unified community in which all of us looked after each other.

While, naturally, our Catholic parish had weakness and imperfection, I preferred the life it offered to the life offered by the dominant culture. I opposed feminism, abortion, and the promotion of casual sex, porn consumption, and promiscuity. I opposed the demonization of men, whether it came to disparaging their masculinity or labeling them inherently sexist and misogynistic. And I opposed the inferior attitude toward women who, rather than pursue a professional career, chose to be homemakers and mothers.

The way I saw it, my podcast with Tara was the perfect opportunity to discuss the importance of traditional values. No force, false promises, or manipulation was involved. People were free to choose their own path. But in witnessing the nihilism and overall unhappiness of many of my fellow millennials who walked the path of the dominant culture, I felt the need to promote an alternative path.

Tara and I decided to title our podcast *Virtue of the West*. We interviewed a range of political figures, from Lauren Southern to Tommy Robinson to James O'Keefe. Tara chose half of the guest list, while I chose the other half. Ultimately, we were open to interviewing anyone, activists with small followings, and even activists who we had political and religious disagreements with. Fortunately, after only a few episodes, my shyness abated. I found myself able to relax and was self-assured enough to entertain our guests, while at the same time asking questions that paved the way for compelling discussions.

Virtue of the West enjoyed several months of success. This was largely due to the fact that Tara was one of the most organized people I had ever met. Her notes were always neatly presented and well-researched, and even more importantly, she always showed up on time to film. At some point, however, I figured I should also venture out into the real world, attending and perhaps even filming on-the-ground events. As far as political strategies went, a combination of online and offline activism was the most effective. Eventually, I got my wish in the form of an invitation to speak at the Patriot's Day Rally on April 15th, 2017.[63]

My father insisted on chaperoning me. He knew Berkeley was a predominately leftist area, frequented by Antifa members, and wouldn't hear of me going alone. I didn't argue with him. My father is one of the kindest people you will ever meet, but upon first glance, he has a stern, almost severe air about him. I felt safer with him than anyone else.

"Don't leave my side," my father said, as we pulled from the driveway of our house in Gilroy and took the fastest highway route to Berkeley. "If shit hits the fan with Antifa, stay behind me and do what I say."

"I will," I promised. My tone was distracted, but not because I was concerned about Antifa. I had never attended a political rally before, nor had I ever given a political speech. My nervous excitement manifested into a smile as I turned the speech over in my mind. Hours I had spent planning it out, fine-tuning and memorizing each word. I hoped the rally attendees would like it.

A group of armed men in black and yellow shirts awaited us at a parking garage outside the rally. They were members of the Oath Keepers, a non-partisan association of current and former military, police, and first responders who had volunteered to provide security for the event.[64] The Oath Keepers closed ranks around my dad and me, guiding us safely to the Martin Luther King, Jr., Civic Center Park where the rally was scheduled to take place. Outside the doors, I was greeted by the sight of a senior-aged man slumped on the curb, his hands knotted around a bloody gash on his face. Three or four men were crouched around him, tending to him with a first-aid kit.

"Everything okay here?" my dad asked. "What happened to him?"

"Antifa attack," was all the Oath Keepers said.

My dad put his hand on my shoulder, guiding me into a crowded park shaded by leafy trees, and said, "We should leave as soon as your speech is over."

I didn't want to leave so early. There were political activists I had planned to meet up with, but in the end, I didn't argue. More Antifa were arriving by the minute, spilling down the sidewalks, wielding hammer and sickle flags. They seemed to always move in packs, like wolves on the hunt for weaker prey. Sporting dark clothes and thuggish masks, they advanced on the park, amassing at the borders as if they intended to box us in. The only barrier between them and the rally attendees was a sparse layer of Oath Keepers.

The energy in the park was palpable. I kept close to the stage, where a microphone and a speaker system had been setup. A banner hung from the trunk of a tree at center stage, listing the names of the speakers. Many speakers had signed their names along the border of the banner, and I added my own. Then I searched for familiar faces and was happy to spot the Canadian journalist, Lauren Southern. As we exchanged greetings, catching up on all that had happened since we had met at the Deploraball, I quickly got the sense that I hadn't dressed for the occasion. In contrast to my formal dress and lace shoes, Lauren wore military-style boots and a tank-top. A respirator hung loosely from her neck, and a helmet, branded with a giant MAGA sticker, protected her head. I had come prepared to give a speech, while she and many others had come prepared to go to war.

Lauren's speech was slated in the lineup just before mine. As I watched her take the stage, earning cheers from the crowd, something strange happened: all of my nervousness abated. I found myself able to speak loudly and clearly, emphasizing the importance of our first amendment right and the numerous ways in which it was currently under attack.

If you had asked me afterwards how my speech had gone, I would have told you that it had gone well. I didn't grasp how truly chaotic the atmosphere had been until days later, when I watched a video with clips from my speech on YouTube.[65] With a mission to disrupt the event, Anita set off a barrage of M80s—huge, zinging firecrackers that popped in the air like gunshots. The rally attendees shrank away from the blasts, their angry shouts cutting sharply through the smoke-bunged air. I couldn't believe I hadn't noticed any of it.

But the M80s were merely a foreshadowing of what was to come. In spite of the heavy law-enforcement presence, the police failed to deescalate tensions and the rally flared into a riot. I still remember the way the crowd swelled with hostile energy, before shouts escalated into shoves; before shoves escalated into beatings with rocks and bats and fists. In the chaos of pepper spray and tear gas, a rally attendee was nearly killed. His alleged assaulter was a college professor named Eric Clanton.[66]

In footage of the assault, which can be found on YouTube, Clanton is shown cracking a bike-lock over the skull of a rally attendee.[67] The rally attendee appears too shocked to process the fact that he's been hit. Cradling his head in his hands, his face slick with blood, he stumbles around in a daze. A horrific sight.

As a penalty, Eric Clanton got a light slap on the wrist. He was sentenced to three years of probation for nearly murdering an innocent man.[68] He would never even so much as see the inside of a prison cell, as if perpetrators of violence can expect leniency from the California court system as long as those perpetrating the violence have leftist ideological views.

"Let's get you home," my dad said toward the end of the rally. "At this point, I don't trust the police to protect anyone."

I followed my dad to the car, grinning in spite of my rapid pulse and the odors of pepper spray wafting from my clothes. My instincts had been right: I was hindering my effectiveness by restricting my work to the online sphere. During various conversations at the rally, I had learned that many political activists were dividing their work between social media and the streets. They attended patriotic rallies, reported on political events across the country, and some even conducted investigative journalism. Still reeling from the experience, my heart full of adolescent hope, I felt myself longing to join them. To create change through my actions, not just my words. Perhaps, finally, I had found the path I had been searching for.

NIGHT-CRAWLING IN PARIS

Over the next six weeks, I barely saw my family. Life became a whirlwind. I traveled to Los Angeles for a speaking engagement at a pro-Trump rally. I also returned to Berkeley with a group of activists on April 27, 2017, to speak in place of conservative author, Ann Coulter, who had cancelled her speech after losing the backing of conservative groups that had initially sponsored her appearance.[69] From there, I finally got the opportunity to transition into a field that interested me: independent journalism.

While I didn't regard myself as a proper journalist, considering I had a clear bias, I figured that since the mainstream media was chock-full of leftist activists, the alternative media needed a few right-wing activists of their own. Unlike the mainstream media, though, I was fully transparent with my audience about my political beliefs.

For my first journalistic project, I covered the 2017 French Presidential Election in Paris, France. Fought between Emmanuel Macron of the En Marche! party and Marine Le Pen of the National Front party, the election ultimately saw Emmanuel Macron take the victory.

During my three-day visit to France, I met with Lauren Southern, Tim Pool, and a few other independent journalists. The most eventful moments didn't relate to the election itself, but to the Victory Day March on May 9, 2017, and even more so, to a police brutality protest in a suburb of Paris called the 91st arrondissement.[70]

It was the first time I had inhaled tear gas, and it felt as if the oxygen in my lungs had caught fire. Heaps of garbage littered the streets, blowing around in the breeze of passing cabs, and pools of glass busted from car windows crunched beneath the boots of policemen and rioters. Like an idiot, I wore the same lace shoes I had worn at Berkeley, meaning one wrong step could have left me with a serious injury. For hours, I hopped along street curbs, using the light from my cellphone to maneuver between shards of glass. First thing the next morning, I bought a proper pair of sneakers.

At least three-hundred migrants attended the protest. A local French journalist informed me that the migrants were protesting a case of alleged police brutality. Apparently, a young migrant had died while trying to evade arrest by the French police. But the police hadn't actually killed the young migrant; he had collided with a bus while attempting to escape.

"You girls should cover your hair," the French journalist warned Lauren and me. "It's attracting too much attention…especially Lauren's blonde hair."

He didn't need to explain further. We had noticed the migrants watching us since our arrival. I dug a beanie from my rucksack, more annoyed than concerned. We were in France. Since when had it become dangerous for women to show their hair in *France*? In that moment, I realized it probably hadn't been wise to attend the protest. Most of the migrants weren't willing to speak with us, anyway. In fact, they spent most of the night yelling at us.

"Get out of our neighborhood! This is *our* turf."

We managed only a few minutes of footage before a young migrant boy broke from the mob and aimed for us, waving his hands in warning to back off. He pulled our translator aside and they exchanged words in French. A feeling of unease came over me as I watched our translator's features stiffen into an expression of fear.

I'll never forget the light catch in his voice as he said, "We need to get out of here."

"Why?" Lauren asked. "What happened?"

"*Now!*"

Huddling together in a tight circle, we cautiously retreated. I later learned the migrant boy had told our translator that 'things were about to pop off.' If we didn't want to get hurt, we needed to do two things: turn off our cameras and leave immediately. The migrants hated being filmed and would interpret the action as an invitation to attack.

I risked a final glance over my shoulder as we left. The migrants had united in an aggressive swarm and were howling, jumping around, and smashing glass bottles against the pavement. My first instinct was to run, but I listened to my second instinct, which was to stay put. Running would only draw more unwanted attention. Our translator advised us not to take a getaway car either. We would be sitting ducks if the migrants tried to cut us off and box us in.

Lightheaded with adrenaline, I kept in stride with Lauren as we navigated the dark streets. She locked her arm in mine, her face lost in the shadows, but I knew she shared my worry. At this point, we barely knew each other, couldn't even be called friends, yet having one another for support was a stabilizing comfort. Every so often, I scoped our parameters, concerned that the migrants had followed us. Fortunately, none of them had, and we eventually reached a section of the city where the French police were staking out.

"You're mad for going into that mob," the police told our translator. "Absolutely mad."

"Yeah," he admitted. "But that's what journalists do."

Some of the journalists broke off and continued filming the protest, hoping to get some useful footage, but given that we'd distanced ourselves from the main source of action, most of their footage fell flat.

In retrospect, I'm grateful for having this particular experience in France. Personally, I'm not opposed to immigration in general. However, on top of being legal, it must be limited and controlled, meaning it must not have a negative or transformative cultural, ideological, or economic impact on the native population. Immigrants must have a will to not only assimilate, but to contribute to society in a meaningful way. Immigrants can assimilate, for example, by embracing the language, culture and traditions of their host country, participating in their local communities, respecting the rule of law, and working to earn their living as opposed to relying on welfare. They must also have a sense of loyalty and love for their host country.

In many ways, this is unfortunately not happening in Europe. The mainstream media can continue to insist that Europe is progressing, thriving under the benefits of multiculturalism, but that night, I saw the dramatic effect with my own eyes. The experience led me to start considering the concept of assimilation on a deeper level. Back then, I believed assimilation was possible for all immigrants. I have since changed my mind; however, I don't view an unwillingness or inability to assimilate as abnormal. On the contrary, having an indissoluble tie to one's native language, culture, traditions, and values is not only healthy; it is natural. It's natural for people to want to see their own ethnicities, cultures, religions, and native languages represented in government, entertainment, education, media, and so on. For this reason, I don't disparage immigrants who struggle to assimilate, or even those who find it impossible to do so. For them, assimilating would be akin to destroying an innate and invaluable part of themselves. And this is precisely why honesty regarding the consequences of mass immigration is so imperative. Western governments need to start being honest with their native populations about the colossal changes their countries are and will continue to undergo as a result of mass immigration. No more lying, no more gaslighting, and no more persecuting those who shed light on or who oppose these changes. We need an open and sincere debate, one that poses the question of whether or not the native populations *want* their countries to change. Up until this point, only those who support mass immigration have been given a say. But there are millions of others—arguably the majority in Western countries—who have been cast aside, and who to this day remain desperate for a representative voice.

THE RIGHT-WING FRACTURE

I chose not to return home after my trip to France. Instead, I continued traveling for the next two months, reporting on patriotic rallies in various cities across the United States. One weekend I flew to New York City, the next to Chantilly, the next to Portland, and the next to Los Angeles. Although traveling required a lot of time, energy and money, I was determined to attend as many rallies as I could. Often, the rallies made national news, so I felt it was important to livestream unedited footage via the mobile app, Periscope, of what was occurring: patriotic speeches, leftist counterprotests, Antifa violence, and so on. With each new rally I attended, the presence of Antifa and other leftist activists grew larger and more hostile. Often, a sparse row of law enforcement was the only buffer between the rightist and leftist attendees. Granted, Antifa incited the vast majority of the violence, and most of the right-wing attendees showed up with the intention of being peaceful, but others showed up either to brawl or to film the brawling in the hopes of racking up YouTube views.

Ultimately, my experience left me questioning the effectiveness of the political rallies. In general, political rallies have the *potential* to be effective, but only if they are planned with detail and precision. Hierarchy, organization, and discipline are essential. Unfortunately, back then, we had no leader or unified movement; we were simply a loose coalition of patriots whose primary common ground was that we had voted for Donald Trump. So far, we had managed to avoid a disaster, but I strongly felt that, sooner or later, someone was going to get killed.

Additionally, I was starting to grow wary of the changing political landscape. It's often said that, in a society creeping toward totalitarianism, humor is the first casualty. I was largely discovering this to be true. The fun and easy humor of the presidential election was starting to fade. The laughter, jokes, shit-posting, memes…much of it was being stifled by an air of severity and disunity. Certain public figures proved incapable of putting aside their personal beefs for the sake of the greater cause. Sure, the drama was entertaining—it garnered a lot of attention and YouTube views—but it too often resulted in splintering the right into smaller and smaller factions. It was in witnessing these divides that I first came to understand the importance of trust. The political arena is packed with shapeshifting opportunists. Many of these people value loyalty only insofar as it serves their personal agenda. Should a personal dispute ever arise, these trusted allies won't hesitate to air out your dirty laundry; some even resort to blackmail. I witnessed multiple journalists and activists gossiping behind each other's backs, leaking private messages, or secretly recording one another. As I watched it all unfold, I felt the ground that had once seemed so stable, rock beneath me. Most of these people weren't my friends. Most of them would turn on me the moment it became in their best interest to do so. I'll admit, this realization was a bitter pill to swallow. For the first time, the conviction I had felt after Donald Trump's inauguration was deeply shaken.

The final political rally I attended in the United States took place in

Portland, Oregon. It was held at the Terry Schrunk Plaza, a grassy outdoor park near City Hall, and to this day, remains one of the most dangerous rallies I've ever experienced. The Portland Antifa are among the most radical in the country, oftentimes going so far as to assault the police.

I declined a speaking role in favor of livestreaming the rally. Cut off by Antifa and leftist Portland residents, we were blocked from entering or exiting the park. Our only choice was to stay put until the rally ended, to hope that the Antifa didn't breach the police barricade. Thankfully, the police presence was heavier than usual. Apart from the Portland Police Bureau, the FBI and Homeland Security had also been recruited.

Violence broke out halfway through the rally. Beneath their blood-red Communist flags, the Antifa members launched a volley of rocks at the police. The police leapt onto the hoods of cars and returned fire with pepper-spray projectiles and stun grenades.

I don't know why the Antifa acted so aggressively toward the police. My best guess is because the police had confiscated their weapons: brass knuckles, sticks, shields, clubs and bricks. These were but a few of the 'accessories' that Antifa members had attempted to smuggle in to the rally.

From that day on, the true motives of Antifa were clear to me. Protesting our ideas wasn't their goal. In their eyes, our ideological differences were irreconcilable, meaning their goal was to injure, even to kill us if they thought they could get away with it. And yet, to this day, the mainstream media still refuses to condemn their movement, to call them out for what they are: a domestic terrorist organization. Instead, the mainstream media continues to shamelessly promote Antifa, penning articles with headlines like: 'As Neo-Nazis grow bolder, the 'Antifa' has emerged to fight them.'[71]

A NEW BEGINNING

After the rally in Portland, I finally flew home—not to California, but to Idaho. My family had recently moved, which made me happy because Idaho is a conservative state filled with homesteaders and veterans. The only downside was that I had no friends in the area. Not to mention, it was a political dead-zone.

But I didn't mind the isolation. In fact, I was happy for a break from the endless blur of airplane flights, hotels, meetings, interviews, video projects, and live-streamed events. Looking back, it's difficult to recall those months with much clarity. In a way, you could say that I spent the majority of the time on autopilot.

Thanks to the comfortable familiarity of home, I was able to break out of this state, and the sudden wave of clarity that hit me afterwards was jarring. I hadn't realized it during my travels, but I had lost over ten pounds. Because of the daily stress and lack of sleep, my face had also flared up with acne. It was fitting; I felt no different on the inside than I looked on the outside.

A week after I had returned home, on a late morning when I was still lying in bed, Nicole called to me from her bedroom. "Hey Britt, can I have your help for a minute?"

Sluggishly, I pulled on a grey sweatshirt, rubbing the sleep from my eyes as I walked into her bedroom. There, I found her sitting on the floor, sorting through a heap of old clothes.

"What are you doing?" I asked.

"I'm donating a bunch of this stuff to Goodwill," Nicole answered. "Is there anything you want before I donate it?"

I glanced over the clothes, about to say no, when I caught sight of my old Trump hat peeking from the pile. Red, with white lettering, the hat was stitched above the visor with the phrase 'Make America Great Again.' Picking it up, I traced my fingers along its edge, smiling as I recalled how often I had worn it during the election. I missed the certainty I had had while campaigning for Trump, the brazenness, the determination. At the same time, I understood that the only culprit at fault for my crippled optimism was myself. *I* was the one who had been foolish enough to place all of my faith in people, when I should've been placing my faith in ideas. Humans are corruptible, blackmailable, and at the very least, *all* of us inevitably err. Personally, I was guilty of my fair share of mistakes, so I was in no place to judge, much less to criticize. Despite my naïve expectations, the Trump Movement wasn't perfect. From activists to commentators to journalists, everyone had their own share of struggles. It wasn't easy to stay cheerful and unified amidst a constant barrage of censorship, character assassinations, assaults on their livelihoods, and accusations of guilt by association. Ultimately, I admitted, I was being much too hard on them.

"I'll keep this," I told Nicole, motioning to the Trump hat. "The rest you can donate."

I turned around, about to return to my bedroom, when Nicole asked, "Do you regret not leaving politics when I did?"

I stumbled to a halt, slightly taken aback. The question seemed random, like it had emerged from nowhere, but only until I reminded myself that Nicole wasn't stupid. Even without voicing my disillusionment, it hadn't been difficult for her to notice. My whole family had noticed. Granted, my hardened state-of-mind was a natural defense mechanism against the constant slander, attacks and life-or-death situations, but I regretted how much it negatively affected Nicole. I rarely spent time with her anymore, or if I did, I was either tired or in a bad mood.

"No, I don't regret my decision," I replied. With my old Trump hat still in hand, I sat cross-legged on the ground beside her. "But I do regret jumping in too fast. I've been thinking that maybe I should slow down a bit. Maybe even take a break altogether."

"I think it would be really good for you," Nicole said. "You've exhausted yourself, Britt—traveling, staying up all night, posting three or four YouTube videos a week. There's more to life than politics. You have friends, family…"

"I'm sorry that I haven't spent much time with you lately," I said.

Nicole's face softened, showing traces of a smile. "Let's spend some time together now."

I smiled back, filling with relief. "We can grab coffee," I suggested. "I'll help you drop the clothes off to Goodwill on the way."

It turned out to be the perfect time to take a break. Tara McCarthy and I had just two pre-recorded podcasts left to publish, and after that, we had mutually decided to go our separate ways. As we grew and matured in our beliefs, we diverged too much on important political issues. We weren't interested in interviewing the same people, and we disagreed on the subject of video topics. A year or so later, Tara converted to Catholicism, which led her to morally reconsider and eventually change many of her political views. She stepped away from politics in 2018, and now spends her days focusing on her family and her Catholic faith.

During my political break, I poured all of my focus into rebuilding. Having failed to pray much during my travels, I made an effort to return to Church. I forced myself to eat healthier foods, to exercise, and to get daily sunshine. The time I normally dedicated to social media and making videos, I instead spent with my family, especially Nicole. We had a blast talking away the nights, swimming in the Spokane River, and hiking the trails in the woods nearby. In a way, it felt like the old days...before either of us had been political activists.

I also made an effort to spend more time with friends: Nick Monroe, a political and video game journalist whom I had recently met through Twitter; and also, my old friend, Baldwin, who finally trusted me enough to reveal his identity.

By the end of June, I felt much happier and healthier. The acne on my face hadn't fully cleared, but my complexion had resumed a healthy color, and I had gained back most of the weight I had lost. With my energy restored, I managed to recapture the youthful passion and starry-eyed idealism that had seemed so distant during the past several weeks. It finally seemed like the right time to return to making YouTube videos full-time.

Going forward, though, I promised myself that I wouldn't allow politics to interfere with familial priorities or my mental and physical health. As difficult as it was, I needed to maintain a balanced schedule.

In the midst of settling into my new routine, I noticed that Lauren Southern had sent me a message on Twitter. Having not spoken to her since our adventures together in France, I was surprised that she had reached out. But perhaps even more surprising was the message itself— an invitation to travel to Europe with her in July, where we would report on a mission called Defend Europe, in which several members of a European patriotic movement called Generation Identity planned to charter a ship in the Mediterranean, with the goal of shedding light on illegal migrant crossings into Italy.

I took my time replying to Lauren's message. I knew little about the movement, Generation Identity. A quick Google search informed me that they were a pan-European, identitarian youth movement opposed to mass migration and the Islamization of Europe. Their movement had become popular as a result of the Europe's struggle with the 2015 Migrant Crisis, which had seen over a million largely Syrian, Afghan and Iraqi migrants cross into the European Union from overland and overseas.[72]

Founded in France in September of 2012 under the name Génération Identitaire, the movement had since expanded to several European countries and had become one of the leading patriotic youth resistances. It was comprised of several hundred young male and female activists. Online photos showed the identitarians demonstrating in energetic marches, hoisting banners with patriotic slogans and black-and-yellow flags marked with the symbol of their movement: the Greek lambda. Overall, they seemed well-dressed, well-spoken, and well-educated. In fact, like many other third-party right-wingers, I felt myself drawn to them right away. Which is why I wasn't surprised to discover that the mainstream media despised them. Article after article revealed a common thread: hit pieces that unanimously labeled Generation Identity 'far-right.'

Mistrustful of my research, I decided the only way I could know for sure was if I met them myself. Call it intuition, even a gut feeling, but I sensed I would be making a mistake if I turned down Lauren's invitation.

Sure, I'd love to go! I wrote. *Send me the dates, so I can grab a flight.*

I hoped I had made the right decision. After all, I could always fly home early.

I could never have predicted the adventures the Defend Europe mission had in store. I could never have predicted how many remarkable people I would meet, or how much one of them in particular would forever change my life.

4

We sometimes encounter people, even perfect strangers,
who begin to interest us at first sight, somehow suddenly,
all at once, before a word has been spoken.
  —Fyodor Dostoevsky

BELFAST, NORTHERN IRELAND
JULY 2017

My Europe trip kicked off on July 10, 2017, with a flight to Belfast, the capitol of Northern Ireland. Lauren, who was traveling with two other independent journalists, had arranged a meeting in the city with some political contacts.

Since I was still relatively new to the journalistic scene, I tagged along shyly, keeping mostly in the background, capturing footage wherever I could. We happened to be in Belfast for the anniversary of the Battle of the Boyne, so half of the city was in celebration. Parades flowed through the streets, led by Orangemen marchers toting banners and drums and flags. Fires blazed on gigantic pyres, emitting waves of heat that pressed back the gathering crowds. Dwarfed by the largest bonfire, which seemed to tower a hundred feet, its smoke mingling with the clouds, I thought it was one of the most incredible sights I had ever seen.

The main downside of the Belfast trip was that the Icelandair Airline lost my suitcase. After spending three days in the same unwashed jeans and sweater, I swore I would never again travel without hand luggage.

I also caught a nasty summer cold. Thankfully, in my renewed mental state, neither the lost luggage nor the cold was enough to dampen my spirits. I enjoyed my time in Belfast, and I enjoyed the company of the people I met.

On July 13, Lauren and her journalist friends spontaneously flew to France for two days. Since I hadn't yet recovered my luggage, I was forced to stay behind, but I didn't mind being alone. I had a blast exploring the city, dipping in and out of random shops, until I finally got the call that my luggage had been found.

"Thank God." I remember practically hugging my suitcase when an employee rolled it out of the airport storage-room.

On July 14, I boarded a flight to the sunny, ocean-side city of Catania, Sicily. I was the first member of the group to arrive, so I rented a room in a small yet charming hotel called the Suite Inn Catania. Jewel-green ivy curtained the walls and balconies, its curling vines somehow perky and fresh in the wilting summer heat.

I spent a full day indoors, recovering from my cold, before venturing out into the city. The stereotype about Italy that proved to be true is that Italians are among the friendliest people in the world. It caught me a bit off guard at first. I wasn't used to striking up conversations with strangers in the street. I wasn't used to having lunch with them either.

The stranger I lunched with was a Sicilian man named Alfonso. Around age sixty, wearing a wide-brimmed sun hat and warm smile that remains fresh in my mind, Alfonso spent his afternoons strolling through the city, introducing himself to new people in the hopes of making friends. Like an angel sent from heaven, he intervened when a group of migrants accosted me in the city square.

"We go now to nice bar. You want to come with us?" the migrants asked.

"No, thank you," I replied.

"Awww, don't be like that. We promise you have good time."

"I'd rather not go," I repeated.

"But it's just around the corner," they persisted.

None of the migrants threatened me. One could certainly argue that they had no bad intentions, but on the other hand, they had to be nuts if they thought I was going to walk off with a group of strange men. Not to mention, I didn't appreciate their obstinacy. How many times, I wondered, would I have to refuse their invitation before they finally left me alone?

Alfonso approached me with an air of familiarity, pretending we knew each other and that we had planned to meet. "Ciao, Bella signora," he greeted warmly. "I'm sorry I kept you waiting so long."

Alfonso and I lunched in a café on the edge of the square, in full view of a hundred other people in case he, too, decided to breach any personal boundaries. During our meal, I didn't mention politics. In fact, Alfonso had no idea I was in Catania for political reasons.

"There are too many of them in Catania," he told me, gesturing toward the city square fountain, where the same group of migrants who had harassed me still stood. "They are arriving here by boats...more and more of them all the time."

I stopped looking over my menu, and asked, "Do a lot of Sicilians feel the same?"

"We do." He nodded. "But don't get me wrong...we don't mind helping some of the migrants. And we didn't mind having them here at the beginning, but there's just too many now. We don't have enough space, enough jobs."

I pitied Alfonso, for although I agreed with him, I understood how much of the wider world would spit on his opinion. "Racist," they would call him for daring to want to preserve his way of life.

"Are you ready to order?" a waiter asked us, stopping beside our table with a notepad and pen.

"Yes. I'll have the pasta à la Norma," I replied.

"Vorrei gli Spaghetti ai Ricci," Alfonso added.

After placing our orders, Alfonso's and my conversation drifted away from politics. But even as we branched off into different subjects, such as the areas of Sicily I should visit, his initial comments stayed with me.

The question "Do genuine refugees deserve help?" has always been a no-brainer for me. Yes, I believe they do. The problem is that even the mainstream media itself admits it's nearly impossible to distinguish between refugees and economic migrants.[73] While refugees are genuinely fleeing persecution, economic migrants simply wish to take advantage of the opportunities and benefits that Europe offers. Does the world truly expect Europe to fling open its borders and welcome in every single person who asks?

Figures from the International Organization for Migration show that around 120,000 migrants arrived in Italy exclusively by sea in 2017, with the government putting the cost of taking them in at €4.2 billion.[74] In 2016, the number was even higher, with Italy announcing a record of 181,000 migrants having crossed the Mediterranean.[75]

If Europe does decide to fully open its borders, I wonder at what point it will be enough. Ten million migrants? Twenty million? Moreover, who is to say which migrants should be helped and which should be abandoned? Even with ten million migrants helped, millions more remain.

If a borderless Europe is truly the goal, then Europe will soon meet the same abject fate of the war-torn Middle Eastern countries abandoned by the migrants. The European people don't owe this debt. No country owes such a debt. If the Middle East requires assistance, I support granting it to them, but the majority of it should be done through reasonable humanitarian methods like foreign aid.

I also support putting an end to interventionist wars of regime change that have been destabilizing the Middle East for so long. I, for one, never voted for these wars. And I strongly believe that we need to leave the Middle Easterners in peace, to allow them to foster their own unique cultures, identities, and societies. This way, few of them will have to travel to Europe. They will be free to rule over their own countries as they see fit, far from the grasping, blood-soaked hands of Western political elites and their warmongering special interests.

MEETING MARTIN SELLNER

Lauren and the Generation Identity crew arrived in Catania on July 17, 2017. Martin Sellner, the young Austrian who had been selected to lead the Defend Europe mission, messaged me on Twitter in the early afternoon.

Hi Brittany, he wrote. *Thank you for your interest in our mission. I've seen some of your videos, and I'm happy you're able to join us. Are you free now to meet? I can explain to you all the details.*

I'd love to meet now, I replied. *But I already told Lauren I'd have lunch with her. Let's talk about mission's the details at the group meeting tonight.*

Lauren and I lunched in the City Center, in the Elephant Square, on the outdoor patio of a café called Caffe del Duomo. Bustling with native Sicilians, tourists and migrants, the café had a pleasant atmosphere, with beautiful potted shrubs and boxes of colorful flowers. Striped sun canopies provided shade from the scorching heat, while built-in sprinklers misted cool water onto our faces and hands.

Our lunch began with talk about Defend Europe—what types of collaborative videos we should film, which members of the crew we should interview, whether or not we should join the crew on the ship— but, by the end, the conversation took an unexpected turn.

"Have you met Martin Sellner yet?" Lauren asked, as she sipped the last of her wine.

"Not yet. He wanted to meet now, but I came to lunch with you instead."

"He's single, you know." I heard a smile in her tone. "Actually, now that I think about it, you two would really be perfect together."

Her words left me feeling reluctant. "I'm sure he's great, but I don't like set-ups," I said.

Getting the hint, she steered the conversation back toward politics, but not before adding, "Something tells me you'll change your mind."

After lunch, I spent the rest of the afternoon switching hotels. The identitarians had rented two apartments, one for the men and one for the women. Because Lauren had decided to stay in her own hotel, I shared my apartment with only one other girl, a beautiful Italian named Eleonora Cassella. With her sultry eyes and thick glossy hair, Eleonora looked more like a fashion model than a political activist. Rather than live an ordinary life like most other eighteen-year-olds, she was risking her reputation for an important political cause. Even more impressive was that she didn't do so for fame or financial gain. She worked in the background, arranging media communication and other logistical aspects of the mission.

Just after sunset, I went to the men's apartment to attend the official crew meeting. I'll never forget the beauty of Catania by night. Stars broke up the black sky, glittering over the velvet-blue ocean like a million hovering jellyfish. The cobbled streets, still warm and dusty from the afternoon heat, seemed to wander aimlessly around the misting fountains and spiring baroque architecture. In another life, I wouldn't have visited the city for a political mission, but to write a book. I arrived at the men's apartment an hour before Lauren, who had been held up with business calls.

The air hummed with excitement as identitarian activists from all over Europe darted about, finalizing preparations for the mission. French. German. English. Italian. I couldn't keep up with all the languages being spoken at once. Some of the men worked on arranging a press conference; others updated social media; and still more organized the arrival of the ship they had chartered for the mission, the C-Star.

"Hey Clement, how did the interviews go?" someone asked.

"Martin and I are professionals," Clement assured in a lilting French accent. Grabbing a towel from the back of a chair, he headed toward the showers, looking sleepy as a bear. He and Martin had spent the entire afternoon interviewing with the mainstream media, who had, to no one's surprise, taken a strong interest in Defend Europe.

I was first introduced to a big and burly Swiss named Jean-David Cattin, whose job was to help coordinate all the mission's press releases, press conferences, and media communications. Despite having been one of the original founders of the French Generation Identity branch, he often worked humbly in the background, a hidden yet effective political force. After that, I was introduced to a second Frenchman named Damien Rieu, who had worked for Marine Le Pen. Tall and green-eyed, with neatly-trimmed facial hair, Damien had a suave and smooth edge about him, one that I found to be common amongst the French.

My initial reaction to Generation Identity was fascination. Like a scientist discovering a new species, it was unlike any other political movement I had come across. Their optics were stellar, their hierarchy strict, their activists disciplined, and their rules non-negotiable. If a new recruit wished to join, they were subjected to a thorough vetting process. Recruits needed to prove themselves, to show that they were willing to adhere to the movement's objectives, before they were granted the status of activist. More than a few recruits had been kicked out over the years.

The identitarians also maintained a strong focus on education. Activists were encouraged to form weekly reading circles, and to gain a thorough understanding of political theory, philosophy, history, marketing and nonviolent political protest. As a result, each activist was prepared to debate every point of his ideology, and even to plan and execute his own political demonstrations and campaigns.

Within half an hour, the apartment was filled with activists. I don't remember exactly how many people were present. At least fifteen, maybe more.

Martin was last to arrive.

The first time I saw him, cheerful and energetic, even after a long day of interviews, was a moment I will never forget. He wore a brilliant blue shirt with 'Defend Europe' inscribed on it that emphasized his muscled frame, and his black hair, styled in an undercut, looked freshly washed. Striding confidently into the room, he spared time to greet each activist. Raw and unruly, his charm was like the charisma of animals. Whether he was speaking German, French, or English, he managed to generate a contagious enthusiasm, a magnetic force that captured every eye, pulling the whole world toward him, including me.

I straightened up as he walked my way, doing my best to appear self-assured. Unfortunately, my heart was already starting to race, my face flooding with heat. Even at the age of twenty-four, I was a stranger to such feelings. Uncertain how to react, I defaulted to a friendly smile, hoping I didn't look as nervous as I felt.

"Hello, Brittany," he greeted, in a thick Austrian accent. "I'm Martin Sellner. It's good to finally meet you."

"It's nice to meet you, too," I replied, shaking his hand. "I'm looking forward to finally hearing about the mission."

"Yes, I'll tell you soon," he assured. "We have an interview with a journalist in about an hour at a local bar. We can discuss the details there."

"A bar?"

"Of course." He grinned. "We're Europeans, after all."

DEFEND EUROPE LAUNCHES

An hour later, Lauren and I joined the identitarians at a local outdoor bar for an interview with a conservative British journalist named Katie Hopkins. She had traveled all the way from England for the sole purpose of writing an article about Defend Europe.

On the way, Martin and I walked ahead of the group, telling each other how we had first come to be interested in politics. What struck me most about him was his sincerity, not just toward me, but toward all those he interacted with. Nothing about him, from his unwavering cheerfulness to the way he walked on my left side to separate me from passing cars in the street, was artificial. He made direct eye contact when he spoke, something I wasn't used to. Most people, myself included, are incapable of it. Feeling too vulnerable, too exposed, our eyes focus on everything except for the eyes of the person we're actually speaking to.

By the time we reached the bar, I began to understand why so many people admired Martin, why he had such an avid support base.

The identitarians, Lauren and me spent most of the night chatting with Katie Hopkins. Meeting her was a memorable experience in itself. She spoke about a million miles per hour—her words broken up by sudden, spirited laughs—and she always had a joke up her sleeve. At one point, I recall her flinging her notebook into the air with a scream because she was so excited about the details of Defend Europe.

Like Katie, I was also fascinated by the mission. I soon came to learn its three primary goals:

> To monitor Non-governmental organizations (NGOs) suspected of colluding with smugglers in the criminal trafficking of human beings.
> To destroy empty smuggling boats so the boats couldn't be recovered and reused by the smuggler mafia.
> If necessary, to save any migrants in danger of drowning and to bring them to the nearest non-European safe port.

As I came to understand the goals of Defend Europe, I also came to understand why the mainstream media had taken such an interest in reporting on it. The mission, if successful, had the potential to disrupt more than a few powerful people and organizations. It was no amateur racket that the identitarians had picked a fight with; it was a multi-million-dollar industry. I realized then that the mission would not be easy, nor would it be safe. The identitarians were in for the battle of their lives.

We passed the following days doing little more than work. To no one's surprise, the mainstream media had done all in their power to pervert the mission's objective, publishing articles slanted with outrageous lies such as: 'A European alt-right group wants to take to the sea to stop rescuers from saving immigrants,'[76] and even worse, 'Alt-right group wants to hunt immigrants at sea.'[77] The mainstream media liked to claim that Generation Identity opposed mass immigration simply because they 'didn't like non-white people,' which is utterly false. Generation Identity opposes mass immigration regardless of ethnicity. For example, the German identitarians would be just as opposed to taking in millions of Swedish immigrants as they would millions of Turkish immigrants, because both actions would have the same result: the erosion of the German identity, language, and culture.

My Twitter inbox filled with interview requests from mainstream media journalists. I didn't bother responding. While I hadn't been able to attest to Generation Identity's character before meeting its activists, I saw the lies in the mainstream media articles now. None of the identitarians were far-right extremists. Ironically enough, I suspected that the mainstream media themselves knew this. The problem was that if the mainstream media told the truth about the identitarians, accurately reporting on their political beliefs and goals, millions would have likely joined their cause. And this, of course, was the last thing the mainstream media wanted.

Thankfully, a healthy portion of the public didn't buy into their lies. Thousands of people, from Europe to America, rose up in support of the identitarians. The fundraiser for their mission, launched on an alternative fundraising site called Wesearchr, ended up raising around $200,000. While $200,000 is admittedly a large sum of money, it disappeared quickly over the course of the mission. The cost of chartering the ship, the C-Star, was 105,000 euros, which didn't include port costs and fuel costs (about 70,000 euros). Salaries were also paid to the ship's captain and its Sri-Lankan crew.

I spent my time doing a variety of different work: filming videos with Lauren, auditing the identitarians' organizational conferences, challenging the mainstream media's lies through social media, and updating the American supporters on how the mission was progressing. One strange way I ended up being of service was when I smuggled a dozen of the identitarians' laptops to a separate hotel in the middle of the night and guarded them until morning. The Sicilian secret police had taken a keen interest in the mission and had begun tailing the crew. In the event that the Sicilian police launched a surprise raid, storing the laptops at a different location reduced the risk of confiscation.

I also interviewed a few members of the mission: the Italian identitarian Elenora, an Austrian identitarian named Patrick Lenart, and, of course, Martin Sellner. While I had attempted to keep our interview professional, asking only questions that concerned the mission, both my mother and twin sister called me a few hours after I published it on YouTube.

"So…when's the wedding?" Nicole teased.

"Who's the Austrian guy? Are you two dating?" my mom asked.

Martin and I didn't have much time get to know each other in Catania. The mission kept us both busy, especially Martin. Feeling the weight of his responsibilities, he maintained a laser-sharp focus. Thousands upon thousands of people were counting on the mission being a success. He needed to prove that their faith in him was well-placed.

As leader of Defend Europe, he was tasked with the bulk of the planning. Hours he spent in a rented conference room in Catania, arranging for the safe docking of the C-Star, live-streaming a press conference and planning the launch of the mission with the crew. Plan A ended up going way off-course. So did Plan B. By the time the mission had ended, Martin and the crew were executing Plan Z.

The only free time Martin and I had to talk was when the crew gathered for meals, or when Martin offered to walk me back to my apartment in the evenings. It was then that he dropped his strict demeanor—one he had learned in the Austrian military, no doubt—and exchanged it for a relaxed smile. Naturally, these walks were my favorite part of the day. We discussed topics ranging from philosophy to poetry to our pasts. I learned that we shared a similar upbringing. Not only did we both come from large conservative families, we were both Catholic.

"Defend Europe was your idea, right?" I asked one night, when he was walking me home. "Is that why you're leading it?"

"Yes," Martin replied. "Normally, the Generation Identity branches keep to their own countries. But since the issue of mass migration is a problem that concerns all of Europe, we decided to combine our resources for this political action. It's by far the biggest one we've ever attempted."

"It's definitely impressive," I admitted. "Your movement is full of young people, yet all of you are so organized and motivated. I guess I didn't expect to find a resistance like yours in Europe."

"It's necessary," he said. "If we left the issue of mass migration up to our politicians, it would never get resolved. In fact, it would likely only worsen. As patriots, it's our duty to engage in provocative yet peaceful acts of civil disobedience that put pressure on our politicians, forcing them to address the issues we're pointing out."

"Do you think you'll still be a political activist ten years from now?" I asked.

"It depends on the state of Europe. I won't stop until the issues of mass migration and Islamization are solved."

I searched his eyes, noting his seriousness. Having started political activism when he was fifteen, here he was twelve years later, still an activist and still in possession of a drive more passionate and idealistic than any I had ever witnessed. On the other hand, however, I knew that the political activist life wasn't what he truly wanted. He had very different hopes and dreams: finishing law school, achieving a master's degree in philosophy, writing books. But, like me, he had realized that unless we were prepared to turn a blind eye to the devastating state of our countries, living a normal life wasn't possible.

"We have a mission meeting tomorrow morning at seven," Martin told me, when we arrived at my apartment. "You're welcome to join us."

"I will. Goodnight, Martin," I said, with a smile.

As I climbed the steps to the door, I found myself regretful of the limited time we had together. It almost made me wish that we had met under different circumstances, perhaps at a political rally or even randomly on the street. Any place that would've allowed for us to have a few free days together. However, I've since changed my mind. I wouldn't trade our first meeting for anything. Defend Europe was a mini-encapsulation of our political struggle.

I also spent a lot of time with Lauren in Catania. Having known little about her before Defend Europe, I was happy for the opportunity to learn more. A fierce and dedicated journalist, she had a habit of plunging headfirst into even the most precarious of situations. If she was afraid, she never showed it publicly. Her outer shell was solid, seemingly devoid of an Achilles heel. But, of course, the longer I spoke with her, the more I came to realize that, like all people, she had her vulnerabilities. Her projection of fearlessness was simply a defense mechanism—one that, in my view, made her journalistic efforts all the more admirable. In reality, she was a fun-loving and deeply compassionate 22-year-old who was simply trying to find her place in the world as she fought for what she believed was right.

Lauren and I filmed a handful of videos together, some about the mission and others about cultural issues. At times, we could barely get through our talking points without having to restart the camera. One of us either said or did something silly, oftentimes unintentionally, causing us both to burst out laughing. Perhaps the main reason we got along so well was because we shared similar personality types. Even though our backgrounds weren't similar, our life goals were: dedicate ourselves to fighting for political change, and if we were fortunate enough to meet the right man, get married and have a family.

I miss these carefree moments with Lauren. The adventures we shared and the memories we made. The boundless creativity we possessed for political projects, and our steadfast certainty in the fact that we would be working together for years to come. But I've since come to accept that, sooner or later, life changes. Old phases end and new ones begin, and sometimes, even the best things must come to an end.

MY FIRST INTERROGATION

Thanks to lies from the mainstream media, the attention on the tiny city of Catania exploded internationally, which created obstacles for Defend Europe. Soon, not only were the Sicilian secret police tracking the identitarians' every move, but the Mayor of Catania, a man named Enzo Bianco, got involved.

"I've told authorities that allowing the ship to dock in our port would be very dangerous for public order," Bianco said in a statement to *The Guardian*.[78]

Lorenzo Fiato, a perpetually sanguine Italian with a head of curly brown hair, who at the time led the Italian branch of Generation Identity, responded, "The mayor can do what he wants within the limits of his city, but the water is not his territory. It's up to the coastguard and we haven't received any information about this. The mayor doesn't have the power to do anything."[79]

The identitarians weren't discouraged by this setback. Martin devised a new plan in which the crew would secretly board the C-Star from Cyprus, Greece instead of Catania, Sicily. In the meantime, everyone was ordered to only share photos from Catania on their social media accounts. A few of the identitarians even decided to stay behind, giving interviews to the mainstream media as if the mission was progressing normally.

At this point, I acknowledged that my role in the mission was no longer exclusively journalistic in nature. Somewhere along the way, I had become an active supporter. Wanting to be honest, I made my thoughts known to my social media following. Most of them reacted positively because they supported the mission as well.

When we arrived at the Catania airport, we were greeted by the chief of the Sicilian police. Flanked by a row of officers in crisp blue uniforms, he stopped Martin and a few of the other identitarians at the check-in.

"Passports, please," he said.

I listened in on the conversation from a different check-in line. I couldn't make out much of what was said, but assumed Martin's answers satisfied the police, for we were soon on our way to the city of Larnaca, Cyprus. Since Lauren had booked an earlier flight than the rest of us, she managed to evade the second wave of police that laid in wait for us.

This time, all of us were stopped at passport control. Our passports were seized, and we were escorted to a large holding room at the back of the airport. Rather than question all of us at once, the border police separated us into different rooms, questioning us individually about our plans in Cyprus. It was clear they wanted to determine if our responses matched up.

"What should I tell them?" I asked Martin.

"You can tell them the truth," Martin assured. "We're doing nothing illegal."

He was right. If the identitarians had in fact been breaking the law, the mission would have been shut down a long time ago. Because of the international attention they had generated, every move they made was being scrutinized.

I was the only member of the group who was questioned by a female border agent, a strategic tactic, no doubt. If I didn't feel intimidated, maybe I would let down my guard and give up information. She was kind enough and smartly dressed, with her blonde hair let down in curls. The starched fabric of her shirt crinkled each time she leaned in to ask a new question.

"Why did you come to Cyprus? What is the purpose of Defend Europe? How did you come to be involved in the mission? What is your phone number?"

The questions went on and on, poking and prodding at my innermost thoughts and motivations. The woman regarded me strangely, as if being wary of illegal and mass migration was a shocking concept. In her eyes, my beliefs made me alien, something to be placed under a microscope and studied. She detained me for thirty minutes before giving me permission to leave. I plopped onto a bench outside the holding room, reeling from my first interrogation. It wouldn't be the last.

The complete interrogation of the identitarians lasted approximately six hours. On top of that, we were forced to wait another hour for a final decision from the higherups on whether or not we would be allowed into the country. I'll admit I probably would've laughed at the irony if they had ended up deporting us.

Approved.

Cheers and clapping erupted from the group as the border agents returned our passports. Relieved, I collected my passport and hurried out of the airport without looking back.

"We shouldn't drive to the hotel together," Martin suggested, once we had gathered on the busy sidewalk outside. The air was a bath of heat, even though the sun was setting, lengthening the shadows on the street.

"You're right," a German identitarian agreed. Bearded, with a slight build and square-rimmed glasses, the German's name was Robert Timm. "The Cyprus police are surely monitoring us. It'd be smarter if we split up into groups of two."

"Exactly. It's less likely the police will be able to follow all of us if we're in multiple groups," someone else added.

"We'll follow Robert's plan," Martin decided. "Each group will go to dinner and then walk around the city for at least an hour before going to the hotel. If any of you notice you're being followed, don't come to the main hotel. Rent a room someplace different."

Everyone nodded in agreement, pleased with the plan—me most of all because Martin was my partner.

A taxi driver dropped us off at a random restaurant on the edge of Larnaca; it was snug and small, with a little doorway wreathed in pink Bougainvillea vines. The restaurant owner gave us a welcome unlike any I had ever experienced. He didn't give us menus, didn't ask us what we wanted to eat; instead, he served us every dish his restaurant had to offer. Our table was filled with food three times over. I'll never forget how hard Martin and I laughed as the owner kept reappearing with plate after plate after plate.

At this point, I was starting to suspect that Martin felt the same way about me that I felt about him. While he hadn't yet told me in words, he didn't exactly have to. Since our first meeting, he had treated me in a protective manner. Always making sure I felt safe and secure. Never allowing me to walk back to my hotel alone. Keeping me close when we were out and about. I knew he would tell me eventually. It was just a matter of waiting.

ALLEGATIONS AND ARRESTS

The following days brought more struggles. The identitarians left Larnaca and crossed the border from the Greek to the Turkish side of Famagusta, a city on the east coast of Cyprus which enjoys the deepest harbor of the entire island. For a while, the prospect of finally launching Defend Europe looked bright. The C-Star arrived at the port of Famagusta, complete with its captain and crew, and waited for the identitarians to board.

Unfortunately, the mission took a turn for the worst when Martin got word from the one of the port agents, a shady fellow by the name of Marco, that the C-Star had encountered some 'slight trouble' at Turkish customs. The identitarians had booked a hotel in Famagusta for the night, planning to set sail early the next morning, but Martin didn't trust that the trouble with Turkish customs would be sorted out as quickly as Marco claimed. Deciding it would be too dangerous to stay, Martin arranged a driver to bring him and the rest of the identitarians back to the Greek side of Famagusta.

Martin's intuition proved to be spot on. The Turkish authorities arrested the entire crew, including the captain of the C-Star later that same evening. The wildest part was the accusation behind the arrest: trafficking of humans, weapons, and drugs.

Obviously, the accusations were false. The captain and crew of the C-Star had never engaged in weapon, drug or human trafficking; on the contrary, human trafficking was the very crime they were trying to prevent with Defend Europe.

The identitarians spent the next few days bargaining for the release of the C-Star's captain and crew. But each day we stayed was a risk—the city was swarming with secret police, who watched our every move—and so we made the decision to hide out in a tourist resort on the southern coast of Cyprus called Ayia Napa.

Ayia Napa was a hotspot party destination. Its bars and strip clubs were packed to capacity with young people in swimsuits and flip-flops, its beaches spangled with colorful sun-umbrellas. A theme park was built at the heart of resort, it's neon lights flashing to the beat of hip-hop music that blared late into the nights. With its never-ending flow of tourists, Ayia Napa proved to be a good hide-out. The secret police couldn't locate us in all the commotion.

By now, the identitarians had decided it would be wisest if Lauren and I didn't join them on the C-Star. At any point during the mission, smugglers could attack the ship, many of which were armed with guns and other weapons. The C-Star, on the other hand, wasn't permitted to have weapons aboard. Plus, the identitarians didn't know what dangerous lengths they might have to go to when it came time to board the C-Star.

Lauren and I respected the wishes of the crew, but by now I was starting to get worried—not just for Martin, for all of the identitarians. Over the last few weeks, I had formed friendships with the entire crew: Lorenzo Fiato from Italy. Clément Gandelin from France. Robert Timm from Germany. Patrick Lenart from Austria. Damien Rieu from France. Thorsten Görke from Germany. I was well-aware that any one of them could end up injured, arrested or worse. But I also knew better than to voice my concerns and interfere. They were intent on completing their mission, no matter the risk. They had made promises to their supporters in their home countries and needed to do all in their power to follow through.

Lauren decided to return home to Canada. Since she would no longer be joining the crew on the C-Star, she didn't see a reason to stay. I was happy when she suggested we meet again in the future for a new project.

"You were right about Martin," I told her before she left.

She hugged me tightly, not bothering to hide her smile. "I know."

I remained with the identitarians in Ayia Napa for three more days. The living conditions were hardly anything to brag about. Lying on a rock-hard bed in a cramped room with no air-conditioning, I remember thinking it would probably have been more comfortable if I slept on the stoop outside. But in the end, I didn't mind too much. The crew would have to endure far worse when they were finally aboard the C-Star.

My strangest experience in Ayia Napa was a meeting with Martin and Marco at a bar on the beach. I don't remember what day it was, only that it was sometime around three in the morning. Marco was a port agent in Famagusta, and in his own words, he managed the buying and selling of goods. Bearded, with eyes like rolling marbles, he was animated to say the least. Arms waving, body bucking with laughter, it was like watching a performance. Hours he spent downing drinks and smoking cigarette after cigarette.

"We get the C-Star back. It's no issue, cross my heart," Marco promised.

The phrase 'it's no issue, cross my heart' seemed to be his favorite in the English language. He used it at least fifty times throughout the course of the night. At one point, he leaned in and told me that if I ever needed a job done, anywhere in the world, I should call him. I never took him up on his offer.

THE BATTLE FOR THE C-STAR

The next morning, the identitarians woke to more bad news. Contrary to Marco's claim that freeing the C-Star's captain and crew was 'no issue,' they remained locked up. Worse, the Turkish authorities were considering transporting the prisoners to Turkey to be tried in front of a Turkish court.

A bleak mood hung in the air. Weary and disheartened, some of the identitarians questioned whether it was worth it to continue. If Martin was also discouraged, he didn't show it. Still smiling, he tried lifting the spirits of those who needed it. I suspected that, as the leader of the mission, Martin knew he would be the face of its failure if they chose to give up.

"Will you do me a favor, Brittany?" Martin asked, after the identitarians agreed they would stay the course.

"Absolutely."

"Will you take a flight home tomorrow morning?"

My heart sank. It was the last thing I had expected him to ask. As much as I wanted to stay, to support them until the moment they stepped onto the deck of the C-Star, I couldn't deny that he had a point. The mission was getting more dangerous by the day. I risked getting arrested or kidnapped or worse. Plus, I knew it was an extra burden on Martin to have to constantly worry about my safety.

"I'll book a flight," I agreed.

Later that evening, the night before I flew home, Martin finally told me how he felt about me. He explained how his younger brother had introduced him to my political work a few months earlier, and that he liked my work so much he had reached out to me, both in an email and on Facebook, introducing himself and asking if we could do an interview together. He confessed that he had fallen for me on the first day, but had tried to ignore his feelings because he needed to focus on the mission. His words, shy yet ardent from the purest soul, felt like a seal on my fate. From that moment on, I knew that there was no human being I would dedicate myself to or sacrifice for more.

I took the earliest flight from Larnaca to the United States. The combined three flights plus the layover time lasted over twenty hours, but eventually I saw the winding blue rivers and forested mountains of Idaho from my airplane window. As soon as the wheels touched down, my internet connection was restored and my inbox flooded with messages. The identitarians had managed to board the C-Star. Defend Europe was finally ago. The bogus accusations of trafficking had been dismissed, and the Turkish authorities had agreed to release the C-Star's captain and crew. The C-Star left the port of Famagusta and met the identitarians off the coast of Limassol, a city on the southern coast of Cyprus.

Desperate to make their final attempt a success, the identitarians rented a boat and sailed out to meet the C-Star in the middle of the night, battling stormy waters and turbulent winds. The secret police arrived on the coast at the exact same moment and briefly detained the Austrian identitarian, Patrick Lenart, who had decided to remain ashore to help with communications during the mission.

I still remember the breathless mixture of fear and bliss I felt when I realized Martin had sent me a final message.

If everything works, then this could be my last message for quite a while, he wrote. *You are the best thing that has happened to me yet.*

EUROPE DEFENDED

I spent the next four weeks praying like I had never prayed before. Every day, every hour, every minute. Sometimes I managed to ease my worry; other times it threatened to crush me. I began to understand how my parents felt whenever I attended a dangerous political event.

The identitarians had no internet connection for most of the mission. The only way I could monitor Martin was through an app called Marine Traffic, which allowed me to track the location of the C-Star via its AIS system. I nearly drove myself crazy obsessing over that app. Late at night, buried beneath the large comforter on my bed, I followed the tiny turquoise boat that represented the C-Star, hoping Martin was safe.

While I had assumed that living aboard the C-Star would be rough, I could never have predicted just *how* rough. Cramped and hot, the sleep quarter was nothing more than a musky hallway loaded with sweat-stained beds. The shower, tucked inside a squalid washroom belowdecks, reeked of foul odors like mold and rust; the identitarians couldn't be inside longer than a few minutes without getting sick. Without sufficient protection from the sun, most of them sustained severe sunburns. In fact, Martin suffered heatstroke toward the mission's end.

But worst of all was the sea-sickness—brought on by a seaquake and the fact that the ship was unbalanced because they were unable to refill their ballast tank in Famagusta. Half of the identitarians spent the first few days vomiting over the side of ship or into the dingy bathroom toilet. The other half collapsed into their beds, feeling like their skulls were going to explode every time the ship crested a new wave. Throughout history, sailors have been known to cast themselves into the sea, happy to die by drowning rather than have to endure another moment of sea sickness. Notwithstanding those hellish circumstances, the identitarians remained in good spirits. In every photo and video posted on social media, their smiles were cheeky and their eyes shone despite sun-roughened faces. They had made it this far. Nothing could stop them now.

But still the mainstream media tried. Day after day, they published false articles, the worst of which was entitled: 'Stranded anti-immigration ship gets help from refugee rescue boat.'[80] In short, the claim was that the C-Star had been rescued by an NGO ship following a distress call. What truly happened was that, due to water being mixed inside the fuel tank, the C-Star's engine malfunctioned and the ship lost control, drifting off course. In an effort to follow Maritime Law, the captain made a distress call, which informed nearby ships that the C-Star had lost the ability to steer and cautioned them not to sail too close. The distress call ended up alerting an NGO ship, which offered its help, but the identitarians refused. After a few hours' work, they fixed the issue on their own.

I spent several weeks tracking the mainstream media, challenging the lies about the C-Star that they presented as facts. The skills of my good friend, Nick Monroe, who was a political and video game journalist, were invaluable. From the moment I met Nick, I was struck by his meticulousness and efficiency. I wondered why he didn't have a bigger social media following. At the time, he had around seven thousand Twitter followers, although I suspected he would go on to amass much more. He had the talent, the patience, and most importantly, he had an irrepressible drive to expose false and biased reporting. Pumped up on rock music and energy drinks, he crafted dozens of well-sourced Twitter threads that put the mainstream media's lies to shame.

Nick and I spent hours on Skype each day, trying to help the identitarians in any way we could, cracking jokes to lighten the mood. His laughter and upbeat mood were contagious, coaxing me to smile even in the midst of my increasing worry.

"Seems to me that Generation Identity has been a positive example for the American right-wing," Nick told me. "Ever since Trump's election, they've been fracturing more and more."

"I've actually already noticed certain parts of the American right-wing adopting Generation Identity's tactics," I replied. "Some of them have even started to use the term 'identitarian' to describe themselves. I'm not sure if the same type of movement will work here in the states, though."

"I guess time will tell. I didn't vote for Trump, but even I can see that he's stagnating on a few of his biggest campaign promises. Some right-wingers are dropping their support of him because of it."

I had noticed the discontent among certain right-wingers as well. It had largely started following Trump's decision to carry out a missile strike Syria in early April. The attack had been justified by the allegation that Bashar al-Assad, the president of Syria, had used chemical weapons on his own citizens.[81] Assad denied the allegation, but either way, many Americans believed it wasn't our job to police the entire world. We wanted Trump to bring an end to the constant interventionist wars of regime change. Not only have these wars cost our country trillions of dollars and thousands of American lives, they have created considerable destabilization, death and suffering in the countries we have occupied. Like many others, I supported a complete withdrawal from the Middle East, and I believed we should instead be focusing our money, resources and energy on our own nation's issues—of which there were (and still are) many. During his presidential campaign, Trump had promised to stop the forever wars, to withdraw from the Middle East and to focus on putting America first. It was high time for him to start acting on these promises.

On August 23, 2017, nearly a month after setting sail, the identitarians announced on social media that the Defend Europe mission had been successful. The C-Star had spent two weeks following an NGO ship called the Aquarius, documenting its actions and making certain that the crew didn't accept any transfers of illegal migrants from smugglers. They also encountered a second NGO ship called the Golfo Azzuro, which ended up being stopped by the Libyan coastguard near the Libyan Search and Rescue (SAR) Zone.

The following is a rough transcript of a recorded conversation between the Libyan coastguard and the Golfo Azzuro, posted on YouTube by the identitarians:

> "You are causing a big problem. You are acting like an assistance to smugglers. You are acting like a transporter, like a service to smugglers," the Libyan coastguard told the Golfo Azzuro.
> "Ok. Copy the message. We are going North. Just to remind you, we are here to save lives," the Golfo Azzuro replied.
> "We understand," the Libyan coastguard assured. "But you are putting a lot of lives in danger because you are staying here, smugglers know that. You are in this area, so they are sending more and more and more every time.
> "Copy that message. We go north and out of communication," the Golfo Azzuro promised.

"Go ahead and never come back. I repeat: never come back!" the Libyan coastguard shouted. "We will not warn you again."[82]

During Defend Europe, illegal migration into Italy dropped by approximately fifty percent. The mainstream media argued that the reason for the abrupt decline in illegal migration was likely the result of a 'more aggressive turnaround policy by the Libyan navy and coastguard, backed by improved boats and equipment—funded by the European Union—and Italian-led training.'[83] Therefore, it still remains up for debate how much credit Defend Europe should actually receive.

But at the very least, Defend Europe should be credited with pressuring the Italian parliament to take measures to defend its border. On August 2nd, in the midst of international attention on the C-Star, Italy's parliament approved a plan to send two naval boats to Libya as part of an effort to stop migrants from crossing the Mediterranean Sea and entering illegally into Italy.[84]

It wasn't until a year later, in June 2018, that Defend Europe was finally and fully vindicated. Matteo Salvini, who was Italy's Interior Minister at the time, published a statement that NGO-operated ships carrying migrants would not be allowed to dock at Italian ports.

"Italy no longer wants to be an accomplice of human traffickers and contribute to the business of illegal immigration," Salvini said in a Facebook post. "As a father and as a minister, they can attack and threaten me all they want, but I won't give up and I'm doing it for everybody's sake."[85]

If Generation Identity taught me anything, it's that solely relying on politicians to create political change is not only naïve, but it is strategically bankrupt. The vast majority of politicians cannot be trusted to fulfill their campaign promises without external pressure. And this is where political activism plays an invaluable role. Most patriots accept that their duty to their countries extends beyond casting votes during elections. But only a few of these patriots are willing to go beyond this passive participation to an active participation, dedicating themselves to acts of peaceful yet effective political activism that put inexorable pressure on politicians, forcing them to acknowledge and to react to the issues at hand. This is what Generation Identity managed to accomplish with Defend Europe, and what they would go on to accomplish with many of their future actions. However, in witnessing the identitarians' growing popularity and ambition, the left wasn't about to continue allowing them to do so without a fight.

OPERATION CASSANDRA

With Defend Europe now complete, the identitarians searched for a port at which to safely dock the C-Star. The problem was that ports in both Crete and Tunisia were refusing to grant them access.

The identitarians' final hope was Malta, a Southern European island country in the Mediterranean Sea. Low on fuel, and even lower on food and water, they were unable to sail further. Still, in an act of sadistic cruelty, the Maltese government denied them port entry and placed an embargo on the C-Star,[86] forbidding anyone from replenishing their supplies. The identitarians later informed me that the Maltese government had done this in the hope that the identitarians would become so desperate, so overwhelmed by hunger and thirst, that they would humiliate themselves by sending out an SOS signal, thus having to be rescued by an NGO ship.

Using Nick Monroe's research skills, he and I managed to locate and contact an organization on Malta called the Maltese Patriots, who strongly supported the identitarians' cause and wanted to see the Defend Europe mission succeed. Communicating through a message group, Nick and I helped the patriots coordinate a campaign to collect donations for a fresh supply of food and water. Then, in a courageous act that can only be described as a middle finger to the Maltese government, the patriots rode out towards the C-Star in speed-boats, breaking the embargo and resupplying the identitarians with food and water.[87]

I still remember the photos from that day. Elderly men with bushy beards and sunbaked skin, smiling and waving as they zoomed up alongside the C-Star. Their boats were so small that Martin had to dangle off the edge of the ship to receive the supplies. The courageous act of the Maltese Patriots reminded me that, no matter how evil or corrupt a government might be, one can always find goodness amongst its citizens.

Since the food and water was only enough to last a few days, the identitarians needed to devise a plan quickly. How could they get off the C-Star?

Originally, the identitarians joked that they had escaped by lassoing a dozen sea turtles and riding them ashore. Obviously, this was a silly cover for the truth, but the identitarians had wanted to protect the names of their true rescuers. Since the names of these rescuers have since been made public, I see no issue in sharing them. The rescue mission, entitled Operation Cassandra, was helmed by the very same Maltese Patriots who broke the embargo to resupply the C-Star with food and water.

Too anxious to sleep, Nick and I stayed awake the night before the operation, as well as my mom and Nicole, who tried to support me through the rescue. No number of encouraging words were enough to ease my nail-biting worry. The whole situation was utterly new to me. I had never before faced the possible reality of watching someone I cared about get hurt. I was helpless—a feeling I never wanted to experience again.

"Why don't we say a prayer?" Nick suggested over Skype. "At the very least, it'll get your mind off Martin."

"I've already prayed a lot tonight, but you're right. We should pray some more," I replied. Grabbing my rosary from my desk drawer, I moved the beads through my fingers as I whispered under my breath. "Hail Mary, full of grace, the Lord is with thee..."

As always, praying helped, granting me a few minutes of peace before the worry kicked in again. But Nick, kind as he was, refused to hang up the Skype call the whole night, even when I had to leave the room for a new cup of coffee or a breath of fresh air. He stayed on the line until sunrise, distracting me with all sorts of interesting stories, such as his role in the infamous internet controversy, GamerGate. How strange it was that people who met on the internet could go on to become such good friends. But in all honesty, Nick was more loyal than friends I had known in my childhood, standing true through hardships, disagreements, even through dangers. He was the sort of person who gave to give, not so that he would receive something in return. And he cared so deeply about his friends that he put them before all else—his work, his vacation, and even before himself. I hoped we would have the chance to meet in real life one day.

One of the Maltese Patriots, an older man named Stephen Florian, who had mastered the art of sending the perfect GIF for every situation, fed Nick and I updates throughout the night.

Your friends are EU citizens and therefore part of the Schengen agreement, Stephen wrote to us on Facebook. *The actions of our government are a scandal. But don't worry. Our boats are ready to help your friends. We are just finishing some last-minute preparations.*

Then Stephen sent me a GIF of a dancing starfish, telling me that a 'sea-star' would soon be safely on the shore.

Before sunrise on August 27, 2017, nearly one week after the C-Star had been denied entry into Malta, the Maltese Patriots rescued the identitarians from the C-Star undetected. No one, not the border patrol, the media or the Maltese government, knew that the identitarians had been brought ashore.

In a glorious act of trolling, the identitarians and the Maltese Patriots took photos of themselves outside the Prime Minister of Malta's office, hoisting a giant banner printed with the slogan 'Defend Europe.' When I saw the photos, I laughed until my face was sore. After how callously the Maltese government had treated the identitarians, I felt more than justified in my low opinion of them. While I already knew they were corrupt, they would soon go on to prove their hypocrisy. In 2018, one year after Defend Europe, the very same Maltese government that had labeled the identitarians racist for wanting to put a stop to illegal immigration, closed their ports to migrant NGO ships.

"Malta's ports will no longer allow entry to ships carrying migrants that are operated by NGOs," a government spokesman confirmed to *Times of Malta*. "Malta needs to ascertain that operations being conducted by entities using its port services and operating within the area of Maltese responsibility, are in accordance to national and international rules."[88]

In other words, the Maltese government's condemnation of Defend Europe was nothing more than a cowardly virtue signal, a bending of the knee to the globalist mob.

The identitarians waited until they had purchased flights and landed safely in Italy before publicizing news of their escape. Hours I spent by the phone, heart pounding in anticipation, before Martin called me from a hotel in Rome. The sound of his familiar Austrian accent was like a switch, releasing all the emotions that had built up inside me over the past four weeks. If I hadn't been so shocked, in such an utter state of disbelief that all the danger and the worry and the longing were finally over, I probably would have cried.

"I didn't forget the promise I made you," he said, a smile in his tone. "I just hope your government likes me better than the Maltese's."

5

The darkest places in hell are reserved for those who
maintain their neutrality in times of moral crisis.
                              —Dante Alighieri

IDAHO, UNITED STATES
SEPTEMBER 2017

Martin returned to his home country, Austria, before visiting me in the
States (not to enjoy a well-earned rest but to tackle the mountain of
work that awaited him in Vienna). From the day it launched, Defend
Europe had created powerful ripples across the continent. Even
Sebastian Kurz, who was Austria's foreign minister at the time, had
called on Italy to tackle the migration problem.

Kurz announced he had told his Italian counterpart, Angelino
Alfano, that "rescue missions in the Mediterranean cannot be seen as a
ticket to central Europe," on the sidelines of an OSCE meeting in
Vienna. "We hope that ferry services for illegal migrants will be halted
between Italian islands like Lampedusa and the Italian mainland."[89]

Martin spent the next two weeks buried in work. Dozens of
journalists, in his own country and around the world, reached out for
interviews. He arranged a series of meetings with his largest supporters,
thanking each one individually. Then there were YouTube videos to
film, demonstrations to attend, and he had also promised to record the
audiobook for his newest book, *Identitär!* which required him to drive
to Germany.

We kept in contact through Skype. I told him that, after a long search, I had finally managed to locate the message he had sent me over Facebook:

Hi Brittany,

I'm from Europe, Austria. I'm an activist in the identitarian movement. I also make YouTube videos. I just discovered your channel and thought that we maybe could make a video together someday. What do you think?

Greetings from Vienna,

Martin

I was embarrassed that I hadn't responded, but in a way, I was grateful Martin and I had met in person rather than online.

"Look what I made for you," Martin said shyly over Skype. His face was tanned and slightly wind-burnt, and his bright, boyish smile just as handsome as I remembered.

He sent me a photo of the C-Star's foremast, which was strung with an array of colored flags. The flags were International Maritime signal flags, used to communicate with other ships. While there are various ways the flags can be used as signals, one of the main ways is by spelling out a message. In decoding Martin's message, I learned the flags spelled out my name. Without a doubt, it was the most romantic thing anyone had ever done for me.

As I got to know Martin better, I learned he had been a part of the nationalist scene from age fifteen to eighteen. In Austria and Germany, the nationalist scene consists of several small, often subcultural, and sometimes even extremist groups, that range from patriots, to skinheads, to actual national socialists. In countries like the United States, being a nationalist is a common and acceptable political position, but nationalism has had a different meaning in Western European countries like Austria and Germany since World War II: those who label themselves nationalists are often understood to be sympathetic to national socialism.

For many young patriotic men in Austria and Germany, it's easy to get lost in these circles—to become part of a futile and politically meaningless parallel society. After a few years in these circles, Martin saw the errors of their ways and their thinking. He encountered the thinking school of the 'New Right', which led him to revise his views. His goal ultimately became to create a new kind of patriotic movement, a platform for young Austrians that was democratic, peaceful, and based on right-wing views, without being connected to the old-right subculture.

Several years later, in 2012, Martin and two fellow Austrians, Patrick Lenart and Alexander Markovic, launched a new branch of Generation Identity in Austria, known as the Identitäre Bewegung Österreich.

Martin's controversial past didn't bother me; he had turned his life around since his teenage years. Still, I knew the mainstream media would forever use his past as ammunition against him. A decade later, at age twenty-seven, he was everything a patriot should be, and he had endured far more hardship for his political activism than I had. He had been the subject of countless false articles, lies, and slander. In 2016, he had been attacked by a gang of Antifa in a subway station, and after defending himself with a pepper spray gun, had been served with a weapon's ban, which was eventually overturned in 2019. Antifa had hunted down his parent's home and firebombed their car. They had plastered posters and stickers of his face all over Austria, labeling him a Nazi. They had even graffitied death threats outside his Vienna apartment. But somehow, against an endless stream of setbacks, he always wore a smile. Never wavering and never complaining, he managed to make light of every difficulty, overcoming even the most hopeless of situations with his positive attitude.

I had witnessed this fortitude during Defend Europe, and I continue to witness it now. In truth, it highlighted my personal weakness. I hadn't suffered half of what Martin had, and yet, I sometimes faltered in the face of negative political experiences. For example, every now and again, I struggled with the fact that the mainstream media and leftist activists had deceitfully and maliciously tarnished my reputation. Lies about me—such as me being a white supremacist and a racist—were but a mere Google search away, easy for my relatives and school friends to stumble across. I couldn't necessarily blame my relatives and school friends for believing such lies about me, as most of them were presented in the form of mainstream media articles, or relatively trusted information sites. For example, a defamatory Wikipedia page about me was published in 2017. A few of my prominent political friends asked Wikipedia to remove the false information, and Wikipedia kindly obliged. However, since the majority of the information on my Wikipedia page was false, there wasn't enough information left to justify the existence of the page, and the page was deleted entirely. Unfortunately, someone—likely a leftist activist—transferred all of the false information to a new page about me on Rational Wiki.

I also sometimes struggled with the fact that I had to deal with attacks from right-wingers—people I considered to be on my own side. While the majority of right-wingers treated me fairly and kindly, some criticized me for not holding all the exact same beliefs as they did, or engaged in peddling gossip about my private life.

As difficult as my struggles were, however, they were nothing compared to what Martin had endured. In truth, the price I had thus far paid for being a political dissident amounted to less than the bare minimum. At this realization, I made the decision to stop complaining. I resolved to dig my heels in and press on. One day in the future, I would likely leave politics—for example, when I got married and had a family of my own—but until then, I promised to hold myself to a higher standard, to never again allow the difficulties of the political world to cause me to lose my sense of self or my inner peace.

On September 15, Martin finally came to visit me in Idaho. It was early evening at the Spokane airport, the wind was blowing cold and crisp, and the leaves were breaking from the trees. I waited for him at the baggage claim, where only a few pieces of luggage wheeled around on the conveyor belt. I tried my best to remain patient, but my eagerness was growing with each passing moment, flooding me with excitement, until I was practically bouncing up and down. The lack of control over my emotions was new, perhaps because I had never found myself so captivated by a man before. The main difference between my relationship with Martin and those I had experienced in the past was my certainty. It was a certainty that hadn't taken me long to understand, but had been instantaneous, from the very first moment. Martin and I hadn't met by chance.

When I finally saw him in the crowd, smiling with a big bouquet of roses, my heart gave a painful leap. My feet were moving before I realized I was running. The distance and danger of the past six weeks had made reuniting seem impossible. And yet here we were, back in each other's arms, suspended somewhere between joy and relief.

I never wanted to let him go again.

My family took to Martin right away. My dad, who had always been overly protective of the five girls in my family, surprised me with how quickly he gave his approval. Of all the things my dad could have been doing, he was cleaning his guns in the garage when Martin asked him for permission to date me.

"I felt like I was in one of those movies where the dad sits on the front porch, guarding his daughters with a gun," Martin later told me with a laugh.

THE BERKELEY BREAK-IN

Martin and I remained at my parent's house in Idaho for a week, before taking a road trip to California. Conservative author and pundit, Milo Yiannopoulos, had announced a 'Free Speech Week' in Berkeley, an event where several prominent right-wing figures would give speeches, seminars, and host discussion panels. Unfortunately, the event encountered setbacks and was eventually cancelled a few days before it was scheduled to take place.[90]

A few of my political friends, who had already booked flights and accommodations, traveled to Berkeley, anyway. Wanting to introduce Martin to the American political sphere, we agreed to join them. I figured it was a good opportunity for him to make contacts, plus I wanted to collaborate on a few YouTube videos with Lauren Southern.

After renting a car at the Spokane airport, Martin and I set off on our road trip to Berkeley. Apart from our evening walks in Sicily and Cyprus, it was the first time we had ever been alone together. We spent the hours diving deep into our pasts. I told him about my rebellious phase as an early teenager, during which I had constantly clashed with my parents. He also told me about his own rebellious phase, during which he had been drawn to radical right-wing politics and had turned away from Catholicism.

Every few hours, we made a short break at a fast-food restaurant. Martin, who had learned about our fast-food culture from American television, wanted to try as many different types as possible: Dairy Queen, Arby's, In-N-Out Burger, Five Guys, and more.

"What should I order?" Martin often asked me.

"I don't know. I've never eaten here."

"What do you mean? Americans are supposed to love fast food."

"I did when I was a teenager, but then I got chubby."

"I doubt you were ever chubby."

I laughed. "Wait until you see the pictures."

In between our conversations, Martin introduced me to some of his favorite music: a mix of classical, folk, synthwave, and German hip-hop. Having learned a few of the songs from a foreign exchange student in high school, I was able to sing along. Rolling down the window, the wind tangling my hair, I smiled so big that my face ached. I felt happier and freer since the day we had said goodbye in Cyprus.

"What are some of the most important German words I should know?" I asked Martin.

"The first word you need to learn is 'Oida'" he replied. "It doesn't exactly mean anything, it's more of an exclamation when you're frustrated or surprised."

"Oida," I repeated the word, having never heard it before. While I had spent a few months in Berlin back in 2013, I had forgotten most of the German I had learned. Plus, it was quite different from Austrian

German, not just when it came to words, but the dialect as well.

Fifteen hours later, sleepy and full of fast food, Martin and I pulled into the driveway of a bustling Airbnb in Berkeley. The political meetup turned out to be larger than expected. Some of the most prominent online political commentators and activists showed up, all crammed together in one house. I won't reveal most names, as I suspect certain people would prefer not to be mentioned, but our time together proved to be memorable. Most of the people in the house had right-wing sympathies. However, there were still a lot of political disagreements, making for a slew of interesting debates.

The wildest night of the trip occurred when the men went to see a movie at the theater, leaving me, Lauren, and a journalist friend named Cassandra Fairbanks alone at the Airbnb. Back then, I knew Cassandra better from her online image than in real life. Beautiful, with olive skin and blue eyes, which were often lined in heavy makeup, she never hesitated to say exactly what was on her mind. If she didn't like a particular person, she would let that person know, often with the help of a few curse words. Personally, I found her authenticity refreshing. She was a splash of cool water in a dry desert climate where many were either too fearful or too dishonest to say what they were truly thinking.

Lauren, Cassandra, and I were gathered in the back bedroom, dressing up to go out to eat, when we heard something shatter in the front of the Airbnb. It sounded like someone had hurled a rock through the sliding glass door. The patter of footsteps followed, as if someone was running through the Airbnb.

"Lock the door," Lauren gasped, and then lunged to do it herself.

"Is it a burglar? Or Antifa? Holy shit, what if it's Antifa?" Cassandra darted around the bedroom, searching for her phone.

"Out the window, out the window," Lauren cried. She leapt onto the bed, swinging her legs over the window ledge. Cassandra followed. Her form-fitting dress, clinched tight around her thighs, almost ripping as she scrambled onto the roof.

There wasn't time to look for my shoes. Barefoot, with a pink comb in hand, I hopped out the window after them. The comb wasn't sharp, but I figured that, if necessary, I could use it to cause a scratch or two.

"What do we do now?" Lauren whispered hoarsely.

"Over there." Cassandra nodded at a low wall on the edge of the roof. "Let's hide."

Tiptoeing across the roof, the three of us took cover behind the wall, me moving so fast I almost pitched headlong to the ground. Down on our bellies, the wall hiding us from view of the bedroom, we took a moment to catch our breath. I was nervous being so close to the ledge; the drop to the sidewalk was at least thirty feet, enough to crack my skull.

Risking a glance over the wall, I searched for signs of movement in the house. Since it was late in the evening, and all the lights inside the house were off except for the one in the bedroom, I couldn't make out much, not even the silhouette of a body. But every so often, we did hear noises resounding from somewhere inside.

"What makes you think it's Antifa?" I asked Cassandra, keeping my voice low.

"They've been searching for our Airbnb since the day we got here." Tears streamed down Cassandra's face as she wrestled with the keypad on her phone, trying to dial the police, while Lauren messaged the men at the movie theater, pleading for them to help us. Cassandra ended up being too hysterical to talk with the police, so I offered to do it myself.

"How many intruders are in the house, ma'am?" the policewoman asked.

"I'm not sure. At least one, maybe two," I said. "My friends and I are hiding on the roof. If they find us out here, there's nowhere for us to go. Please send help quickly."

I gave the policewoman our address and then handed the phone back to Cassandra. We spent the next ten minutes in a tense waiting game, the silence interrupted by a few muffled sobs from Lauren and Cassandra.

"It's going to be okay," I promised. For some reason, my panic button had failed to activate. At one point, I even started laughing, which caused Cassandra and Lauren to turn on me with irritated glares. I tried to shut myself up by covering my mouth with my hands, even tried biting my lips, but without success. Laughter has often been my way to cope with fear—laughter or an eerie mask of calm. Fear eventually does hit me, but it's always well after the fact, when the danger has passed, and I'm already safe.

"Shut up, Britt. It's not funny," Lauren said.

"What the hell is wrong with you?" Cassandra demanded. "We could die."

I pressed my palms more tightly over my mouth, feeling like some sort of monster.

The Berkeley police took over ten minutes to arrive. When their sirens could finally be heard wailing in the distance, and a series of flashing strobe lights could be seen weaving through the oncoming traffic, I shrank back in embarrassment and suddenly wished I had the ability to teleport back to Idaho. Not only had the Berkeley police dispatched five police cars; they had also called in a *fire truck*.

The men arrived at the same time, car tires screeching as the driver braked on the curb. They poured onto the street, their faces tight with anger, ready to take down whoever had broken into the house. When Martin caught sight of me, waving to him from the ledge of the roof, his expression became confused.

"Are you all right?" he shouted.

I nodded. Part of me felt guilty for the scene we had caused, and the other part felt humiliated by how stupid I looked, stranded on a rooftop in the dark, dressed in a black cocktail dress with bare feet, holding a pink comb.

The firemen launched a hook ladder onto the roof, then directed us to climb down. I knotted my dress between my legs before stepping onto the ladder, not wanting the crowds that had gathered below to get a view of my underwear. I hoped no Antifa were hiding out in the conflux of police, firemen, and spectators. I also hoped that no one had cameras. To my knowledge, the only person who filmed the spectacle was one of the men in our group, a prominent British political commentator.

Martin caught me in a hug when I stepped safely onto the sidewalk. He refused to let me go until the Berkeley police had finished sweeping the house. If you think we were embarrassed before, imagine how embarrassed we were when the police found *no traces* of anyone inside the Airbnb. Lauren, Cassandra, and I insisted we hadn't imagined the break-in. We *had* heard a loud sound like shattering glass, and we had also heard footsteps. Of course, the Berkeley police thought we were crazy. So did our male friends. One of them even spent thirty minutes walking us through the whole scenario logically, explaining to us how it was impossible that anyone could have been inside the house.

Looking back, that night is now a comical memory, especially during a time when the stakes were lower, when the political world seemed less cruel, and it was still easy to laugh in the face of the average threat.

AN AMERICAN IN EUROPE

Martin and I flew to Austria at the end of September. Since we were serious about our relationship, we wanted to spend as much time together as possible. I planned to continue my political work from Austria. However, being in Europe, I figured the most practical use of my time would be to report on European news. By now, the right-wing movement in the United States had exploded in growth. Dozens of political commentators had created YouTube channels and were pumping out multiple videos a day related to American news. In Europe, on the other hand, few English-speaking alternative media outlets and independent journalists covered the news.

It was my first visit to Austria. From the moment I arrived in the capital city of Vienna, I was captivated. Rolling green mountains hid the setting sun, and the evening alpenglow cast romantic shadows across the city. Its famous Jugendstil buildings with their sinuous curves and ornate façades were nothing short of majestic. Like the Italian culture, the Austrian culture was much more relaxed than I was accustomed to. Often, the Austrians would spend their mornings or afternoons lounging inside cozy cafes, reading the daily paper, smoking cigarettes, and drinking piping hot Melanges, which is the Viennese version of a cappuccino.

Martin's family welcomed me as one of their own. I had once been told it was impossible to get an accurate sense of someone without first meeting their family. In meeting Martin's parents and brothers, I was further convinced of Martin's good character. The family placed value on keeping together as a strong unit, acquiring a university degree, having personal integrity and ambition, and, most importantly, their Catholic faith.

Martin also introduced me to his friends. Most were members of Generation Identity, known in Austria as Identitäre Bewegung Österreich. In Austria, the movement was both influential and successful, boasting hundreds of activists and thousands of sympathizers. All under age thirty, the activists understood their hierarchical roles and always exercised discipline when carrying them out. Some planned peaceful demonstrations, info-zones, and banner actions, during which other activists took photos and filmed footage. The photos and footage were then edited into slick, professional videos and posted publicly online.

I was nervous, even a bit intimidated, when I first met the Austrian identitarians. Smartly dressed and neatly-groomed, most of the men sported sleek undercuts, while both the men and the women took pride in maintaining their physical fitness. All of them were intelligent and well-educated, capable of speaking multiple languages. Best of all, they were some of the kindest and most welcoming people I had ever met. The mainstream media wanted the world to believe they were a militant faction of violent extremists, but in reality, they were average university students of varying political and religious beliefs who were united under a common cause: stopping mass migration and the Islamization of

Europe. I recall being confused by their excitement to meet me—I wasn't well-known in Austria, after all—but I later found out that this was because they were shocked Martin finally had a girlfriend.

During my first week in Austria, I turned twenty-five. Martin, who wanted to make the day extra special since I couldn't spend it with my family, spared no expense. We breakfasted at the famous Gloriette next to Schönbrunn Palace, and in the afternoon, we took a romantic carriage ride through the bustling Museum Quarter. We explored the city and ended up visiting the Imperial Treasury, which housed the Holy Lance of St. Stephen and the Imperial Crown of the Holy Roman Empire of the German Nation. In the evening, Martin surprised me with a party. And then he gave me a gift which I still treasure to this day: a traditional *dirndl*, which is a dress consisting of a bodice, skirt, blouse, and apron, and it's traditionally worn by women and girls in Austria, southern Germany, Switzerland, Liechtenstein and Alpine regions of Italy. The amount of planning and creativity Martin put into each gift was overwhelming. Outside of my family, I had never been treated with such care. It was the best birthday I ever had.

But we were soon back to work.

We spent the next several weeks on the road, attending various political events across Europe, surviving on fuel station coffee and sandwiches. I filmed videos whenever I could. I wanted to show my American audience on-the-ground footage of the what was happening in Europe. I published a video about the PEGIDA movement, German patriots who had been assembling in Dresden to protest mass Islamic migration since 2014. We went on to attend the Frankfurt Book Fair, where Martin had been invited to present his new book, *Identitär!* The event was ambushed by Antifa, who swarmed the book hall, chanting slogans, blowing whistles, and jostling attendees until the police intervened. Then we traveled to Hungary, where I published an interview with the Mayor of Ásotthalom, László Toroczkai, who was responsible for erecting a border fence that reduced illegal immigration by more than ninety-nine percent.[91] Mayor László revealed that his people had sympathized with the plight of the migrants and wanted to help them. However, they changed their minds when it became clear the migrants were similar to those they had taken in after the Yugoslavian War in the 1990s.

"We had very bad experiences with these migrants," Mayor László explained. He told me his town was poor, but that arriving migrants were full of money because they were aiding human smugglers. "These human smugglers came here from everywhere. We could catch criminals from Italy, from Sicily, from Chechnya, from Pakistan and from all of Arabic countries. This was the biggest international business for the mafia, to organize this immigration. And this is why I say always this immigration is a crime. And those politicians who support this immigration are criminals who cooperate with the mafia, the international mafia."[92]

I wasn't shocked by Mayor László's words. It was no secret that there were other benefits to supporting mass immigration. Not everyone who sought to provide them aid was motivated by humanitarian reasons. For example, in the United States, certain groups like the Democratic Party profit from supporting mass immigration electorally. The vast majority of immigrants vote Democrat, which accounts for an irreplaceable portion of their voter base.[93] Numerous big corporations also make a profit.[94] Using the HB1 visa system, these corporations bring in thousands of immigrants who work for lower wages than regular American citizens, consequently robbing American citizens of their jobs.

MEETING TOMMY ROBINSON

In October 2017, Martin and I traveled to London. Martin had been tasked with overseeing the launch of a new branch of Generation Identity in the United Kingdom, while I had scheduled a handful of interviews with the British punditocracy.

My biggest interview was with independent journalist and anti-Islam activist, Tommy Robinson. Although his birth name was Stephen

Yaxley-Lennon, he had taken on the pseudonym, Tommy Robinson, sometime in the early stages of his career. I had interviewed Tommy over Skype in the past, but it was the first time I had met him in person.

Short, yet stalky, like a bulldog that keeps snapping its leash, Tommy spent his days barreling fearlessly into even the most heated of situations, all for the purpose of journalistic footage and interviews. His colorful past made for a captivating interview, one in which he shared his predictions for the future of Europe.

"If you bring us back six years, and you would've told people that in six years' time this will be happening…children's concerts being blown up, people being mowed down in the streets in cars, women sitting and eating in restaurants in London and people getting up and slitting their throats…people would've been like nah, never, that can't happen," Tommy said.

He went on to clarify that the horrific events mentioned had occurred in the past few months alone. But numerous other attacks had occurred over the past six years: 86 killed and 400 injured during the Bastille Day terror attack in Nice, France.[95] 130 killed and 352 injured during the night of the Bataclan Theatre Massacre terror attack in Paris, France.[96] 32 killed and more than 300 injured during the Brussels Bombings terror attack in Brussels, Belgium.[97] 12 killed and 49 injured during the Christmas market terror attack in Berlin, Germany.[98] The list went on and on.

"That's happened, that's where we're at, and it's only going to get worse," Tommy continued. "I describe it as this is a trailer for a movie that's about to play. And we all know that a trailer is a two-minute clip. Now we've got a mass movie of complete carnage coming our way in Europe."[99]

Only a year earlier, Tommy's prediction would have terrified me. But my time in politics had hardened me in a way that, for better or for worse, left me utterly desensitized to the horrors that occurred on the daily. It wasn't that I didn't care; it was that I had seen too much.

Our interview lasted about fifteen minutes. I wanted to speak with

Tommy longer, particularly about his time in prison, but he was pressed for time. We agreed to meet for another interview the next time I was in London.

Meanwhile, Martin was hard at work launching the UK branch of Generation Identity. Candidates from Britain and Northern Ireland had rented an Airbnb outside of London, where Martin spent two days giving a masterclass about the identitarian movement—the core tenant being that it opposed mass migration and the Islamization of Europe. Private interviews were held with each candidate. Ultimately, not everyone was accepted as an activist, either because they were too extreme in their political views or because they gave off an infiltrator vibe. Martin's instincts regarding infiltration were spot on, for two of the female candidates turned out to be moles. The first woman had secretly recorded footage of our meeting for an ITV Exposure documentary about Britain's far-right. And the second woman was an extremism researcher named Julia Ebner, who went on to publish a book about her experiences infiltrating various right-wing movements. Given that the book was rife with sensationalism, and sometimes even outright falsehood—such as including the provably false rumor that one of Martin's supporters made a Nazi salute at the Frankfurt Book Fair—no one on the right-wing took the book seriously.

The official Generation Identity UK launch took place on Westminster Bridge. Nearly a dozen activists hung a yellow-and-black banner off the side of the bridge bearing the slogan 'Stop Islamization.' Thankfully, no policemen or protestors interfered. I managed to get some useful footage, while a few others snapped professional photos from afar.

Generation Identity UK posted a statement to social media immediately after the action, explaining the symbolism of the location for the stunt.

"On 22 March 2017, a terrorist attack took place on Westminster Bridge. The Islamist inspired attack killed five people and injured more than fifty. London Mayor, Sadiq Khan, believes that the threat of terror attacks are 'part and parcel of living in a big city.'" On the contrary, we think that the source of Islamization lies in mass immigration, which must be stopped."[100]

Shortly after the Generation Identity UK launch, I returned to Idaho. Since I didn't have a visa to live in Austria, I was legally obligated to return to the United States. It was difficult for me to leave Martin, but I reminded myself how lucky I was to have found him. While I don't believe in love at first sight, I do believe in knowing at first sight that you *will* fall in love. That's how it was for me. I was certain from the moment Martin and I met, and every moment afterwards, until, somewhere along the way, it happened—not on a specific day or at a specific time, but somewhere in between the moments.

I've often been asked what it is about Martin that made me fall in love with him. It's a difficult question to answer, as there are too many reasons to give, but admiration is near the top of the list. I admire his goals, his discipline, his perseverance, and strength under pressure. I admire his kindness, his happy warrior attitude, and the fact that he always upholds his words with actions. But perhaps, most importantly, I admire his fearlessness. Whether he is stranded on a ship in the middle of the Mediterranean Sea, rappelling onto the rooftop of the Burgtheater to hang a political banner, or caught in a violent mob of Antifa, he never breaks form. In fact, it's in such dangerous situations that Martin seems to thrive most.

"I want to live my life in a way that if it was a YouTube video, no one would be able to click away," he once told me.

And this is exactly what he does. If there is any hope left for the future of Europe, it's thanks to him and the thousands of other patriots like him who, in the face of every feasible attack, manage to press onward, proving to the rest of the world that there is still strength left in the European spirit.

POLITICAL CENSORSHIP ESCALATES

Homelife in Idaho raced by at a chaotic and blue-streak pace. I made an effort to go on outings with my family, while also keeping myself busy with political projects. My friend, Nick Monroe, and I filmed a six-part video series about the life and work of the billionaire investor, George Soros. Nick worked for weeks to compile the necessary research, after which we spent over one-hundred hours filming and editing.

On the sidelines of the Soros project, I managed to maintain my weekly schedule of interviewing right-wing political activists. As far as I was concerned, I should've been allowed to interview anyone, from people I disagreed with to people I disliked on a personal level. The problem was that leftists were in the midst of incorporating a guilt-by-association narrative into politics. This resulted in countless conservatives breaking away from one another, afraid of being held accountable for one other's words and actions—even if, in private, the average conservative agreed that the notion of guilt-by-association was ridiculous. Simply chatting with or interviewing another person didn't equate to endorsing all of that person's beliefs. In a world with such a standard, nobody would be speaking to anyone. Political, religious, and cultural discourse would cease to exist altogether.

President Trump, meanwhile, was on the tail-end of his first year in office. Reports from the White House revealed a slew of positive achievements such as withdrawing from the Trans-Pacific Partnership, declaring a nationwide public health emergency on the opioid epidemic, and enacting historic tax and regulatory reform that contributed to economic growth and pushed the stock market to record heights.[101] But despite these achievements, many Americans were eager for him to start safeguarding our first amendment rights.

Leftists, having realized they would face no consequences for weaponizing political censorship, were intensifying their attacks. New days brought new bans, with countless rightists being purged from big tech platforms like YouTube, Facebook, Twitter, and Instagram. Many of us suspected that leftists would eventually seek to expand their censorship tactics, and we were ultimately proven correct. Overtime, the censorship escalated, with right-wing patriots being denied access to payment processing platforms such as PayPal and Stripe, and even to their own private banks. Companies like Uber, Lyft, Airbnb and Mailchimp also followed suit. The fact that American politicians were standing by as thousands of their countrymen were effectively being 'un-personed' for having the wrong ideological views was a scandal in itself.

Personally, during the course of my own political career, I was banned from Patreon, PayPal, GoFundMe, DonorBox, and Mailchimp. I was also banned twice from Instagram; however, my account was reinstated on both occasions due to the fact that I never broke terms of service.

Martin, on the other hand, has been the target of an unprecedented censorship. Between the years 2017 and 2020, he was banned from nineteen separate bank accounts, as well as every major social media and fundraising platform: YouTube, Facebook, Twitter, Instagram, Stripe, PayPal, Mailchimp, TikTok, Kickstarter, and more.[102] The strategy was always the same: leftists who detested Martin painted slanderous and deceitful portraits of him in the form of media articles or reports, which they then used to pressure Big Tech platforms into banning him. The strategy proved effective—so effective, in fact, that even pictures of Martin's face appear to now be banned on Facebook and Instagram. I say 'appeared to be' because Facebook and Instagram never released an official statement on the matter. While a few people can still get away with posting photos of Martin, many others, myself included, were forced to remove all our personal photos of Martin under the claim that he fell into the category of 'dangerous persons and organizations.'[103] To this day, I can't get over the reprehensible dishonesty of this claim. Martin isn't dangerous, nor is he a criminal. He's never committed a crime or encouraged violence in his entire life. On the contrary, he only advocates for peaceful political activism. The reality is that the left knows they don't stand a chance against his ideas.

If they allowed him a level playing field, he would win over too many minds and gain too much support. He would be too much of a threat.

To no one's surprise, since leftists weren't on the receiving end of the censorship, the majority of them reacted to our bans with celebratory applause. They argued that big tech companies like YouTube and Twitter were free to censor speech as they saw fit given that they were private platforms. In response, rightists argued that big tech companies were acting as publishers rather than platforms; therefore, at the very least, they should lose their protection status under Section 230 of the Communications Decency Act, which states that platforms cannot be held legally liable for the content posted by their users.

There was also the undeniable fact that the big tech companies were monopolized. What was the alternative to YouTube and Twitter? To PayPal and Stripe? Efforts were made to launch alternative platforms such as Gab, SubscribeStar and BitChute, but none of these companies were able to gain a strong foothold because the mainstream media smeared them as platforms for extremists.

The truth was that the power to control speech had become radically concentrated. And worse, the few elites who wielded this power weren't politically neutral. Most of them were leftists, with zero interest in protecting the rights of those they ideologically disagreed with, which proved to be disastrous for the long-term health and civility of political discourse. Leftists fostered extremist online communities, often even openly advocating for violence,[104] with little to no repercussions, while the right was forced to tip-toe about. Granted, some right-wingers were similarly extreme, for which they deserved condemnation, but these extremists were largely on the fringes, devoid of significant influence on mainstream politics. Many of us feared how such biased censorship would not only affect our livelihoods and our ability to achieve our political goals, but also the outcome of the 2020 presidential election. In our view, the only feasible solution was for Congress or the White House to start regulating big tech. Relentlessly we campaigned for such measures, but our efforts fell on deaf ears.

THE FREEDOM PARTY

I remained in Idaho until I was legally allowed reentry into Austria. I enjoyed the months I spent with my family, especially my parents and Nicole, but I also felt torn—between two countries, between two very different worlds. Fortunately, my family had grown accustomed to my absence. Often, they were worried for my safety, but I was grateful they saw the value in my political work. They also trusted Martin would take care of me.

The first half of my stay in Vienna was peaceful. Taking a break in my routine of constant travel, I opted to stay in one place for a change. I wanted to become familiar with the city and spent days exploring, getting lost in the rich Viennese art and culture. Some of my favorite tourist spots were the Volksgarten and the Türkenschanzpark. I frequented a few cozy cafés where I dedicated free time to writing, researching, and reading. As strange as it was, I quickly came to feel at home in Austria, not just when it came to the country, but to the people and the culture as well. The sole obstacle was the language barrier, but I knew that if I applied myself, I would be able to learn.

In the midst of studying German, I also educated myself on Austrian politics. I learned that Austria, which was a parliamentary democracy, had a president who served as the head of state and a Chancellor who served as the head of government. At the time, the two most powerful political parties were the Austrian People's Party (ÖVP) and the Freedom Party (FPÖ). In December 2017, these two parties had formed a government coalition, with Sebastian Kurz of the Austrian People's Party serving as Chancellor and Heinz-Christian Strache of the the Freedom Party serving as Vice-Chancellor.

Chancellor Sebastian Kurz and his party were conservatives. At just thirty-one years old, Kurz's youthful charisma seemed to appeal to the average Austrian. Blue-eyed and baby-faced, he was often listed among the world's most handsome leaders. In my opinion, however, like most politicians, Kurz was more of an opportunist than a genuine actor. He often seemed to wish to appease the mainstream media, and even worse, to piggy-back off of political trends. Before 2017, Kurz's party had been liberal and socialistic. But leading up to the 2017 election, Kurz's party had shifted dramatically to the right. The reason for this was that many Austrians no longer supported pro-migration policies due to their negative experiences with the 2015 Migrant Crisis. While many right-wingers initially believed this shift to be a good thing, it proved to be ineffective in the long-term because it was superficial. Rather than enact strong policies against mass migration and the abuse of the asylum system, Kurz instead contented himself with enacting watered-down versions of these policies.

Vice-Chancellor Heinz-Christian Strache and the Freedom Party, meanwhile, were right-wing populists. At nearly age fifty, Strache still radiated a boyish energy. He grinned brightly in most media photos, wearing posh suits, trademark black-rimmed glasses, and sometimes a colorful scarf. Despite rumors that he was a bit of a diva, his political positions seemed to be much more consistent and genuine than Kurz's: preventing mass migration, the population replacement of the Austrian people, the abuse of the asylum system and the Islamization of Europe. In fact, much of the Freedom Party's political positions were similar to those of Generation Identity's. And therein lied the reason why the mainstream media despised them. Not only did the mainstream media relentlessly attack the Freedom Party with hit pieces and smears, they also attempted to connect them to Generation Identity in an effort to damage their reputation. Unfortunately for the mainstream media, however, no such evidence existed. The Freedom Party and Generation Identity kept a healthy distance at all times. Generation Identity had no interest in getting involved in party politics. In their view, their job was to fight on the metapolitical level.

Overall, I felt politically secure in Austria. Like the United States, Austria's right-wing government seemed to wish to thwart the totalitarian agenda of the left. At least for a time, their pledge to uphold freedom and democracy seemed as if it was destined to last.

120 DECIBELS

Sometime in February 2018, a new movement called '120 Decibels' caught my attention. The movement, comprised of young Austrian and German women, spoke out against the rape and murder of European women by migrants. I soon learned that they had chosen the title 120 Decibels because it's the pitch of a standard pocket alarm. Apparently, many European women had taken to carrying these pocket alarms as a way to signal for help in emergencies.

Before lending my voice to the movement, I took some time to get to know the activists involved. Most of the girls were in their late teens and twenties. Some had become politized by the 2015 Migrant Crisis, while others had taken an interest in politics much earlier on. None of them held extreme views, such as all migrants being violent rapists, they were simply tired of being ignored, of witnessing the crimes committed against European women overlooked by their politicians and silenced by their media. Many of them felt they had no choice but to take matters into their own hands.

I agreed with the girls' concerns, so I made it a goal to help promote their message. Together, we managed to make one of 120 Decibels' videos go viral, which naturally prompted an angry reaction from the mainstream media. 'Far-right activists and 'alt-right' trolls are using the #MeToo movement to bolster their xenophobia,' *Salon* published in a headline.[105]

I remember being shocked when I read the *Salon* article, which referred to migrant sexual assault as a 'nonexistent European crimewave.' I also remember thinking that the mainstream media's flat-out denial of these copious crimes was exactly what made 120 Decibels so important. The famed #MeToo movement, which protested sexual assault, had barely acknowledged the existence of migrant sexual assault. There have been numerous cases across Europe over the years,[106] with little reporting on the topic; however, in the eyes of the left, acknowledging the existence of migrant sexual assault is 'an act of racism.' This flawed trend of thought led police in the United Kingdom to spend years covering for rape gangs. In January 2020, a detective-ranked whistleblower published a 145-page report which accused the Greater Manchester Police of turning a blind eye to crimes of a rape gang that consisted predominantly of Pakistani men.[107] Allegedly, the gang allowed 97 men to freely abuse 57 young British girls. The Greater Manchester Police were 'aware of sensitive community issues' and the 'incitement of racial hatred in the area at the time.' In other words, the police were worried that the arrests would 'stoke racial tensions.'[108]

Since 2016, a number of people have questioned my focus on migrant sexual assault, with some even deeming it xenophobic, which is utterly ridiculous. My motivations are both straightforward and reasonable. I focus on spotlighting migrant sexual assault because it's underreported and often denied altogether by the mainstream media.

That said, I strongly oppose *all* forms of sexual assault, regardless of the ethnicity and political affiliation of the perpetrator. Which is why I was initially happy about the birth of the #MeToo movement. Despite the fact that the majority of #MeToo's activists were leftists, I still believed that a movement in which thousands of men and women were uniting for the sole purpose of campaigning against sexual assault was remarkable. One of the most well-known #MeToo cases involved former Hollywood film producer, Harvey Weinstein, who was accused by 87 different people of 'inappropriate to criminal behavior ranging from requests for massages to intimidating sexual advances to rape.'[109] Most disturbingly, Weinstein's predatory nature was an open secret in Hollywood for years, with many reportedly being aware of his alleged crimes, but doing nothing to intervene.[110]

On the heels of Harvey Weinstein's downfall, the #MeToo movement experienced worldwide attention and success…at least for a time. Here and there, it suffered blows to its credibility over false or wildly exaggerated allegations made in its name; however, the most significant blow came when the #MeToo movement started to be weaponized for political gain. For example, the case of Associate Supreme Court Justice, Brett

Kavanaugh, who endured a grueling smear campaign spearheaded by the Democrats during his confirmation hearings in late 2018. I call it a smear campaign because, despite multiple women accusing Kavanaugh of having committed sexual misconduct, the FBI were unable to find any evidence to substantiate the allegations.[111] Further, some of Kavanaugh's accusers ultimately recanted.[112]

Another example occurred in early 2020, when Democratic presidential candidate, Joe Biden, was accused of sexual harassment and sexual assault by eight different women.[113] Personally, I consider the allegations against Joe Biden credible, but I also believe that he deserves due process—a guilty conviction is not for the mob, but for the courts to establish. The #MeToo movement, on the other hand, largely brushed aside the allegations. Had they simply disbelieved the allegations, that would've been one thing. However, due to the fact that the #MeToo movement had coined the slogan 'Believe All Women,' many people found their reaction to be hypocritical. One of #MeToo's most popular activists, Hollywood actress Alyssa Milano, announced that she still supported and admired Biden despite the allegations.[114] Many others followed suit, with one female author penning an article for the *New York Times* entitled 'Believe All Women is a Right-Wing Trap.'[115] And another female author penning an article for the *New York Times*, in which she stated: 'Compared with the good Mr. Biden can do, the cost of dismissing Tara Reade (one of Biden's accusers)— and, worse, weakening the voices of future survivors—is worth it.'[116]

In the end, no one but the #MeToo movement was to blame for the loss of its credibility. The #MeToo activists themselves were the ones who killed it.

SPEAKER'S CORNER

In March 2018, Martin was invited to deliver a speech in the United Kingdom by the youth branch of the UKIP political party, entitled Young Independence. Martin had received a similar invitation by the same group a few months earlier, but the event had been cancelled due to threats from Antifa.[117] Since Antifa had succeeded in shutting down the event the first time, I was hardly surprised when a representative of Young Independence informed Martin that the event had been threatened a second time, causing the venue to pull out.

In a statement, Young Independence said, "It is with deep regret that we have been forced to cancel our Free Speech Conference this Saturday, once more due to security threats from the far left. Despite booking the venue and informing them of our planned speakers well in advance, they have blocked our conference from taking place and decided to inform us just six days before it was due to take place, leaving us with no time to rearrange with another venue."[118]

In my view, the cancellation was a challenge that intensified my determination to make it to the United Kingdom. I was tired of Antifa using intimidation tactics to shut down our events. I wasn't afraid of them, not to mention, I had already arranged interviews with Tommy Robinson and a British classical liberal named Carl Benjamin, who used the pseudonym 'Sargon of Akkad' in his YouTube videos.

"We should go to the UK, and you should still give your speech," I told Martin. "We just need to find a new venue."

"I don't need a new venue," Martin replied. "I'll give my speech at Speaker's Corner."

Located in London, Speaker's Corner was an area on the northeast corner of Hyde Park instituted for public-speaking and debate. Historical figures such as George Orwell and Karl Marx had spoken there in the past. Among many London residents, it was understood to be a 'last bastion of free speech.'

Martin and I agreed on the idea. We arranged for the Generation Identity UK members to provide security for the event, and then filmed a YouTube video, announcing our plans and inviting our subscribers to attend.

The month was early March 2018. Nothing particularly crazy had happened to us yet that year, except for one incident in January, when

Antifa firebombed Martin's car. Having grown accustomed to peaceful days, I think it's safe to say that Martin and I were both unprepared for the catastrophe that awaited us in London.

6

We shall soon be in a world in which a man may be howled
down for saying that two and two make four, in which people
will persecute the heresy of calling a triangle a three-sided figure,
and hang a man for maddening a mob with the news that grass is green.
—G.K. Chesterton

VIENNA, EUROPE
MARCH 2018

Before sunrise on Friday, March 9, Martin and I boarded a train to the
Vienna International Airport. The morning showed no hint of trouble.
A late-winter fog covered the blooming countryside, where cows had
been let out to graze. Huddled together in the train cabin, Martin and
I spent the morning drinking coffee and laughing over hilarious tweets.

We arrived over an hour early for our flight. Relaxing inside an
airport café, we ordered a hot breakfast of ham and eggs. I recall being
acutely aware of German being spoken around me as we ate.

"Servus. Wie geht es dir?" (Hello. How are you?)

"Möchtest du einen Kaffee?" (Would you like a coffee?)

"Um wie viel Uhr geht dein Flug?" (What time is your flight?)

I was getting used to hearing German spoken on a daily basis, but
the loud hum of a bar or restaurant could still be overwhelming. I
chalked this up to the fact that I was only at a beginner's level. After
another year or two of study, I hoped it would sound as familiar to my
ears as English.

An Austrian fan recognized Martin on our way through airport security.

"What a coincidence to meet you." The man laughed. "I'm on my way to London to watch your speech."

The run-in felt like a positive omen, a sign that we had made the right decision to go ahead with the speech. I didn't for one moment consider the possibility that the UK Home Office might have watched Martin's and my YouTube video about Speaker's Corner and that they were lying in wait for our arrival.

I felt a rush of enthusiasm on the flight. After a lengthy break from political-related traveling, I was looking forward to getting back in the arena. Although I had reservations about being in the public eye, Martin's presence eased my discomfort. He offered security and leadership, born from years of experience, that I hadn't previously known. I eventually came to trust that, no matter how formidable the path ahead might become, I was no longer alone in walking it. He would always be beside me.

The morning was still early when Martin and I landed at the Luton Airport. The chilly weather echoed that of Vienna, though the surrounding landscape was dreary, like a painting in a hundred shades of gray. The long, wet runway quivered with smog that seemed to choke the life out of anything resembling a plant. The goliath airport, with its sterile fixtures and glaring white walls, felt more like a prison than a structure where one was allowed to freely come and go. I wondered how it was possible for employees to work in such a place long-term without getting depressed.

Martin and I were forced to separate at passport control. Since Martin was an EU citizen and I was a non-EU citizen, we had to pass through different security lines. It was for this reason that I failed to notice the border police confiscate Martin's passport and instruct him to take a seat in the waiting section.

"Are you traveling alone?" they asked him. "Where's your girlfriend?"

Martin didn't respond. He hoped that, unlike him, the border police didn't have my name on a watchlist. When Martin caught sight of me in line, he gestured for me to go through passport control alone. I knew he was just trying to look out for me, but I wasn't about to abandon him. Plus, if the border police had detained him, they were likely to detain me, as well. I might as well save everyone time.

"I'm Martin's girlfriend," I answered, stepping out of line. "Is there a problem?"

"Give me your passport, ma'am," one of the border police said.

I did as he instructed and then followed the border policeman to the waiting section. He placed me in a chair at the opposite end of the row where Martin sat. For some reason, he didn't want us within talking distance of one another.

"Don't speak to one another or use your cell phones," he warned.

I tried to keep a polite smile. The way the border policeman regarded Martin and me, with a twisted smirk of contempt, suggested that he had been briefed on our political work. The fact that he was a foreigner, either an immigrant or the descendent of immigrants, didn't help matters. He had probably been fed the lie that we were 'racists who hated people like him.'

Eyeing the wall-clock, I was alarmed to find that my interview with the political YouTuber, Sargon of Akkad, was scheduled to take place in less than two hours. Even if I made it through passport control, I still needed to check into my hotel, freshen up, and then travel to the interview meeting point.

"I have an appointment in a few hours," I told the border policeman. "Is there a chance we'll be free before then?"

The border policeman shrugged.

I sank back in my chair, accepting the fact that, for the time being, I wasn't going to get any straight answers. The border police likely didn't know any more about the situation than I did. They were just underlings, after all. The final decision would be made by the higher ups at the Home Office.

I passed the time reading a book. Every so often, I stole a glance at

Martin, who was watching me with a smile.

"Are you okay?" He mouthed the question so the border police wouldn't hear.

"Yes, don't worry," I mouthed back.

An hour passed.

I managed to sneak my phone from my pocket and send a quick text message to my friend Michael. Martin and I had arranged to meet him and two other friends, Lucy and Suzanna, at the baggage claim. I assumed they were worried since our flight had landed over an hour ago.

Martin and I have been detained at the border, I wrote. *Can't make it to the interview. Please tell Sargon I'm sorry.*

Not a moment after I had pressed 'send,' the border police returned and confiscated our rucksacks and cell phones.

"Come with us," they said. "We need to search your belongings."

The border police helped us retrieve our luggage and then led us into a poorly ventilated room arranged with long metal tables. The tabletops looked like they hadn't been cleaned in weeks. Alarmed, I watched one of the border police rifle through my wallet as if it were his own. He inspected the receipts inside.

"What do you plan to do in London? he asked.

"Interviews, mostly," I replied. "One with Tommy Robinson and a few other political activists."

"Do you also plan to interview members of the Ku Klux Klan?" he asked.

It was an effort to keep from laughing. Clearly, the man didn't actually know what Tommy believed. He had likely gotten his information about Tommy from the lying mainstream media, but regardless, his statement made him look stupid. Raising awareness about the negatives of Islam, as Tommy did, had nothing to do with the KKK.

The border police searched my suitcase from top to bottom: my camera case, my make-up bag, my clothes—down to the lint in my pockets. I looked over my possessions, strewn like innards across the tabletop, abhorring the invasion of my privacy. The border police were clearly hunting for a controversial item that could be used as grounds to ban me from the country. Unfortunately for them, the most controversial item in my possession was a sticker that read: Stand Your Ground.

Once the luggage search was complete, I was locked inside a windowless interrogation room, shaped like a square, with walls the color of old cardboard. Aside from a table and two plastic chairs, there were no other fixtures.

I took a seat at the table, grateful for a brief respite. What a bizarre turn the day had taken. At that very moment, I was supposed to be interviewing Sargon of Akkad, but instead I was locked away in the Luton Airport, being interrogated for a 'thought crime.'

I felt no anxiety over the outcome. The situation was too ridiculous to be taken seriously. My only concern was for my family, whom I suspected were sick with worry, but it was impossible for me to call them since the border police had confiscated my phone.

Five minutes later, my interrogator arrived. He looked young, perhaps even close to my age. With his scruffy crew cut and wrinkled button-down, he exuded a nervous energy that made me wonder if it was his first day on the job. Booting the door open with his shoe, he shuffled inside with a pen, a notepad, and a coffee-stained paper cup.

"Do you know where my boyfriend is?" I asked.

"He's also being questioned," the man answered, taking the second chair.

I knew Martin was more experienced than me. I knew he was infinitely better equipped to handle the situation, but still, I couldn't help but worry.

"Why did you come to England?" the interrogator began.

"To film my boyfriend's speech," I replied. "I also want to interview Tommy Robinson and a political YouTuber named Sargon of Akkad."

The interrogator scribbled my response onto his notepad before moving on. "Are you a member of Generation Identity?"

"No, the movement is strictly for Europeans. It doesn't exist in America. But I often report on the movement's demonstrations. I also support it."

The interrogator nodded, and then took a big swallow of coffee. For about thirty minutes, his questions rolled out in the same fashion: "What is Generation Identity? What are your political views? Why do you want to interview Tommy Robinson? What questions do you plan to ask Tommy Robinson?"

His final questions left me bewildered. Why should anyone care why I wanted to interview Tommy? He had been interviewed by dozens of mainstream media outlets in the past. Why was it suddenly a problem when I wanted to interview him?

Following the interrogation, the man fingerprinted me with a kit of pungent black ink and then locked me in a holding room. Martin, who had also completed his interrogation, stood in a holding room opposite mine. Apparently, it would still take a few more hours before the final decision regarding our entry into the UK was made. At this point, I already knew the answer would be no. The border police were clearly stalling in order to give the Home Office enough time to invent a plausible reason to ban us.

My holding room was small and poorly lit. In one corner was a bathroom stall with a thin privacy curtain; in another, stretched a long couch, bookended by two squishy beanbag chairs. The wall-television was broken, but there was a bookshelf that offered an acceptable replacement. The room had a single door, which the border police kept locked, and one window, through which I could see into Martin's holding room.

Figuring I would be locked up a while, I made myself comfortable on one of the bean-bag chairs. My mood was calm, my stress-level was low, but I wished I had my phone. Unfortunately, my only options were to read, eat from a bowl of snacks, or make use of a notepad I had found on the windowsill. I settled on the notepad, using it to scribble down some random thoughts.

Martin, who also had a notepad, used his for a very different purpose. Sketching out silly pictures and funny notes, he pressed them against the window for me to read. His antics kept a smile on my face the whole night. I was convinced that, even if we somehow ended up in a situation where we were on the brink of death, he would find a way to make me laugh.

THE UNITED KINGDOM BAN

"Wake up, Miss Pettibone." A deep, accented voice, roused me from sleep. I sat up in the beanbag chair, blinking my eyes until the hazy outline of a uniformed immigration officer sharpened into focus. I wondered how late it was, how long I had been sleeping. I didn't even remember falling asleep. "You've been denied entry into the United Kingdom," the officer continued. "All the information you need is listed in this document."

> Immigration Act of 1971
> Notice of Refusal of Leave to Enter
> To: Brittany Alicia Merced Pettibone
> You have asked for leave to enter the United Kingdom as a visitor for five day but as you stated in your interview, I have reasons to believe that you are seeking admission to the United Kingdom to interview Tommy Robinson—a far right leader whose materials and speeches incite racial hatred.
> You stated at the interview that you will be filming your boyfriend Martin Sellner speech at speakers corner in London Hyde Park. Your boyfriend admitted at the interview to being a co-founder of the Austrian branch of 'Generation Identity' which is viewed in the UK as a right wing organization.
> Furthermore, your boyfriend have in his possession the Leaflets with scenarios regarding possible violence at his speech.
> I believe that your planned activities whilst in the United

Kingdom bear a serious threat to the fundamental interests of society and are likely to insight tensions between local communities in the United Kingdom.

You have not sought entry under any other provisions under the immigration rules.

I therefore refuse you leave to enter the United Kingdom.

My first thought was that whoever had typed the document wasn't a native English speaker. Highly unprofessional, it was riddled with spelling errors. My second thought was that it was the most groundless document I had ever read. Tommy Robinson wasn't an inciter of 'racial hatred.' He opposed the religion of Islam, which was an ideology, not a race. As for Martin, what was wrong with him being a member of a right-wing movement? Had the United Kingdom suddenly become off-limits to right-wingers? If so, the UK authorities would need to start locking up several million of their own citizens.

I also noted how the document mentioned that Martin had been in possession of 'leaflets with scenarios regarding possible violence at his speech.' The Home Office knew perfectly well that these leaflets didn't encourage violence. They knew perfectly well that the leaflets were simply guidelines explaining how one should react and defend oneself in the event that Antifa violently disrupted the speech. The fact that the Home Office had used these leaflets as a reason to ban us was in itself proof that they weren't acting in good faith.

I pocketed the document, wondering whether I should be angry or flattered. Clearly, the Home Office had wanted to ban us by any means necessary. But without a legitimate reason to do so, they had been reduced to lying and twisting our words. Before that moment, I hadn't realized how not only totalitarian, but how weak the UK government was—a weakness that could only be held together by force. Any appearance of freedom was merely a simulation, constructed for the purpose of keeping the population docile. Behave yourself, and the simulation would continue, even until the end of your life. But should you ever decide to start asking the wrong questions—or worse, challenging these questions and sharing their answers with others—the hammer would come down, shattering the illusion.

"No problem," I assured. "Martin and I will take a flight back to Vienna tonight."

"That's not possible," the immigration officer said. "You and your boyfriend will be taken to an immigration removal facility until Sunday evening."

Sunday evening. But it was only Friday night. And we had already been in holding for an entire day. My family would go wild with worry if I waited another two days to contact them.

Martin and I bargained with the immigration officer, trying to convince him to allow us to book an earlier flight. But apparently, there was a rule that stipulated we couldn't leave the UK unless it was on the same airline that we had used to arrive: EasyJet.

There were no existing EasyJet flights from the Luton Airport to Vienna, at least not until Sunday evening. But there were a few EasyJet flights to Vienna early the next morning from a different airport, Heathrow.

"I can't allow you to fly out from a different airport," the immigration officer said. "The transfer will require too much paperwork."

Our final option was to book a flight to Germany for later that evening. Once again, the immigration officer refused, citing the excuse that he didn't want to risk Germany deporting me back to the UK since I wasn't an EU citizen. It was a garbage excuse. I had flown to Germany several times over the past year, never with any issues. It was almost as if he *wanted* to lock us up, as if he hoped the experience would scare and humiliate us. We weren't about to give him the satisfaction.

"Both of you will be taken to the immigration removal facility later this evening," he said.

"Can we travel together?" I asked.

"It's against protocol for men and women to travel together in the same vehicle. But we will bring you to the facility at the same time in separate vehicles."

"Fine," I agreed, glancing at Martin. He smiled, as if to assure me everything would be okay, and I returned the gesture. Frankly, I was more bewildered than afraid. All the rules, all the protocol. It seemed excessive that we weren't even allowed to speak to one another. It wasn't as if we were planning some kind of jailbreak.

The border police locked me back in the holding room where I sank onto the beanbag chair. I don't recall how long I stayed awake, only that when I did wake, it no longer felt like evening. My back was stiff and sore, as if I had been lying on the beanbag chair for hours. Eyelids sleep-heavy, my makeup a crusty film on my face, I peeled off my coat, wishing for a shower. When I checked the wall-clock, I was startled to find that it was seven in the morning. I knocked on the door of the holding room.

"May I speak to whoever's in charge?" I called.

A border policeman answered. "What's the matter, ma'am?"

"Why wasn't I taken to the detention facility last night?"

"My apologies. We had one free vehicle, so we only brought your boyfriend," he explained. "We'll bring you later today."

A hard knot formed in my throat. I was angry that I had been lied to, that Martin had been transported to the facility without my knowledge, but I couldn't bring myself to yell at the border policeman. He had nothing to do with Martin's transfer. Not to mention, he was a thousand times kinder than any of the people I had encountered the day before.

"I appreciate your help, sir," I said. "I have one more question: what's the facility I'm being taken to?"

"Colnbrook Immigration Removal Centre."

The name had no significance to me. It wasn't until days later, when I did some research, that I realized the Colnbrook Immigration Removal Centre had been built to the standard of Class B prisons, making it one of the highest security immigration removal centers in the United Kingdom.[119] In the past, detainees had been seriously injured and even murdered while in custody.[120] To this day, I'm thankful that Martin and I weren't aware of this information during our detainment. Sometimes, it's better not to know you've been swimming with sharks until you're standing safely on shore.

THE WARDEN'S WARNING

About seven hours later, an armored van arrived to transport me to the Colnbrook Immigration Removal Centre.

"Protocol dictates that I place you in handcuffs," the friendly border policeman told me. "But I really don't see it as necessary. Please hurry and get into the van, though. If I'm caught breaking the rules, I could lose my job."

I thanked the border policeman, was even tempted to shake his hand. He was the first person at Luton Airport who hadn't treated me like a criminal.

The armored van resembled a cage. I was the sole detainee in the vehicle, separated from the driver and his partner by a set of metal bars. The journey lasted nearly an hour. All the while, my mind raced with concern for Martin. Was he safe? Would I be allowed to see him? I did my best to distract myself by speaking to the driver and his partner. To my surprise, they turned out to be pro-Brexit.

When I told them the details of my detainment, their eyes widened in shock. I sensed they didn't believe me.

"How can you stand living in such a totalitarian country?" I asked.

"We Brits tend to suffer in silence."

I found this to be a sad excuse. Suffering in silence wasn't going to fix the United Kingdom. On the contrary, ignoring the country's problems would only see those problems become permanent. And in my experience, the driver was mistaken. None of the Brits I knew had agreed to suffer in silence. They were making their voices heard.

At the Colnbrook Immigration Removal Centre, our vehicle underwent a security probe. The guards used search mirrors to conduct a full inspection, including the underside of the vehicle. As far as I knew, the search mirrors were used to ensure that no explosives, weapons, drugs, or any other contraband were being smuggled into the facility.

Approved.

We drove through dual layers of towering security gates and then parked in an empty lot outside the facility.

"Am I allowed to bring a change of clothes?" I asked.

"Just one," the driver said. "All of your other possessions, including electronics, will be documented, separated into plastic bags, and kept locked up overnight."

I had expected as much.

The driver ushered me into the facility, where I immediately met with a doctor for a medical check-up. The doctor asked me a range of questions, from my health history to the possibility of me being pregnant. I would be lying if I said I wasn't tempted to answer "yes" to the pregnancy question. But I decided that I was already in enough trouble as it was.

"No, I'm not pregnant. I'm not on birth control, nor am I currently taking any medication."

I was then made to stand for a photo. The photo was placed on a laminated detainee card, which listed private details about me like: what religious category I belonged to. Lastly, I was given a Nokia-styled cell phone to contact my family and friends. I wasn't surprised to discover that the phone had no internet connection.

"Am I allowed to see my boyfriend?" I asked one of the female staff members.

"That's up to the warden," she replied. "Lucky for you, he's asked to see you. Come this way."

The staff member guided me into a windowed office, where heaps of clutter sat on dusty shelves. The warden was bent over a large wooden desk, his head only slightly visible over reams of documents, used coffee cups, and an assortment of odd knickknacks.

"Miss Pettibone, nice to meet you," he said, shaking my hand with a firm grip.

"I was told that I needed your permission to see my boyfriend."

"Yes, you can meet him in the Visitor's Center once we're finished up here." The warden paced around the room, arms locked behind his back, looking sheepish. Whatever he wanted to say, he seemed to be struggling with the appropriate way to phrase it.

"I've already warned your boyfriend, and I also feel that I should warn you…it's best for everyone involved if you and Martin refrain from revealing who you are or why you're here to any of the other detainees…just to avoid any kind of disturbance."

My hands clenched around the cuffs of my coat. There was no need for the warden to say another word. Obviously, there were Muslims amongst the detainees whom he feared might react with hostility to people like Martin and me.

My first instinct was to yell at him, to demand why he had brought us here. If there was even the slightest chance that we could be assaulted, why had he not placed us in an isolated room? I hated my vulnerability. My helplessness. Not only did I have no power to rectify the situation, but I knew that if I caused a scene, the warden might change his mind about allowing me to see Martin.

"I won't tell anyone who I am," I agreed.

THE MIX-UP

I hurried down the hallway that led to the Visitor's Center, barely resisting the urge to run. The warden's warning had left a cold feeling in the pit of my stomach. I was even more desperate to see Martin to verify his safety. Even now, nearly eight months after we had met, it was difficult to pass a single day without him. Our detainment had enhanced this feeling, providing a glimpse of what life would be like if we were ever forcibly separated.

"Slow down, ma'am," the staff member called. Like a personal shadow, the woman had been ordered to follow me wherever I went. I jolted to a halt, annoyed by her slow stride. I waited for her to catch up and then darted into the Visitor's Center.

The center was a spacious community room, furnished with couches, vending machines and shelves of board games. A sign hung on the wall that read something along the lines of: *No cursing, no kissing, no inappropriate touching.* A variety of couples and young single men lounged about the room, mostly from Eastern Europe and the Middle East.

When I finally saw Martin, my unease turned into fear. He was sitting on one of the sofas, pale-faced and swollen-eyed, as if he hadn't slept the entire night.

"Babe, what's the matter?" I asked.

Martin sprang from the sofa when he caught sight of me and gripped me into a hug. Rough and desperate, he had never held me so fiercely before.

"I thought you'd been kidnapped," he gasped.

"What...what are you talking about?"

"The immigration officer promised they would bring you here at the same time as me. Before the curfew last night, I asked the information desk about you, and they told me you weren't here."

"They kept me at the airport overnight," I explained.

"Yes, that's what I thought until early this morning," Martin admitted. "I asked the information desk again where you were, and they told me you weren't here and that you weren't at the airport either. Since your name wasn't in either system, they told me you'd probably been put on a flight back to the United States."

"Are you serious?" Had I been in Martin's position, I would have lost my mind. How could the UK border police have been so careless? Either they were the most disorganized border force in history, or, God forbid, they had done this to us on purpose.

"Are you okay? Did anyone hurt you?" Martin asked. He was still hugging me, arms clenched around my waist, his expression as relieved as if I had just returned from the dead.

"No one hurt me. I promise I'm fine," I assured. "But this situation is getting way out of hand. I think it's time to start telling everybody what's going on."

FREE SELLNER! FREE PETTIBONE!

The building where I spent the night appeared to be an entirely separate wing of the Colnbrook Immigration Removal Centre. The standards were poor, but passable: a small room with a single barred window that showed a patch of gray sky, a narrow bed with a wool blanket, and a community bathroom with a flimsy curtain-door and no soap.

In contrast, Martin was locked in a building modeled after a high security, Category B prison.[121] Filled with wings of gloomy cells, each cell offered a cold metal bed and a yellow-stained toilet. Due to the warden's warning, I asked that Martin be given his own cell as an extra security precaution. My request was denied.

Once alone in my room, I immediately called my twin sister, Nicole.

"Are you okay?" Nicole asked, when she answered the phone. "This is insane. They're treating you and Martin like criminals."

"Yes, I'm safe at the moment. But I need to contact some of my political friends. The problem is that I don't have any of their phone numbers."

"Most of your friends follow me on Twitter," Nicole pointed out. "I'll get their numbers. I can also ask them to spread the word about your detainment."

"Thanks, Cole. That will help a lot."

While Nicole got to work sending the messages, I asked her how our parents were doing.

"Mom's pretty worried. You should call them."

"I'll do it now."

My parents weren't upset, just concerned for my safety. They told me that in choosing to become a political dissident, they had expected authoritarians to come for me sooner or later. My dad even tried to make light of the situation.

"Hello, am I speaking to prisoner 1323?" he teased.

"As long as you continue doing what is right, we'll support you," my mom added.

I spent the next few hours on the phone with my political friends whose numbers Nicole had provided. As always, Nick Monroe proved himself to be an invaluable friend. He spent the entire night spearheading a Twitter storm until everyone from conservatives to libertarians to nationalists to classical liberals were uniting in raising awareness about our situation. Soon, our names were trending hashtags on Twitter. The UK branch of Generation Identity even held a rally for us at Speaker's Corner, with dozens of attendees holding signs that read: 'Free Sellner' and 'Free Pettibone.'

Among the rally attendees was a young Irish man named Seán, who I hadn't yet met, but who would later become a close friend of mine. He had been interested in politics for a while, content to observe rather than to get involved, but all of this changed on the day of Martin's and my detainment and banning. In Seán's view, the Home Office's treatment of us was a deal-breaker. It was next level censorship and tyranny, which is why he, along with many others, decided to visibly defy their government's actions by attending the support rally for us at Speaker's Corner.

The large show of support encouraged me beyond belief. For the first time, it made me feel like there was some kind of international solidarity amongst the dissident network. Perhaps Martin and I weren't as alone as we had thought.

I managed to contact Tommy Robinson just before curfew. In his eyes, and in the eyes of thousands of others, Martin's and my detainment was unprecedented. The grounds upon which we had been banned were outrageous, not to mention, unethical.[122] Tommy was furious that the UK Home Office had slandered his name, calling him a 'far-right leader whose materials and speeches incite racial hatred.'

"I've booked a flight to Vienna for tomorrow," he told me. "I'll be waiting for you and Martin at the airport with a camera crew."

I didn't sleep much that night. I was too paranoid. The warden's warning continued to haunt me, raising my concern for not only my own safety, but for Martin's, as well. I prayed no one would recognize him, that God would keep him safe. He later told me that the warden's warning had put him on edge, so he had spent the entire night sitting in front of his door, gripping a makeshift weapon—a long sock with a travel-size shampoo bottle inside—just in case any of the detainees recognized him and tried to attack him.

By the time dawn arrived, I couldn't have been more grateful. The nightmare was in its final stages. In just a few hours, I would never have to deal with the border police again...well, at least not with the UK border police.

A driver returned me to the Luton Airport about two hours after Martin. The procedure was roughly the same—an armored van, multiple security checks. The only difference was that this time, I couldn't escape the handcuffs.

I felt so ridiculous, I couldn't help but laugh in spite of the situation. Hands cuffed behind my back, escorted by border police, I was marched through the Luton Airport. Travelers at the baggage claim watched me with curious stares. I could tell they were wondering what kind of crime I had committed to warrant such treatment. In hindsight, I wish one of them had taken the time to snap a photo. It would have been a nice souvenir.

The border police returned Martin and I to the airport holding rooms. We spent four, maybe five hours in lock-up before we were finally given a pair of boarding passes and ushered onto our EasyJet flight.

My eyes blistered with fatigue as I boarded the flight. My unwashed hair felt greasy against my neck, and my body, overheated from the holding room, smelled of sweat. But I spared only a fleeting thought for my appearance. I was too happy to finally be leaving the UK, and even more importantly, to be reunited with Martin. No more having to be locked up in separate rooms. No more monitoring of our movements. No more restrictions on our speech.

We were free.

THE BANNED INTERVIEW

At the airport in Vienna, two Austrian policemen escorted us off the plane. They conversed with Martin as we deboarded. I didn't understand what they said to him, but from their smiles and sympathetic tones, I gathered the exchange was friendly. My suspicion was confirmed when they waved us through passport control without a security check. At this point, I considered the Austrian police a thousand times better than those in the UK.

"How do you feel?" Martin asked, as we collected our luggage.

"Happy to be home."

"You consider Austria a home?"

"At the very least, I consider it a second home," I said with a smile.

Martin took my hand, squeezing it tightly. I could tell my words made him happy.

Outside the custom's gate, our friends had arranged a spectacular surprise. About fifty of them were grouped together, chanting patriotic slogans in German and holding a large banner that read 'Die Gedanken sind Frei' (Thoughts are free). The welcome party was so lively that it drew the attention of all the passersby in the airport.

Tommy Robinson and his camera crew, who had flown to Vienna earlier that day, were among the group. Dressed in a sharp navy-blue suit, Tommy greeted us with handshakes and a caring smile. It was nice to see a friendly face.

Tommy interviewed us briefly about our thoughts on UK detainment and then invited us to his Airbnb to film a longer interview.[123] After spending a few moments talking with our friends, we ordered two large coffees from an airport café and then drove to Tommy's Airbnb. His cameramen had already set up a professional filming area in the living room. Two cameras on tripods were arranged to film us from different angles, while a couple of soft-box lights doused the area in warm light, helping to soften the tired lines on our faces.

Martin and I ended up filming a fifteen-minute interview with Tommy, during which we shared all the details about our UK detainment.[124]

"Have you got a speech prepared?" Tommy asked Martin during the interview.

"I had a speech for Speaker's Corner, but I rewrote it in my prison cell," Martin answered, drawing a wrinkled stack of papers from his pocket.

"If I take this speech," Tommy said, accepting the speech from Martin, "this is the backfiring of the government and the police and what they're attempting to do. Speaker's Corner has a three-hundred-year history from some of the most controversial figures from Karl Marx to George Orwell. Everyone is allowed to speak there, it's part of our country's history. And the fact that they're trying to stop Martin and the fact that we see Islamic preachers coming in every week, I'll deliver this speech on your behalf. I'll read this speech out. So, the government hasn't won."

Martin found Tommy's plan to be the perfect counterattack. As a consequence of the UK government's tyrannical efforts to silence him, Pandora's Box had been opened, drawing allies from all across the world to his defense and magnifying his voice one thousandfold.

The evening ended with a final interview, which as of this moment, still remains on my YouTube channel: 'The Tommy Robinson Interview That Got Me Banned from the U.K.'[125]

I still recall how overwhelmed I felt as I sat across from Tommy, asking him questions that ranged from his experiences in prison to how his outspokenness against Islam had affected his wife and children. After all that I had endured to make it to that moment, the interview seemed larger than life. I almost didn't know how to conduct it anymore.

But somehow, I managed to hold myself together long enough for Tommy to share his story, the story of a man who had suffered through years upon years of systemic abuse as punishment for his political activism: defamation, physical attacks, threats to his family, investigations, trials, and even imprisonment.

Ultimately, Tommy's story made me question what Martin's and my political future held. If we chose to stay in the trenches, fighting against the tyranny of the establishment, would we also come to be the targets of sham investigations and trials?

Yes. I believed that one day we probably would.

Of all the times in my life that I wish I had been wrong, I wish I had been wrong about this prediction the most.

THE BANNED SPEECH

By the time I concluded my interview with Tommy, the only thing I could think about was getting a decent night's sleep. The last three days had left me depleted to the point that I debated taking a few days off. Granted, there would be articles about Martin and me the next morning, but for the most part, we assumed the situation would wind down and that life would soon return to normal. We couldn't have been more wrong.

At around four in the morning, Lauren Southern sent me a message on Twitter. She had been trying to enter the United Kingdom via a bus from France, but had been detained by the police at the border.

Putting me in a detention lock, she wrote. *Not letting me enter. Taking phone now, love ya.*

This was the last message I received from Lauren for several hours. It wasn't until later in the day, to the shock of the entire political right-wing, that we learned the border police had interrogated Lauren under the terrorism act, Schedule 7, due to a social experiment she had spearheaded in England a few months earlier.[126] The social experiment, while admittedly controversial, was intended to highlight the double-standard when it came to making inflammatory statements about Islam and Christianity.

In July 2015, *VICE* had published an article entitled 'Was Jesus Gay?,' which blasphemously insinuated that Jesus Christ was a homosexual.[127] The article, which had been defended on the grounds that it was free speech, remains on *VICE*'s website to this day.

In response, Lauren decided to conduct a social experiment in which she labeled Allah as a gay god. The social experiment wasn't intended to insult Muslims or Islam; rather, Lauren wanted to determine if the statement 'Allah is gay' would be met with same free speech defense as the question 'was Jesus gay?.' In short, it wasn't. Having been present at the social experiment myself, I had a front-row seat to the outrage. The irate cries from onlookers. The panicked expressions of the British police as they scrambled to shut down our booth and confiscate our flyers.

The UK border police ended up interrogating Lauren for several hours, after which the Home Office resolved to deport her to France, informing her that she was permanently banned from the United Kingdom.[128] On the heels of Lauren's ban, the situation exploded into a much larger issue. Prominent conservative commentators such as Tucker Carlson and conservative politicians such as Nigel Farage covered the story, as did left-leaning YouTube giants like Phillip DeFranco.[129] Lauren was even invited to the European Parliament to give a statement about her ban.[130]

A load of journalists and YouTube commentators reached out to Martin and me for interviews, but we only had time to agree to a handful. On top of this, we filmed our own YouTube video about the detainment,[131] and we also responded to hundreds of encouraging e-mails from supporters, which seemed to be flooding our inboxes without end. All in all, I gained about thirty-thousand new followers from the ensuing publicity.

At the end of the day, we took the victory. It didn't matter that mobs of far-left activists were taking to social media to celebrate our ban. It didn't matter that the mainstream media was publishing slanderous articles about us. The support that rallied around us had grown too large to be defeated. And it only grew larger when, a week later, Tommy fulfilled his promise to Martin about delivering his speech at Speaker's Corner.

From all across the United Kingdom, people traveled to hear the speech, an army of patriots standing shoulder-to-shoulder in support of freedom. Cameras were in the hands of every journalist and cell phones were in the hands of every attendee. Flags danced in the wind overhead, but not only to represent England—an Austrian flag represented Martin, a Canadian flag represented Lauren, and the American flag represented me.

My soon-to-be friend, Seán, who was high on the success of the 'Free Sellner! Free Pettibone!' rally, helped Tommy to coordinate the event. The police struggled to keep the Antifa separate from the attendees, so Seán and a few of his friends spent the entire morning helping to secure the area. Seán also handed out hundreds of copies of Martin's speech, until each pair of hands held a copy, ready to read along with Tommy.

When Tommy arrived, the crowd erupted as if with one thunderous voice into shouts of, "Tommy! Tommy! Tommy!"

Moving quickly through the crowd, shaking hands as he walked, Tommy positioned himself in the center of Speaker's Corner. As was tradition, he didn't use a microphone. His sole accessory was a wooden box to stand on, which placed him slightly above the crowd. There, in a loud and resonant voice, Tommy defied the UK government's authority by reading Martin's banned speech.[132]

The final lines read:

> "People of the UK, remember who you are. Remember your glorious past. You are the sons and daughters of knights, of kings, of explorers, philosophers and artists. Who is the sovereign in this country? It's you, the people. You, the silent and invisible majority who said no during Brexit. You can say no again. No to islamization, no to mass immigration and the Great Replacement. And yes to your identity, your security, yes to your heritage and the future of your children. All of this is impossible without freedom of speech. I know that if these words will find their way to the UK and even to Speaker's Corner, it will be victory for our cause. If they did and if you

are hearing them now, I tell you, go further on that winding street. Don't be afraid because we have an ally. Our ally is unbeatable. Our ally is the truth. The battle, our battle for freedom of speech has just begun. And Speaker's Corner will become a symbolic place in that struggle. When you go home, now I want you to bring the spirit of Speaker's Corner with you. Every single person who raised his hand because he could not relate to the moment of fear when he would not dare to speak his mind, promise me, promise yourself this: Next time I will overcome my inner fear. Next time, I will speak up."

7

To control a people you must first control what they think about themselves and how they regard their history and culture. And when your conqueror makes you ashamed of your culture and your history, he needs no prison walls and no chains to hold you.
—John Henrik Clarke

AUSTRIA, EUROPE
APRIL 2018

Tommy's speech reading sparked a weekly tradition. Every Sunday, crowds of people assembled at Speaker's Corner in celebration of free speech. Although not always big, the gatherings happened nonetheless—an outpouring of courageous solidarity from the English that I was proud to witness from afar.

Within a week, the publicity surrounding Martin's and my UK detainment wound down. Grateful for time to ourselves, we spent a few days exploring Vienna: hiking in the fresh mountain air, visiting popular tourist attractions, enjoying drinks with friends, and eating late-night sausages at the famous Viennese Würstelstands.

I'll admit that, during that first year or so of dating Martin, he remained a bit of a mystery. His character, with its perpetual cheerfulness and optimism, often seemed too good to be true. Of course, like all humans, he had his own imperfections, but there wasn't a fundamental quality about him that I didn't admire.

I admired how he planned each day with precision, his schedule kept intact not by an outward structure, but by the strength of his own discipline. I admired how much he loved his family, how he always made an effort to spend time with his parents, brothers, and grandma. I admired his love for Austria. Not content to merely speak about this love, he lived it daily, dedicating his life to preserving Austria's culture and identity. And, contrary to the monster that the mainstream media makes him out to be, he always maintained a benevolent kindness toward others, even when he felt tired, overwhelmed, or sick. I recall him once giving a pregnant girl a thousand euros upon learning that her boyfriend had abandoned her and their child. There was no doubt in my mind he was the only person in the world whom I would leave home for.

Our break ended after a few short days because Martin needed to prepare for a new mission—a sequel to Defend Europe called 'Defend Europe Alps.' This time, the mission would take place in France, at the Col de l'Échelle near Briançon. The Col de l'Échelle was a popular mountain pass where migrants routinely crossed the Italian border illegally into France. Since the French authorities had failed to establish an efficient border patrol at the Col de l'Échelle, Generation Identity planned to construct their own.

Lauren Southern and I agreed to report on the mission. Since it wasn't scheduled to take place until mid-April, I returned to the States to visit my family. Months had passed since I had last seen them. Before becoming a political activist, I hardly left home. The wildest adventures I had ever experienced were the ones that took place in my head as I wrote science-fiction stories. I understood my new life was a jarring transition for my family because it was jarring for me, too. Coupled with the fact that I was constantly away from home, often getting caught in dangerous situations, I was grateful to still have their support.

The days passed quietly, peacefully. Northern Idaho is magnificent in spring. A cozy gray fog blows over the river near our house on early mornings, but by afternoon, the water is speckled with swimming ducks and glistening with warm sunlight. I spent those mornings discussing politics with my dad as we ate breakfast; afternoons taking cooking lessons from my mother, during which she often reminded me how important it was to keep my Catholic faith strong in the midst of my political work; and late nights laughing with my twin sister, going out into neighboring cities or staying at home in our pajamas to watch movies.

I also tried my best to maintain a consistent political schedule. On YouTube, the political sphere was rapidly changing. Leftist YouTubers were popping up all over, many of which quickly gained large followings. Right-wing YouTubers, on the other hand, were losing access to the freedom of expression we had enjoyed in 2016 and 2017. This was largely due to pressure from influential American 'anti-hate' organizations like the Southern Poverty Law Center (SPLC) and the Anti-Defamation League (ADL), or to a clique of leftist activists who labeled themselves 'far-right researchers.' These far-right researchers spent their days lobbying YouTube and other social media platforms to silence political voices which they personally deemed extreme. Granted, there are some extremists on the right. I don't deny this reality. In my view, right-wing extremism is an issue that all right-wingers have a duty to criticize and condemn. However, when it comes to extremism, the mainstream media and leftist activists don't have the moral high ground. Despite claiming to uphold an anti-extremist stance, they shamelessly defend and promote violent left-wing extremist movements such as Antifa.

Furthermore, these far-right researchers are often guilty of misrepresentation. For the most part, far-right is a meaningless term, which far-right researchers deceitfully apply to all political dissent: libertarians, classical liberals, nationalists, and so on. Acting as if all these political groups see eye-to-eye is dishonest. I am a traditional conservative and an America-first nationalist, yet despite my political stance, I have fundamental disagreements with other types of right-wingers. For example, I oppose neo-conservativism, which is a sort of enlightenment-inspired conservatism that stands for America as being a tool of progress—one that has a historic mission to further mankind. By nature, neo-conservativism believes in the supremacy of its nation and also desires to police other nations, hence why the majority of neoconservatives are warmongers.

I believe there are different nations of different peoples, none of which are inherently superior, and none of which should be judged according to America's moral standards—particularly because the United States itself is guilty of innumerable atrocities, such as slaughtering sixty-two million of its own unborn babies.[133]

The United States doesn't have the duty, much less the right, to forcibly spread democracy or to police other nations. As an America-first nationalist, I believe that Americans should put the interests of the United States over the interests of foreign countries. I believe in defending America's freedom, culture, and identity against all globalist systems.

Regarding immigration, I am not an anti-immigration activist as certain far-right researchers have claimed. I have no issue with limited immigration. However, I am staunchly opposed to mass immigration—in other words, when the number of immigrants is so high that it threatens to replace native populations in their own countries. In the same way that I support the right for the Japanese, Africans, Jews, Chinese, and every other ethnic group to remain the majority in their homelands, I support this same right for Europeans.

In all honestly, I don't like to talk about race. As a Catholic, I believe that every soul is equal and that all of us are precious in the eyes of God. Not to mention, in the grand scheme of things, race is of minor importance. However, as a fellow political YouTube commentator once wisely stated, "You may not care about race, but race cares about you."

This statement has proved to be alarmingly true.

Day in and day out, radical left-wing activists insist upon poisoning our political discourse, our media, our entertainment, our schools and universities, and even our government with harmful ideologies such as Critical Race Theory,[134] which *Britannica* defines as the view that the law and legal institutions are inherently racist and that race itself, instead of being biologically grounded and natural, is a socially constructed concept that is used by white people to further their economic and political interests at the expense of people of color.[135]

Radical left-wing activists also insist upon spinning deceptive lies about white privilege, about how white people are inherently racist, and about how white people have hereditary culpability for the crimes of their ancestors. 'Whiteness is a Pandemic' stated an article for *The Root*,[136] and 'Abolishing whiteness has never been more urgent', claimed an article for *Al Jazeera*.[137] Meanwhile, a public school in NYC asked parents to 'reflect on their whiteness', passing out literature that encouraged them to become 'white traitors' and 'white abolitionists.'[138] Somewhere between the years 2016 and 2021, it became acceptable on a mainstream level to be racist toward white people, to blame them for all the world's problems, and even to deny them the right to stand up for themselves. For example, a group of current and former teachers in Virginia compiled a long list of parents who had spoken out against the destructive teachings of Critical Race Theory, in order to 'infiltrate', use 'hackers' to silence parents' communications, and 'expose these people publicly.'[139] Most worryingly, at least in the Western world, it's white people alone that are being singled out and disparaged by the mainstream media, Hollywood, the education system, and Big Tech. The negative treatment applied to white people isn't being applied to any other ethnic group—at least not by powerful and influential figures and institutions. On the contrary, all other ethnic groups are protected.

If, like me, you decide to speak out against the anti-white rhetoric, you will be slandered as a white supremacist, a Neo-Nazi, and a racist. This has happened to people like Martin Sellner, Tommy Robinson, and many others. To avoid such character assassination, you will have to accept all of the fallacious accusations leveled against white people, publicly wallow in guilt, and spend your days actively promoting lies such as the United States and Europe are systemically racist towards ethnic minorities.

But this, I will never do. In the same way that I would never single out or attack another group for their ethnicity, I expect the same treatment in return. I'm not ashamed of what I am. Not my ethnicity, my beliefs, or my Catholic faith.

My refusal to be ashamed is why 'far-right researchers' and mainstream journalists decided to put me on their radar. Never, at any point, were they interested in my genuine beliefs, my arguments, or a nuanced discussion. For example, not one of the 'far-right researchers' ever reached out to me to ask about my beliefs. As for the mainstream journalists, every single one of them acted extremely kind, fair and balanced towards me in private, while in public, the articles they published about me were chock-full of lies and misrepresentation. Ultimately, I decided to stop interviewing with the mainstream media altogether. I realized that these 'far-right researchers' and mainstream journalists—along with numerous other leftist activists and organizations—were only interested in one thing: shutting me down and all those who think like me. This escalating repression against the right troubled me. I wasn't so much concerned with repression itself, but rather, what it might lead to. In America, we were told that we had freedom of speech. We were told that we had a political path to correcting the wretched state of our countries. And yet, countless right-wingers were being censored as a consequence of peacefully expressing their beliefs. On top of the censorship, their reputations and livelihoods were targeted, leaving them struggling to provide for themselves and their families. When right-wingers wished to peacefully meet in real life, Antifa harassed their venues, which either resulted in the events being cancelled or violently attacked. Few influential systems and institutions stood up for us, and even fewer represented us fairly. For most of us, freedom was a simulation…unless of course, we decided to bend the knee to the ruling ideology. Overall, right-wing patriots were being backed into a corner, and I could see that some of them were becoming disheartened, angry resentful and even radicalized as a result. In some ways, I think certain leftists wanted this to happen. They wanted right-wing radicalization, and perhaps even right-wing violence. Both would supply them with the ammunition they needed to crack down on the right even more.

Martin had once told me that he feared this repression would lead to right-wing terrorism in Europe. Perhaps in America, as well. Both of us rejected such violence. It was never justifiable to target innocents. In fearing such an outcome, Martin often spoke out against it in his YouTube videos. Instead of condoning violence, he offered an alternative solution in which patriots could engage in activism that would peacefully yet effectively fight the metapolitical battle. Being a political activist was difficult, yes. One would almost certainly face an onslaught of repression. However, if we had any hope of saving our countries, such sacrifices were necessary.

DEFEND EUROPE ALPS

During my time in Idaho, I applied for a Russian visa at the Consulate General of Russia in Seattle, Washington. Lauren and I had debated making a trip to Russia in early May. Due to escalating tensions between Russia, Syria, and the United States, we hoped to interview a variety of Russian politicians and public figures so we could share their point of view with our American and Canadian audiences. At the time, all the Russian embassies in the United States were closed, apart from the embassy in Washington, D.C., which left me wondering if I would be able to secure a visa in time. Lauren also encountered difficulties. In Canada, the employees at the Russian Consulate forced her to participate in a string of interviews and background checks. By some miracle, we both managed to acquire visas just a few days before our flights to France. We took this as a sign that we should go ahead with the trip.

On April 18, I flew to Lyon, France. Having been unable to locate a flight with a long enough layover for me to pass through customs, I was forced to buy two separate flights: the first was from Seattle to London and the second was from London to Lyon.

Returning to London was a mistake.

At the Gatwick Airport, I realized that, in order to collect my luggage from the baggage claim, I somehow needed to make it through passport control. While I didn't want to enter the United Kingdom—I simply wanted to pick up my luggage and check it in for my next flight—the border police refused to let me through.

"We can't let you enter the United Kingdom," they said sternly. "We also can't get your luggage and bring it to you."

An eight-hour stand-off followed. Throughout the debate over my luggage, the border police asked me a series of questions. I felt like I was back in an interrogation room, except that this time, the questions were eerily invasive.

"How much money is in your bank account?" one of the border police asked me.

"You're crazy if you think I'm going to answer that," I replied.

The woman flared her nose, affronted by my response. But how did she expect me to respond? Their questions not only violated my privacy; they had no right to ask them. I wasn't trying to enter the UK for a visit; I simply wanted my luggage back.

Eight exhausting hours later, the border police finally let me go. They agreed to send someone to fetch my luggage from the baggage claim, despite having claimed numerous times that collecting it for me was against the rules.

"I was never given specific details about my ban," I told the border police before I boarded my flight. "But I'm guessing I'm permanently banned from the UK?"

"No. You can try returning in about six months, once the publicity surrounding your and your boyfriend's detainment has died off."

To this day, I have not attempted to re-enter the UK. The UK government is not only biased and untrustworthy; it's among the most totalitarian of the Western governments. Perhaps, some people wouldn't agree. I think this is because, as the saying goes, you only notice your chains when you move.

Once in Lyon, I quickly forgot my bad experience at the UK Passport Control. Wandering along the cobbled streets, with Martin by my side, I marveled at the splendor of that historic city—a city whose every sun-warmed street had sights and secrets in store. Rows of high-peaked terracotta rooftops hovered over carefully tended trees, their branches bursting with chandeliers of green leaves. The long University Bridge, spanning the sparkling waters of the Rhône River, gleamed in the quiet night, its moonlit appearance akin to a tintype photograph.

Lyon was also the city where the French identitarians had been established their headquarters. Complete with a bar, a meeting room, and a workout center, the headquarters made for an attractive youth hangout.

Martin and I stopped at a pizzeria for a midnight pizza with a few of the French identitarians. At the time, the French branch of Generation Identity, known in France as 'Génération Identitaire,' was comprised of several hundred activists. A healthy number of young women had joined, but the majority was male, some of whom were married or already fathers.

I had met a few of the French activists during the first Defend Europe mission, so we took the meal as an opportunity to catch up. They explained that the second Defend Europe mission would be shorter in length but greater in size than the previous one.

"We have over one-hundred activists from France, Austria, Germany, Italy, Hungary, Denmark, and the United Kingdom," one of the French identitarians explained. "We also have two helicopters... even an airplane."

"That's impressive," I said. If Defend Europe Alps turned out to be half as effective as its predecessor, the mission was in for a lot of media attacks and misrepresentation.

Next morning, on April 20, our convoy traveled two hours to the commune of Briançon, located about twenty kilometers from Col de l'Échelle. The further we drove into the mountains, the colder the air became, so that tiny flakes of ice began to form on the edges of the windows. The weather had cleared, unveiling a soft blue sky interrupted by only the occasional wisp of cloud. I kept watch out the window, taking in the storied beauty of the Alps. I had always loved France, though my time in politics had altered the way I viewed it—not just France, but all of Europe and the United States, as well. I no longer viewed the various peoples, nature, architecture, and cultures with an innocent awe; I viewed them as something that needed protecting, something that was in danger of being lost.

Our convoy stopped at a hotel on the edge of Briançon. Since the mission had over one hundred activists, the French identitarians had rented out the entire space. Privacy was needed to conduct last-minute preparations; not to mention, they didn't want to risk infiltrators, like journalists, renting rooms in the hotel.

The organization of Defend Europe Alps was impeccable. Activists were divided into groups, and each group was delegated a specific task. The French identitarians held meetings where they discussed and plotted the mission step-by-step. They also relayed instructions on how to react in the event that Antifa disrupted the mission or the police shut it down. Similar to the uniformed t-shirts from the previous mission, the French identitarians wore matching coats. I'll never forget that spectacular sight—a wave of young activists in bright blue puffer coats, emblazoned with the Defend Europe Alps logo, fanning across the snowy ridges of the mountain.

On April 21, the mission officially began. The majority of the activists drove to the Col de l'Échelle Mountain Pass in a long convoy of trucks, whose hoods were mounted with Defend Europe Alps flags. There, the activists scaled the mountain in snow shoes, their backs laden with equipment to construct the border patrol.

Martin and I didn't join them. Along with two other activists, we traveled to a nearby private airport where two helicopters awaited. Customized with Defend Europe Alps logos, the helicopters shimmered in the slanting afternoon sun.

"Have you ever ridden in a helicopter before?" the pilot asked me.

"Never. I'm a bit nervous to be honest."

He winked. "No need to be nervous. I'm a great pilot."

I climbed into the passenger seat of the helicopter, while a young French activist swung into the seat behind me. I took the next few minutes to prepare my camera. Those of us who rode in the helicopters had been tasked with capturing aerial footage of the Defend Europe Alps action. The best footage would later be posted on social media.

"You need to protect your ears," our pilot told us. He handed us each a padded headset, and added, "It gets louder in the cockpit than you might think."

I fitted on the headset and realized that it not only muffled noise; it also allowed the pilot to communicate with us. Riding in the helicopter wasn't as terrifying as I had imagined—at least, it wasn't nearly as terrifying as the way Martin flew. In order to capture clearer footage, he and a French Identitarian named Clément Gandelin chose to fly with the doors of their helicopter open. Strapped securely in harnesses, they filmed against the powerful current of air generated by the whirring rotor blades.

The pilot was right about the noise. I could barely hear myself speak over the operating rotor system. The pilot made an effort to explain the significance of the various locations below, but I was focused on capturing some useful B-roll footage. Soaring above the icy canons and spires of the alps, the shadow of our helicopter darting across the snow, we made for the Col de l'Échelle pass. A cluster of hovering red lights signaled we were close.

Soon, we came within view of twenty activists holding lighted flares. They encircled a large banner that was spread out over the face of the mountain, which read: 'Closed border. You will not make Europe home. Back to your homeland.' The activists waved their flares back and forth, shouting slogans as the two helicopters flew overhead.

I panned my camera across the banner, then down the mountain where nearly a hundred activists patrolled a makeshift border that they had constructed within half a day. Zigzagging between a stand of pine trees, the bright orange border fence came to an end at a set-up of two large tents. Inside the tents, food, water, and extra equipment was stored.

My footage turned out better than expected. I edited the aerial shots with interviews of border activists and then published the video online. Lauren Southern also published a video about the action,[140] but unfortunately, she didn't arrive until the following day. Having missed the helicopter rides, she instead got her footage from the passenger seat of a small airplane that the French identitarians had also rented.

The weekend was largely successful. Only once, the mission was interrupted by the French police, but rather than try to shut it down, they simply asked the activists questions. As for Antifa, they didn't make an appearance until after the mission. Lying in wait at the French border, the Antifa attempted to block the activists from exiting the country. They even smashed the windows of one German activist's car.

Footage of Defend Europe Alps created waves of excitement on social media. Even popular French politician, Marine Le Pen, tweeted in support of the action.[141] But naturally, not all reactions were positive. Leftists criticized the mission, claiming that Generation Identity were simply putting on a show.

"You're just setting up fences and then taking photos," they accused. "You're not actually accomplishing anything."

They were wrong.

Generation Identity's patrol teams spotted several illegal migrants near Montgenèvre and reported their location to the French police, who promptly made arrests. The publicity surrounding the mission put so much pressure on the French Government that they were forced to react. In a press release, Generation Identity stated, "Our continued efforts have shown that it doesn't take much to patrol this area, which hasn't gone unnoticed by the French Government. As a result of our actions, the French Interior Ministry has now pledged to send security forces to the French-Italian border to ensure that it is secured against any illegal migrants trying to cross it."[142]

The success of Defend Europe Alps enraged the far left. Their opposition toward the right of a country to maintain its sovereignty was unyielding. In their eyes, any and all attempts to secure one's border was 'an act of hate,' which is why I imagine they were quite happy when, one year later, three French identitarians were arrested for their participation in Defend Europe Alps. One of the arrested activists, a woman named Anaïs Lignier, who was eight months pregnant at the time, provided a statement to *Breitbart London*.

"This morning, along with two other Génération Identitaire members, I was placed in police custody on the order of the Gap prosecutor, for the absurd motive of 'interference in public service,'" Ms. Lignier said. "In particular, we built a symbolic border at the Col de l'Echelle and flew over the area with helicopters. In fact, Emmanuel Macron's government never forgave us for humiliating him on the 21st of April, when we forced him to send police and gendarmerie reinforcements to secure the Franco-Italian border."[143]

The initial court ruling sided against the French activists. Anaïs Lignier did not face any prison time, but three other French activists were sentenced to six months for 'impersonating members of the security forces to stop migrants crossing a mountain pass from Italy into France,' *The Telegraph* reported. 'The three, Clément Gandelin, Romain Espino and Damien Lefèvre, are all leading figures in the French branch of Generation Identity. Generation Identity was fined €75,000 and the three were each fined €2,000 and barred from exercising civic, civil or family rights for five years.'[144]

Immediately, the French activists appealed the court ruling. Two years later, in December of 2020, the court reached a final verdict: *acquitted*. Ultimately, none of the French activists had to serve prison time, none of them had to pay a fine, and none of them were barred from exercising their civic, civil or family rights.[145]

For a brief moment, I hoped that, in response to Génération Identitaire's acquittal, the French government would acknowledge that Génération Identitaire was operating legally and peacefully, and would stop repressing them. However, the French government chose to do the opposite. On March 3rd, 2021, the French President, Emmanuel Macron, ordered the dissolution and banning of Génération Identitaire[146] on the grounds that they 'incited discrimination, hatred, and violence,' despite the fact that Génération Identitaire firmly opposes violence, and they also hold no hatred for non-French people. They simply want to preserve France as a French country, with a French identity, language and culture.

The message was clear. The French government would refuse to defend its borders, even as thousands of illegals poured in each year. And if any French citizens decided to take it upon themselves to protect the borders, the reward for their patriotism would be investigations, trials and government-enforced bans of their movements. The game was rigged, impossible to win: watch your country fall, or become an enemy of the state in your efforts to defend it.

THE FIRST HOUSE-RAID

After the Defend Europe Alps mission, Lauren joined Martin and me on a road-trip back to Austria. Lauren and I weren't scheduled to fly to Russia for another week, so we decided to vacation at an alpine hut for few days. We hiked mountain trails, and played board games, and passed the night hours in political and philosophical discussion. Lauren and I filmed videos together, but refrained from publicly announcing our Russia trip. We decided it would be wiser to complete all of our interviews and then safely leave the country first.

The alpine hut was small yet cozy. Tucked away on a forested mountain ridge, the rooms offered a view of the cloud-brushing Alps, where ski slopes glittered with freshly fallen snow. Apart from the unforgettable view, the hotel kitchen served some of the best food I had ever tasted. My favorite was the Schlipfkrapfen, a dish of noodles stuffed with potato-garlic-chive filling and topped with butter and alpine cheese. For dessert, I always ordered the Kaiserschmarrn, a sweet caramelized pancake made with rum-soaked raisins and served with powdered sugar, jam, and applesauce. I've never liked beer, but I became fond of a similar drink made from half-beer-half-lemonade called Radler.

I would probably regard the alpine hut as my favorite vacation spot, if not for the bad experiences associated with my visits. One of these experiences occurred the day before Martin, Lauren, and I were scheduled to return to Vienna.

It was early in the morning, around six, when Martin received a phone call from the Austrian secret police. We were in the downstairs lobby, tying on our boots to go hiking. While I enjoy hiking, I'll admit Martin put me to shame. Somehow, he was able to scale even the most challenging mountain trail with little effort, even when burdened with a heavy backpack. Lauren and I, on the other hand, were practically crawling on our hands and knees by the time we reached the top. We took to calling Martin 'the mountain goat.'

Martin's smile faded when he answered the phone. I couldn't make out the exact words he exchanged with the Secret Police; I didn't yet speak German well enough. Thankfully, he gave me a summary.

"Hello, Mr. Sellner. We're outside your flat in Vienna. Are you at home?"

"Not at the moment."

"Okay, we will wait for you for one hour. If you're not home by then, we'll be forced to call a locksmith to change the locks."

"I can't get home by then, I'm in the Alps. It's a seven-hour drive from Vienna."

"Then we'll call the locksmith."

"What's this about?" Martin demanded. "On what grounds are you raiding my house?"

"We have a search warrant. You're being tried on suspicion of forming a criminal organization."

Martin hung up the phone, his mouth pinched into a tight line. He seemed to waver a moment, hovering between denial and acceptance, before settling on the latter. Grabbing his phone, he opened his WhatsApp and Telegram apps and dropped messages into half-a-dozen chat groups, notifying all the Generation Identity members.

"I'm sorry, babe," he said, swiping through his contact list. "We're going to have to cancel the hike. I need to call my lawyer."

I wanted to ask him to wait. I wanted him to explain why the trial was happening and, even more importantly, to assure me the consequences wouldn't be serious. But I knew that any alarm on my end would only put more pressure on him at the moment.

"Do what you have to," I replied. "Let me know if there's anything I can help with."

While Martin phoned his lawyer, I went to Lauren's room and explained what had happened.

"What a farce," she scoffed. "It's obvious the trial is politically motivated."

I couldn't have agreed more. "The mask is slipping," I said. "And not just in Austria. The crackdown's been ramping up all across Europe in the past year."

"It's going to be okay, Britt. Once news goes public, there'll be an outcry. The Freedom Party might even speak out against it."

"You're right. Even if they just make a public statement, condemning the trial, it would help a lot."

I sat on the bed beside her, certain that by now, the Austrian secret police had contacted a locksmith. They were probably raiding Martin's flat as we spoke, confiscating possessions he had accumulated over the past ten years of his life: computers, cameras, microphones, secure digital cards, portable hard-drives, and all of his personal documents.

But it wasn't just Martin.

In total, the Austrian Secret Police raided ten different homes and offices of various identitarian activists that day, including the home of Martin's Generation Identity co-leader, Patrick Lenart.

The prosecuting attorney of the Graz Public Prosecutor's Office, Dr. Christian Kroschl, confirmed the raids occurred with Austrian newspaper

Heute and said the activists were under investigation for the formation of a criminal organization, suspicion of incitement, and property damage.[147]

Martin joined Lauren and me once he had finished consulting with his lawyer. "I can't get a good internet connection up here," he told us. "I think it's better if I drive down to the city. I can film and upload a video much faster there."

"Wait up. I'll come along." Lauren grabbed her coat and purse. "I need to buy a few things."

I decided to stay behind. Still shaken by news of the house raid, I wanted to hide my worry from Martin. I used the time to get a handle on my emotions, telling myself that it was naïve to feel shocked about the raid. Since day one, being politically active, especially as a right-winger, had always come with risks. People in other European countries such as France and Germany had already been prosecuted for their political speech and activism, so it only made sense that similar repression would eventually make its way to Austria. And now that it had, we were simply being put to the test. The following months would determine if, when it came down to it, Martin truly had what it took to stand up for his country and if I truly had what it took to support him. Whatever the outcome of the trial, we had to live with it.

An hour or so later, Lauren sent me a message over Facebook.

Bad news. The police tracked Martin's phone. They picked him up at the café we were working at and questioned him for about an hour. Then they confiscated his laptop and phone. They also searched his car.

I took a deep breath, preparing myself for the worst, and asked, *Did the police arrest Martin?*

No, thank God, Lauren replied. *But they're following our car back up the mountain. They want to search Martin's hotel room. We'll be at the hotel in about five minutes.*

Zipping on my coat, I grabbed my passport and jogged outside to meet them. Martin, Lauren and the police arrived just as I reached the parking lot.

"Are you Brittany Pettibone?" one of the policemen asked.

"Yes," I said, passing an assuring glance to Martin. To my surprise, he didn't look afraid. He was smiling and speaking in a friendly manner to the second policeman.

"Can I see your passport?" the first policeman asked.

I watched him snap a photo of my passport, hoping the situation wouldn't create trouble for me the next time I returned to Austria to visit Martin.

Wanting to avoid a commotion, Martin led the policemen through the back door of the hotel. Thankfully, no hotel staff or guests were in sight. The police were able to complete a search of Martin's room, during which they confiscated several more secure digital cards before anyone noticed their presence.

"The last thing we need are the passwords to your phone and computer," the police told Martin.

Under Austrian law, Martin was allowed to refuse. The only way the police would be able to access his data was if they could successfully crack his devices.

I waited until the police had left before pulling Martin into a hug. The painful sting of worry reminded me of the first Defend Europe mission, when I had endured weeks of sleepless nights wondering if he was safe on the C-Star. Back then, I had hoped I would never have to suffer such worry again.

But here I was.

Our relationship would never be normal. I understood that now. With Martin, I would have to get used to the threat of house-raids, investigations, trials, and, perhaps, even prison. The only question was if I was willing to pay it.

THE MAN BEHIND THE HOUSE RAID

Martin spent the rest of the day giving interviews to various media outlets and making phone calls to his lawyer and Generation Identity activists. It wasn't until later in the evening, when we were eating dinner in the hotel restaurant, that he had time to explain the full situation to Lauren and me.

"There's a public prosecutor from Graz named Winklhofer who's been trying to take down Generation Identity for the past few years," he told us. "Winklhofer started building a case against us after one of our political actions in 2016."

"Which action?" I asked.

"It was an action where we climbed onto the rooftop of the Graz Green Party headquarters and hung a banner that said, 'Islamization kills.'"

I recalled seeing a video of the political action. Martin had explained that it was in response to the Bataclan Theatre Massacre, which had seen radical Muslim terrorists barbarically execute ninety innocent people at the Bataclan theatre in Paris during a concert performed by an American band called the Eagles of Death Metal.[148]

Back in 2017, I also vaguely remembered Martin mentioning Winklhofer and the case he had been building against Generation Identity. I hadn't thought much of the case back then because I didn't see how it had any legs to stand on. But here we were.

"How is it legal for Winklhofer to put Generation Identity on trial for being a criminal organization?" I asked. "I would think he'd have to put you guys on trial individually, because, for example, not everyone in Generation Identity took part in the 'Islamization Kills' Political Action. So how can members who have nothing to do with that action possibly be tried for it?"

"It's because of a 2016 change to one of our laws," Martin explained. "Before 2016, this law was strictly used to prosecute groups as criminal organizations for crimes like racketeering, smuggling, murder, extortion, vandalism, and so on. But then in 2016, the government added a hate speech clause to the law, meaning that groups can now be prosecuted as criminal organizations for committing acts of hate speech."

"You mentioned crimes of vandalism," Lauren said. "Couldn't this

Winklhofer guy technically prosecute you guys as a criminal organization on these grounds alone?"

"No, because the vandalism Winklhofer is accusing us of isn't serious. It's just political stickers on street signs and temporary chalk on the streets, which is *far* less damaging than what Antifa does. Winklhofer needed the hate speech clause to make this trial possible."

Martin went into further detail about the case in an interview for *Breitbart London*. In his statement, Martin claimed that the Graz prosecutor, Winklhofer, was hoping to use evidence found in the house raids to have Generation Identity banned as a criminal organization under Article 278 of the Austrian Penal Code, as well as Article 283, which covered 'incitement to hostile action' against religious and ethnic groups.[149]

"Have any other political movements in Austria been tried under this law?" Lauren asked. She had pushed away her plate of meat and potatoes, leaving half of it untouched, and was swishing her wine in her glass.

"No, we're the first," Martin replied.

"And if you're convicted, what's the sentence? Not prison, right?"

"Yes, prison. Either that or a large fine."

"For how long?"

"Up to three years."

I felt Martin's hand reach for mine under the table. He squeezed it gently, reassuringly, as if he had noticed the shock in my face. I smiled back at him, insisting I was okay, even if, in truth, I didn't feel much like traveling to Russia anymore. More than anything, I wanted to remain in Austria where I could be a support for him. But apart from my commitment to Lauren to accompany her to Russia, I was running out of days to legally remain in Austria. Without a visa, I could only remain for ninety days at a time.

So, I stuck to the original plan and boarded a flight to Moscow with Lauren on May 2, 2018. Before I passed through the security checkpoint, I made sure to let Martin know that I would never leave him, no matter how the trial progressed or what the verdict turned out to be. In the end, the question of whether or not being with him was worth the hardship of a life filled with house raids, investigations, trials, and prison was easily answered. *Yes.* And this answer would never change.

8

Live your questions now, and perhaps even without knowing it,
you will live along some distant day into your answers.
   —Rainer Marie Rilke

RUSSIA, EUROPE
MAY 2018

Visiting Russia had been a dream of mine since early college when I was
introduced to the extraordinary world of Russian literature. Like its
famed novels, Russia haunts you long after you have finished the story,
long after you have left the country.

In Moscow, summer was in full bloom. Cherry-blossom trees, their
sunlit branches hung with copper birdcages, shaded the busy tourist
shops that crowded the Red Square. At sundown, rich smells hung
thickly over the meandering, twinkle-lit streets: steeped tea leaves, sweet
pastries, and roasted meats. Modern architecture of bold and geometric
design was woven with grandiose byzantine churches and palatial
government buildings. The array of striped onion domes made me feel
as if I had stepped into a fantasy land.

Lauren and I booked a room at the Legendary Hotel Sovietsky. Built
in the style of Soviet classicism, the hotel was opulent to say the least.
It was the kind of hotel where waiters wore gloves, and the manager
wasn't too busy to spare time for any guest. I'll admit I felt
uncomfortable at the sight of an oil portrait of the former leader of the
Soviet Union, Joseph Stalin, displayed in the main hall. Apparently, the

hotel had hosted historical figures such as Grigori Rasputin in the past. I hoped that, by some stroke of bad luck, we hadn't happened to book his old suite.

Just as I had always hoped, I liked Moscow, and I liked the Russian people even more, despite the at times austere character of the city. Without a doubt, the average Russian person lives a life of less convenience than the average Westerner. Russians can often seem aloof, but they are profoundly friendly and hospitable once initial barriers are broken. They would invite a stranger to dine at their own table, especially if that stranger speaks their native language.

Russians have deep roots in Orthodox Catholicism. Many women wear fashionable dresses or elegant skirts, even while performing mundane tasks like grocery shopping. Women also wear veils in the churches and clothing that modestly covers their shoulders and knees. Many of the Russian people are patriotic and politically conservative and won't tolerate criticism of their government from foreigners. If you do voice criticism, don't expect a warm reception.

The main downside of the trip was our close proximity to the mainstream media. A crew from *The Atlantic*, who had been filming Lauren's political journey for the past two years, decided to tag along. They told us the footage would be used in a documentary that spotlighted various prominent right-wing figures. While I was far from happy about the situation, I didn't voice my objections. But I did decline to do a professional sit-down interview, meaning I would only appear as a bystander. Ultimately, I appeared in less than five minutes of the final production. The documentary, entitled *White Noise*, was eventually released in October 2020 and primarily featured three very different political figures: Lauren Southern, Mike Cernovich, and Richard Spencer.[150]

As bad as I had expected the documentary to be, it was far worse. The filmmaker, Daniel, had spent several months sweet-talking Lauren, promising to represent her fairly and to provide a nuanced view of her politics. However, the final product offered no such fairness or nuance.

From taking Lauren's quotes out of context to highlighting the most negative moments of her career, the film condemned her at every turn.

I've long had a strict rule about not interviewing with the mainstream media. The reason for this is that I'm aware that the mainstream media isn't interested in understanding people like me. They're not interested in my ideas, beliefs, or arguments. All they're interested in is trying to fit me into a predetermined framework, one that falsely portrays me as a racist, white supremacist extremist. In the end, even if I expected Daniel to be untrustworthy, it was a pity, for I grew to like him over the course of the Russia trip.

During one of the rare moments I spoke with him on camera, I told him about my plan to leave politics. It seemed inappropriate to continue risking my safety, or to travel for political purposes while married with children. Instead, I wanted to prioritize being a wife and a mother.

I still feel this way now. Unfortunately, certain events were soon to occur that would make my political exit impossible. While I have stopped traveling, and generally now only attend local political events and film commentary YouTube videos, I don't plan on fully leaving politics anytime soon. The reason for this is, first and foremost, because I strongly and passionately believe in my political cause. And secondly, because the state of the world has deteriorated at a terrifying rate. Since 2020, millions have been suffering at the hands of a global virus, global lockdowns, mass unemployment, Antifa and Black Lives Matter riots, inflamed racial tensions, threats of civil war, and tyrannical censorship. It's gotten to the point where the stakes are simply too high to walk away. Perhaps, somewhere deep inside, I already understood this back in 2016. I glimpsed the road upon which Western countries were headed and knew that we were on the brink of experiencing tremendously difficult times. But I suppose I also hoped that, by some miracle, there would be an exit route. A future of safety and security somewhere in Austria with Martin. Maybe one day.

THE OLIGARCH AND THE SCAMMER

Lauren and I struggled to navigate Moscow. Very few Russians—apart from teenagers—spoke English, even in the larger tourist hotspots. Another difficulty was that our cameraman was unsuccessful in acquiring a Russian visa. The trip might've been a complete failure had a Russian friend of mine not been kind enough to offer assistance. On top of helping us hire a Russian cameraman, he also acted as our guide and translator.

On May 8, Lauren's Moscow contact arranged for us to interview a Russian oligarch. Under normal circumstances, the interview might have gone smoothly. However, the oligarch postponed the interview at the last minute, rescheduling it for May 9.

"But May 9 is Victory Day," Lauren said to her Moscow contact. "Half the city is going to be blocked off. How are we supposed to get to the oligarch's office?"

"I see your problem, but the oligarch won't reschedule. Either you do the interview tomorrow, or not at all."

"We'll find a way," I told Lauren. "We'll leave early, just in case."

We left our hotel four hours before the interview. As expected, the streets around the Red Square were sectioned off by police barricades, so our taxi driver was forced to drop us off half a mile from the oligarch's office. An impressive parade flowed through the streets, observed by thousands of cheering spectators. Tanks rolled between rows of uniformed soldiers and waving politicians. Even Russian president Vladimir Putin took part. But perhaps most remarkable of all was the Immortal Regiment, a section of the parade in which people from all over the world carried photographs of their deceased ancestors who had fought in World War II.

We followed my Russian friend to Tverskaya Street, which we needed to cross in order to reach the oligarch's office. The problem was that the entire street was gated off.

"Looks like we're going to have to walk *around* the parade," Lauren sighed.

"That could take hours," I said.

We tried anyway. Two hours later, we were footsore, thirsty, and sunburned. It was a hot day, and we hadn't prepared to walk so far on foot. After talking it over, we decided to call off the interview. Lauren phoned her contact.

"The oligarch won't stand for a cancellation," the contact told us warily. "He said you have to come to his office or else."

"Or *else*? Or else what?" I demanded.

"Or else you're going to have problems."

Lauren hung up the phone, her eyes wide with disbelief. "Is this dude serious?" she sputtered. "There's literally *no* way to cross the street."

"We can try joining the parade," my Russian friend suggested.

While it felt disrespectful to join the Immortal Regiment, there didn't seem to be another option. The oligarch had threatened us, after all.

We hopped the gates that blocked off the street and melted into the winding column of marching people. We walked with the parade a while, before ducking onto the other side of the street. The plan was a success, and eventually we made it to the oligarch's office. Faces flushed from the sun, and our clothes damp with sweat, all I wanted was a cold shower, not to conduct an interview. Worse, we were an hour late, but fortunately, so was the oligarch.

Arriving on time would have communicated to us that he was our equal. But, of course, he believed this was not the case. In order to demonstrate his authority and dominance, he had forced us to navigate a near-impossible situation. In his estimation, if we could complete the difficult task, only then would we be worthy of an interview.

The interview went surprisingly well, considering the events leading up to it. Upon meeting us, the oligarch was civil, one could even say charming. He was an elderly man with white-shot hair, and a slow, yet eloquent way of speaking. He sported expensive glasses and a pristine bespoke suit, which he wore naturally, as if it were a comfortable pair of slacks. We mostly discussed the political situation in Syria, nothing controversial or unexpected.

The experience turned out to be one of the calmer moments of the trip.

The scariest moment was when we made the mistake of hailing an unregistered taxi outside the Red Square. Most of the locals knew better than to rent such taxis, for the majority of the drivers were scammers, but unfortunately, we hadn't done our research.

At most, the taxi ride to our hotel lasted between ten and fifteen minutes. Parked curbside outside the Legendary Hotel Sovietsky, the taxi driver smiled pleasantly and gestured to the screen of the taxi fare calculator: *5,500 rubles.*

Lauren and I exchanged confused glances. Five-thousand-five-hundred Russian rubles was the equivalent of eighty-two U.S. dollars.

"Okay bud, there's no way we're paying that," Lauren said. "This is a scam. You're a scammer, aren't you?"

The taxi driver swiveled around in his seat, erupting into angry-sounding Russian. Lauren and I, who had no idea what he was saying, called our Russian friend for help.

"You're right. It's a scam," he said. "Just give him 1000 rubles and leave."

Lauren and I tossed a thousand rubles into the front seat and then tried to exit. *Locked.* The driver had some kind of child-lock system in place.

"You pay the fare, or you don't leave," the taxi driver threatened.

"Oh, so you speak English now, do you?" Lauren challenged. "Why did you pretend you didn't speak any English when we first got in the taxi? Because you knew that if you gave us the fare in English, we would've immediately known you were a scammer?"

I didn't stop trying to unlock the door. The taxi driver, who was growing more and more hostile by the minute, would likely keep us locked in for hours if we didn't pay. Or who knows? Maybe he would even try to hurt us.

It quickly occurred to me that I was wasting time trying to unlock the door when I could simply roll down the window and open the door from the outside. But by then, the taxi driver had stolen Lauren's camera and was holding it hostage until we agreed to pay.

"Come on, Lauren. Let's go," I urged, leaping out onto the sidewalk. "I got the door open."

"No," she said. "I'm not about to let this asshole steal my camera."

I admired that Lauren never allowed herself to be pushed around, but in this particular situation, I feared for her safety. If the taxi driver had no misgivings about fraud and theft, he likely had no misgivings about physical assault.

"Should I go get hotel security?" I asked her.

"Yes, get them quick."

I sprinted into the hotel lobby, where I alerted two security officers.

"Where is your friend now?" they asked.

"Still in the taxi. We need to hurry."

By the time we got outside, the taxi was speeding into a column of moving traffic. Lauren raced down the sidewalk in pursuit, waving her hands and shouting.

"He punched me," she cried, eyes wide with shock. "He actually punched me."

I checked her injuries to make sure they weren't severe. She had a large purpling bruise on her upper thigh. Apparently, the taxi driver had grabbed her by the hip and then taken a swing at her when she had leaned over the seat to take back her camera by force.

"He was likely an illegal immigrant," one of the security officers explained. "Many illegals set up fraud taxi services to scam tourists. Good that you refused to pay him."

Fortunately, Lauren had managed to get a snapshot of the taxi driver's license plate as he fled, so we were able to file a police report. While I hoped the man would be found and arrested, I was most of all grateful that Lauren hadn't been seriously hurt. We were lucky. In fact, we had been lucky one too many times since we had started working together. Sooner or later, I thought, our luck was bound to run out.

Over the next few days, we interviewed a wide range of Russian political figures, but our most prominent interview was the most controversial: Aleksandr Dugin.

An author and political analyst, Dugin is more popular in the United States than he is in Russia. I knew little about him beforehand and had not read any of his writings. Although I agreed with but a few of his ideas, his intricate responses made for a fascinating interview.[151] He was open and honest, if not somewhat severe in appearance. A scraggily beard framed his grim, thin-lipped mouth, and equally bushy eyebrows hung above his pale blue eyes. In some respects, he reminded me of a secular monk. He seemed to me like an anachronism, his voice and demeanor not quite belonging in our modern surroundings. He communicated his ideas with confidence, carefully guiding us along the long, winding road of his thoughts.

Among his most well-known political positions was his support for the geopolitical concept of Eurasianism, which proposed a multipolar world in which continental powers break the current unipolar world hegemony. Many leftists in the United States labeled him a fascist, but in reality, he rejected the political theories of fascism, liberalism, and communism. Instead, he advocated to overcome these former three political theories with a new approach, a fourth political theory.

Lauren and I spent a lot of time together, my personal highlight of the trip. We passed many late nights in our hotel room, tasting different Russian foods on the menu and getting swept away in conversations about our pasts, futures, and private thoughts. Like Martin, Lauren was a fiery idealist, with an irrepressible drive to create political change. She needed a meaningful purpose. For her, no project was too big to take on. She always rose to the challenge, and despite her young age, held her own in the midst of even the most dangerous of situations— traveling to South Africa to make a documentary about the targeted murders of white farmers, being detained and briefly imprisoned in Turkey, and being interrogated in the UK under the terrorism act. But perhaps most meaningful of all was when, in early 2019, her wish for a family finally came true. She married the love of her life, and shortly thereafter, gave birth to a son. To say I'm happy for her would be an understatement. While she still remains active in politics, she has a new life now, as a wife and a mother—a role that many would agree is far more valuable than the political one.

Ultimately, neither Lauren nor I was satisfied with our work in Russia. This is primarily because we had a naïve understanding of the country's national politics, which is why, in the end, I decided against publishing the majority of our interviews. For the past year or so, the footage has remained unedited and untranslated on one of my portable hard-drives.

I don't anticipate traveling again for politics in the future, but if the opportunity does again present itself, I won't repeat the mistakes I made in Russia. I'll do all of the appropriate legwork beforehand. Not just when it comes to understanding the political situation, but when it comes to securing a cameraman, booking interviews, studying the culture, having a guide, and, most importantly of all, making sure there's not a mainstream media journalist in sight.

9

Stand for truth; it is enough.
                    —Ben Johnson

Disclaimer: I cannot recall Martin's 2018 trial in word-for-word detail. Firstly, due to the fact that the trial was in German, and secondly, because recording devices weren't permitted in the courtroom. For this reason, I have relied on Martin's notes, as well as media coverage, to write the following chapter. In the interest of length, minor details have been omitted. Moreover, all of the courtroom dialogue—spoken by the judge, Lehofer, Winklhofer, and the seventeen accused—has either been directly translated or translated with paraphrasing. Lastly, since the judge did not wish for the media to make his identity public at any point during the trial, I have excluded his name and altered the description of his appearance.

IDAHO, UNITED STATES
JUNE 2018

A part of me was happy to leave Russia. I needed familiarity and felt an almost desperate pull toward home. For the first time during my political travels, I was truly homesick. I wanted nothing more than to be back in Idaho with my family, gathered together in our fireside living room overlooking the Spokane River.

Aside from my parents, I missed Nicole the most. Our life paths had significantly diverged since 2016. Having decided not to become a political activist, she spent her days working a part-time job and, in her free time, writing novels. Occasionally, she made cultural commentary videos with me for my YouTube channel, but apart from these rare appearances, she kept a low online profile. I was happy she had chosen a stabler path, that she was able to lead some semblance of a normal life, although she did have her own hardships, as everyone does.

"Do you still not regret getting political?" Nicole asked me one night. We were sitting on the sofa, eating popcorn as we browsed for a movie. She had always been able to read my moods, and I knew she sensed my anxiety over Martin's trial.

"No," I answered honestly. "I still don't regret it…but sometimes I do feel conflicted. It's not something I like doing, and being attacked can get overwhelming sometimes. But quitting would be cowardly. As if I just got too tired and gave up."

Nicole nodded slowly, her fingers absently picking through the popcorn. "I could never see you giving up. It's the right attitude to have, of course, but I'd be lying if I said it didn't worry me sometimes."

I understood how she felt, more than she realized. I knew the pain of seeing Martin suffer. It was the same pain she felt watching me be scrutinized and attacked. I couldn't deny that my political experiences had changed me, in ways both good and bad. I had become more resilient, knowledgeable, and determined to achieve my political goals, but I had also become more isolated, hardened, and mistrustful toward people. The change in me was so drastic that at times it was difficult to relate to others, even to my own family.

Our lives weren't supposed to be this way.

I felt a pang of regret as I recalled the life we used to talk about since we were teenagers: living together in a remote wilderness, in a lighthouse between sea and forest. We had planned to spend our days writing books, with little care for what happened in the outside world. Unfortunately, reality isn't kind to most dreams. Perhaps, if the current state of the world was different, if Western governments were less totalitarian and their leaders less corrupt, I would have been able to pursue this dream. On the other hand, I have come to accept that God dealt me specific cards for a specific reason. To reject them would be to reject His will.

"How would you feel about me visiting you in Vienna this summer?" Nicole asked.

I smiled. Nothing would have made me happier. "Let's look at flights tomorrow."

Over the next month, I hardly slept. Night after night, my mind refused to settle, to stop overanalyzing the allegations of the trial. I had heard rumors that the public prosecutor, Winklhofer, had a reputation for being vindictive. The rumors claimed that his verbal attacks were so vicious he had brought a grown man to tears in court. Anyone who was unfortunate enough to fall into his line of sight ran the risk of being destroyed. He didn't like to lose. This time, though, a victory for Winklhofer would mean a prison sentence for Martin.

Martin and I spoke on the phone almost every day. Since he was in the GMT+1 time zone, nine hours ahead of me, I called him in the middle of the night. He told me that, in total, seventeen members of Generation Identity were being tried: sixteen men and one woman. The date for the trial's commencement was July 4, and it would likely last for the entire month. Fortunately, I was allowed to re-enter to Vienna again on a tourist visa just a few days before the trial began. I would be by Martin's side every step of the way.

I quickly grew tired of lying awake all night. I felt that I was wasting time and decided I needed a new project. The project ended up being this book, *Patriots Not Welcome*. At first, I wondered if drudging up the negative experiences of my political past would take an emotional toll. To my surprise, the process was cathartic. Not only was I able to find closure, I was able to make peace with some of my negative memories. I also enjoyed reliving the positive ones.

As the weeks passed by, I made an effort to pray more. I offered rosaries, novenas, and various other prayers for Martin's acquittal. Knowing that I couldn't bear the burden all on my own, I did what my mother had often told me to do and handed my worries to God. Things got better after that. I came into a much healthier headspace, where I was able to smile, laugh, and plan for Martin's upcoming visit to Idaho.

Martin only stayed in Idaho a few days. The main reason for his visit was to speak privately with my parents. I was asked to stay at home while he went to dinner with each of them individually. What the topic of their discussions were, I didn't know for sure. And I wouldn't find out until almost two months later.

THE TRIAL BEGINS

Martin and I booked the same flight back to Austria. I rested my head on his shoulder for most of the journey, our hands intertwined together between us. His presence, as always, radiated certainty and strength. Still, I figured that, at least on the inside, he had to be concerned. If he was, he would likely never show it. Only once had I ever seen him vulnerable: when I had gone missing during our United Kingdom imprisonment. To him, hiding his vulnerability seemed to be a matter of self-preservation. And even more importantly, a matter of honor.

"We're going to make it," Martin whispered, as I started to nod off, my head still resting on his shoulder.

I glanced up into his face, offering him a sleepy smile. "I know we will."

Although Martin and I had only known each other for one year, it seemed the events we had experienced together could have spanned a lifetime. About half of these events were positive, a treasure trove of memories that were a joy to think back on, but the other half tainted our romance with tragedy. Because both of us were willing to suffer for the other, the suffering brought us closer, bonding us on a level deeper than we had imagined possible.

The mood in the Western world had darkened since 2016 and 2017. Political activists no longer felt the invincibility of the past. What shook our resolve was that, even though we weren't criminals, our enemies were starting to treat us as such. It's like what the chief of the Soviet secret police, Lavrentiy Beria, once said: "You bring me the man; I'll find the crime." This, I realized, was exactly what Martin's political opponents were trying to do to him.

And Martin wasn't alone.

Only a few weeks prior, Tommy Robinson had been imprisoned in England. He had been arrested outside Leeds Crown Court as a consequence of using social media to discuss details of an ongoing gang-rape trial—one that had initially been reported on by local media, but was later put under reporting restrictions. Tommy pleaded guilty to contempt of court, which resulted in him being sentenced to thirteen months in prison.[152]

Upon hearing the news, Martin and I tried to support Tommy in whatever way we could. Martin held a demonstration for him in Vienna, while I filmed a few YouTube videos raising awareness. I also wrote him a couple of encouraging letters.

Ultimately, Martin and I considered that perhaps our goal shouldn't be about surviving long-term, but rather, about staying strong until the end, about living a life, however brief, that we could be proud of.

The days leading up to the trial were quiet, a frustrating calm before an unpredictable future. I was thrilled when my friend, Nick Monroe, traveled to Vienna to support Martin and me during the trial. It was the first time we had met in person, but there was no discomfort, no awkward silences. We had gone through too much together.

Slenderly built, with a close buzzcut and large energetic eyes, Nick seemed to be powered by an invisible engine that never ran out of gas. I was grateful for his optimism, his easy laughter. It was the perfect remedy to lighten the mood.

On July 4, Martin, Nick, and I drove to the city of Graz. When we arrived at the courthouse, the sun was halfway in the morning sky, climbing over a cityscape of red shingled rooftops and emerald patina domes. The sight of Austrian people, chatting as they breakfasted at cafés or rode the tram to work, helped add a sense of normalcy to the day.

Martin and the sixteen other defendants met with their defense attorney, Lehofer, outside the courthouse. Bald, with a baritone voice and a slim athletic build, Lehofer was a husband and a father who enjoyed studying jujitsu in his spare time. He wore a smart gray suit, his tie loosened at the collar, underscoring his professional yet easy-going demeanor.

"Stand back, please. My clients will give no statements at this time," Lehofer told the press, who had gathered outside the courthouse with cameras and microphones. Journalists continued to take photographs, calling out to Martin, asking him why he in particular was refusing to issue a statement. I knew most of the journalists had no interest in seeing him vindicated. On the contrary, for many of them, attending the trial was an obvious act of schadenfreude. Nothing would please them more than to see Martin Sellner off the streets.

One of the most significant shows of support that Martin received came from Heinz-Christian Strache, who was the Austrian Vice-Chancellor at the time. In early May, Strache had shared a video condemning the prosecution of Generation Identity in Austria, calling it 'thought-provoking.'[153]

I hung close to Lehofer as he conversed with Martin and the other defendants, trying to catch what bits of information I could.

"Now, things are getting serious," Lehofer said in German, once the media had left. "Regardless of what you think of Winklhofer on personal grounds, he is *not* to be brushed off or underestimated. He's extremely intelligent. If you think your political knowledge is superior simply because you've read a few dozen political or philosophical books, well, chances are, Winklhofer has read these books, too. Most of you don't stand a chance of outsmarting him, so it's best if none of you try." Lehofer gestured at the courthouse with his thumb, as if in warning. "From this moment forward, your behavior is being scrutinized by everyone—the judge, Wiklhofer, and the media. How you act, whether it be positive or negative, *will* affect the outcome of this trial. So, I'm relying on all of you to stay calm and focused—not just today, but until the trial ends."

His clients nodded their heads, seeming to grasp the gravity of the situation. Martin edged closer to Lehofer and spoke to him in a low voice. I couldn't make out his words, but I didn't have time to ask. The trial was scheduled to begin soon. Wanting to get a good seat, I made my way through the security checkpoint alone. Beyond the security gate was a colonnaded entrance hall, the darkness broken up by beautiful hanging lamps that looked to have come from a bygone era. I wondered how many defendants had walked these halls, both guilty and innocent. How many had received a verdict of true justice? I couldn't help but think, when all was said and done, how Martin would be remembered here. As a criminal? Or as a patriot?

Ten minutes later, Martin and the other defendants arrived. When they filed into the courtroom, a policeman escorted them to a row of chairs at the front. To their left sat the public prosecutor, Winklhofer, and to their right, the defense attorney, Lehofer.

The judge presided over the courtroom from a yellow-wood desk, neatly arranged with documents. Middle-aged, with a pointed black mustache and a wiry build, he donned a uniform of cascading black robes that whispered with his short, clipped strides. He adjusted his glasses as he looked over the documents, his expression neutral. For him, the trial seemed to be business as usual. I caught sight of Martin's book, *Identitär!*, on the edge of his desk. Clearly, he had done his homework. I suspected he had watched all of Martin's YouTube videos, as well.

"What'd I miss?" Nick asked, smiling as he took a seat beside me.

"Nothing yet," I said in a low voice. "Thanks for being here, Nick."

"Don't even mention it." He waved it off. "But I have to say…of all the people I'm friends with, it's you and Martin that are most likely to get me on some kind of watchlist. You two really have crazy lives."

I laughed nervously. "Half the time, it doesn't seem real."

Journalists scattered into seats around us. A few Generation Identity supporters were also in attendance. I envied how they were able to interpret each and every German word spoken, but was equally grateful when one of them offered to translate the important points.

The trial commenced at 9:00 a.m. with a statement from the judge. He began by directing his attention to the seventeen defendants. "Listen closely because I will only say this once: We are *not* here for politics. I do *not* want my courtroom to become a scene for political activism." He then loosened up, addressing the courtroom in full. "Why are we here today? We are here to clearly and accurately examine the actions of the political movement, Generation Identity. The court will determine what the law says in regards to their actions, and a verdict will be reached. In the end, whether you like Generation Identity or not is not up for debate. The only thing up for debate is whether or not they are criminals."

Upon hearing the English translation of the judge's statement, I relaxed in my seat. Perhaps, under his ruling, Generation Identity would get a fair trial. The judge motioned for the court session to continue, shifting focus to the public prosecutor.

A man of older years, Winklhofer was a product of impeccable grooming. His white hair was neatly combed, and his court attire—black velvet robes with a collar trimmed in red—looked newly pressed. He had a firm mouth, which he set in a determined line, and his chin was still strong, despite the aging skin that hung loosely around the edges of his face. The piercing directness of his gaze held my attention from the moment I saw him: there was intent behind it. He struck me as the kind of man who would pursue a goal to the point of obsession.

Rising, Winklhofer formally addressed the courtroom, before launching into his opening plea. He walked the judge through the entire history of Generation Identity, specifying that it had been founded by Martin Sellner, Patrick Lenart, and Alexander Markovic in 2012. He claimed that from the beginning, Generation Identity had been cultivating a hateful environment within its ranks, but that since 2016, the actions that incited hatred of certain groups had intensified, and that Generation Identity wanted to insult and belittle people like foreigners, Muslims, and refugees with the hope of creating a negative public opinion of them.[154]

"The agitation incited by the identitarians has been disregarded for far too long," Winklhofer insisted.[155] He then called attention to the fact that Generation Identity was well-organized. "The identitarians have an almost militarily-strict hierarchical order—a federal leadership, which is followed by state leaders and district leaders. They are also organized in media such as YouTube: constant presentations incite more call to action. This, in turn, stimulates their merchandise sales."[156]

I found it strange that Winklhofer used Martin's merchandise as an angle of attack. Since 2012, Martin and Patrick Lenart had co-owned an online company called Phalanx Europa, which sold political t-shirts, stickers, and the like. In addition, Generation Identity also accepted donations. But why was this controversial? Without money, how else could Generation Identity afford to print giant banners or rent costly equipment such as the ship used in the Defend Europe mission? Did Winklhofer expect them to produce these things out of thin air? Not to mention, many activist movements, including Greenpeace, also accepted donations. It was a standard practice.

Winklhofer went on to highlight the primary indictments of the trial. He accused Generation Identity of forming a criminal organization in accordance with Section 278 of the Austrian Criminal Code, as well as incitement, property damage, and coercion in one case.[157] He also made reference to three of their political actions in particular.

The first action, performed in 2016, saw Generation Identity hang a banner from the rooftop of the Graz Green Party headquarters. The banner, doused with red food dye to create the appearance of blood, bore the slogan 'Islamization kills' and was meant to protest the Bataclan Theatre Massacre during which radical Muslim terrorists had murdered ninety innocent people. In the second action, performed in 2016, Generation Identity interrupted a lecture at the Klagenfurt University in Graz. The lecture was aimed at teaching students how to help migrants integrate into the Austrian labor force,[158] which the identitarians objected to on the grounds that university educations should be politically neutral, not a platform for promoting leftist ideology. The identitarians, half of whom were dressed in burqas, carried a banner onto the lecture stage while shouting slogans through a megaphone. The principal of the university reacted in a rage and latched onto one of the identitarians' jackets. The identitarian, a young man named Luca, responded by pushing the professor away—and for this, Luca faced an assault charge. In the third action, performed in 2017, Generation Identity hung a banner from the rooftop of the Turkish embassy in Vienna that read, 'Erdoğan, take your Turks back home!'

Before concluding his plea, Winklhofer addressed the seventeen defendants directly. "The issue of immigration *cannot* be solved by agitation," he said firmly. "You are not solving the problem of immigration. You are too *lazy*. You are merely boosting your business, the profit of which flows to the people at the top. Your motivation is hatred. In Austria, you can be left, left-left, right, east or west, it does not matter. But you're not allowed to *incite hatred*."[159]

As Winklhofer retook his seat, Nick and I exchanged nervous glances. Even before we heard a precise translation of his plea, we sensed the abrupt change in the courtroom atmosphere, the sudden crackling tension, as if an axe had appeared out of nowhere and was swinging over everyone's heads. Everyone except Lehofer, who calmly finished jotting down his notes. The swift strokes of his pen could be heard even from the back of the room. I assumed he was crafting responses to specific allegations that Winklhofer had made.

Once finished, he rose and addressed the courtroom using the official formalities. His posture was self-assured, his words sure-fire and quick. He didn't seem interested in a tempered rebuttal.

"The prosecution's indictments are a blatant attempt to silence my clients," he declared. "The slogan 'Islamization kills,' used in the 2016 banner action in Graz, was a necessary emphasis for protest and objection.[160] It was crafted in response to the Bataclan Theatre Massacre and was meant to protest a particular radical strain of Islam. To conclude that the identitarians wished to claim that *every* Muslim is a murderer is simply false."

Lehofer likewise declared that the phrase 'Erdoğan, take your Turks back home!,' which was used in the 2017 banner action in Vienna, was *not* directed against all Turks, but rather, against the Turkish president, Erdoğan. Politicians like Chancellor Sebastian Kurz and Efgani Dönmez had also voiced similar opinions.[161]

"The accusation of hatred is completely unhinged," Lehofer continued, speaking with a passion that enriched the meaning of his words. Although he was apolitical, I could see that he was becoming increasingly shocked at the rigidity of the Austrian state. In particular, he criticized Winklhofer's focus on the identitarians' use of chalk in their political actions, saying, "He better now prosecute little girls playing hopscotch in the street for having formed a criminal organization."[162] He further criticized the way in which Austrian police had been dispatched all over the country, hunting down Generation Identity stickers on building walls and street signs in order to photograph and even to fingerprint them.

"It's not only the house-raids that are without merit; this entire *trial* is without merit," Lehofer challenged. "Enshrined within the Austrian Constitution, we have the 'noble value of free speech.'[163] And since the identitarians are a non-violent movement that engages in peaceful activism similar to that of Greenpeace, their activism is protected by this free speech."

Lehofer retook his seat, signaling to the judge that he was finished. The judge responded by announcing that the seventeen defendants would now be individually questioned. Martin, being the founder and co-leader of Generation Identity in Austria, was first in line.

Martin straightened his dark gray suit jacket as he positioned himself before the judge at a small yellow table with a single chair. Mounted on the table was a microphone. Martin sat at his fullest height, his hands folded on the tabletop. I couldn't see his face, only the back of his head, displaying the fresh undercut he had gotten the day before.

"In your own words, what is Generation Identity?" the judge asked him. "What are the goals you hope to accomplish?"

"Generation Identity is a pan-European patriotic youth movement," Martin replied. "We are opposed to mass migration and the Islamization of Europe. The movement was initially founded in France under the name *Génération Identitaire*. But in 2012, I came across online footage of one of their banner protests—it was at the construction site of a mosque in France—and I liked the action. No patriotic youth movements existed in Austria at the time, so I decided to co-found an Austrian branch of Generation Identity with Patrick Lenart and Alexander Markovic, calling it Identitäre Bewegung Österreich" (Identitarian Movement Austria).

"Has Generation Identity ever engaged in violence of any kind?"

"No," Martin assured. "We deliberately founded Generation Identity as a non-violent movement. All of the policies we promote are transparent and peaceful, as are all of our political actions—we always publish photographs and even footage of them online. Some would argue that our political actions are provocative, but that's because the goal is to create attention, to draw the eyes of the public to the issues that we're protesting." Martin paused a moment, as if he had finished with his response, but then added, "In a democratic society, where dozens of left-wing youth movements exist, there also has to be right-wing youth movements. Apart from Generation Identity, no other right-wing youth movements exist in Austria today. We believe that the activism we engage in is an important part of democracy and the political discourse."

"And how many active members are in your movement?" The judge queried.

"We have around three-hundred activists. We also have hundreds of donors and somewhere between ten and twenty-thousand sympathizers."

Nodding, the judge took a moment to refer to his notes. His next question switched gears, probing into Martin's past affiliation with the Austrian nationalist (Nazi) scene. In particular, the judge asked why he had been drawn to the scene in the first place.

"I've never made a secret of the fact that I was a part of these circles when I was young," Martin said. "I've addressed my past in interviews and even in my own YouTube videos. Initially, I was drawn to these circles because they were revolutionary and countercultural and because, at the time, they were the only type of activism offered to right-wing young men."

"You claim you've long since left these circles," the judge challenged. "Why exactly did you leave them?"

"I left them for the same reason I entered—because I wanted to idealistically do something for my country. But I soon discovered that these circles were not the place and that these were not the people who corresponded with my core ideals." Martin explained that the lack of activism options for right-wing young men was what had initially motivated him to launch Generation Identity. "It's a movement that offers a completely new approach to right-wing activism. All of our members are public, engaging in peaceful activism without the use of masks, but with their real faces on display. And in this sense, Generation Identity is an important part of democracy, even preventing real radicalization and extremism of young patriots who want to stand up against mass migration and the population replacement of the Austrian people."

At the corner of my eye, I noticed that Winklhofer seemed to be making detailed notes of Martin's responses. I shifted in my chair, curious to know what he was writing and whether he would also question Martin later that day. I tried to be patient. The court lunchbreak was just minutes away. I might have a chance to ask Martin about the schedule then.

One of the last significant questions posed to Martin by the judge was, "What basic ideas and values does Generation Identity have?"

"We believe in having a healthy consciousness of our people and heritage, while at the same time respecting other nations," Martin replied. "We don't harbor any hatred or supremacist attitudes toward other cultures or races; we simply want to keep our own identity and way of life. And we believe that the current migration policy here in Austria is not allowing for this, so we want a different policy. The problem is that mainstream politics and media refuse to allow this debate to take place. Those who try to talk about it are either shunned or they're not given a platform." As an example, Martin referred to an instance in which Generation Identity paid for posters to be placed on official billboards, but that within one day, the posters were removed. He added that all of the mainstream newspapers and television stations had also refused to accept their advertisements.

"So, the only way for us to create debate surrounding Austria's migration policy is through peaceful grassroots activism in the same vein of movements such as Greenpeace," Martin stated. "As a movement, we have clear political positions that we've always been transparent about. We are opposed to a population replacement here in Austria, and we believe it's well within our right to protest it in a peaceful way—that is, if our society *truly* is a democratic one. All those who disagree with our views, but who believe that democracy should exist in the exchange of ideas, should also be opposed to a ban of Generation Identity."

"You can return to your seat now," the judge told Martin. He then proceeded to announce an hour-long court recess for lunch.

I followed Martin outside the courtroom, eager for a moment to talk. He seemed detached from his surroundings as he moved through the hall, as if he were still mulling over his conversation with the judge. When I caught up with him at the security checkpoint, he told me that Lehofer needed to meet with him during the break.

"Of course." I didn't know why I hadn't assumed this. "Let's talk tonight."

Nick and I bought sandwiches, chips, and sodas from a nearby supermarket, and then sat on a ledge outside the courthouse to eat. Flowering bushes grew over the ledge, their stubby branches doing little to shade us from the hot sun. I regretted wearing such a long dress.

"So…how do you think it's going?" Nick asked, sipping from his soda.

"It's too early to make any real predictions, but I think Martin's doing well so far. Plus, as far as lawyers go, you can't get much better than Lehofer."

"Okay, but hypothetically speaking…let's say that they *do* end up being convicted of being a criminal organization." Nick took a bite of his sandwich. "What exactly would it mean?"

"It wouldn't be good." I handed Nick my soda bottle to open: with my skinny fingers, I could never manage to open bottle caps myself. "If there's a conviction, then a lot of people, far more than the seventeen currently on trial, are going to be in deep trouble. Basically everyone— from those who've publicly supported Generation Identity to those who've donated—will be labeled a part of the criminal organization. In the end, all of the Generation Identity supporters, along with the few hundred activists who aren't a part of this trial, could possibly face convictions of their own."

"Oh, shit," Nick exclaimed.

"I know."

"Wow. I can't even imagine what Martin must be feeling right now."

I couldn't, either. Being the leader and co-founder of Generation Identity, much of the responsibility fell squarely on his shoulders. If convicted, it wouldn't be the movement, but Martin who took most of the blame for dragging hundreds, even thousands, of Austrian patriots into a criminal organization.

"Well, if it makes you feel any better," Nick interjected, "today's the Fourth of July…you know, freedom and all."

I laughed. "But that's just for the USA."

"Even so." Nick raised his soda bottle. "Happy Fourth of July, Britt."

I clanked my bottle against his. "Happy Fourth of July."

An hour later, Nick and I returned to the courthouse, and the trial resumed with more direct questioning of the defendants. I quickly zoned out in the flurry of German words, but every so often, I checked on Martin. He sat up straight, his posture showing no hint of uncertainty. It wasn't until later, when we were in the car driving back to Vienna, surrounded by Fourth of July themed tinsel and streamers that Martin had surprised Nick and me with, that I learned he had a rosary in his pocket and had been praying the entire time.

FREE SPEECH VERSUS HATE SPEECH

After the first exhausting day of trial, Martin suggested it might be better if I didn't accompany him to Graz for the upcoming court dates. Since I couldn't yet understand German, and since Martin needed to focus on the trial, I agreed to remain in Vienna until the day of the verdict.

I tried to keep busy, either filming YouTube videos in my apartment or giving Nick a tour of popular Viennese hotspots. Unfortunately, he soon had to fly home, leaving me to wander the city on my own. Summer was in full swing, hot as a bathhouse sauna, yet somehow still lush as a spring meadow. Bright yellow bees buzzed about the hyacinth flowers, which bloomed across rolling fields that only grew greener as they stretched into the forest.

Sometimes, when the evenings were cool enough, I climbed out my window and onto the rooftop of my apartment. There, while listening to music and drinking hard cider, I drifted in thoughts about the future—not simply about the outcome of the trial, but far beyond that, years ahead. Where would Martin and I be? I hoped we would be married. I hoped we would be living somewhere in the Austrian countryside with a family of our own. While I hadn't spent much of my childhood dreaming about raising a family, since meeting Martin, it had become the life I wanted most.

After each new day in court, Martin called me on his way home from Graz to explain what had happened. Most of the stories he told were grim, but every so often, we were able to laugh. The trial had progressed onto testimonies from the witnesses called to the stand by Winklhofer. One of the witnesses, who was a high-level official from the BVT, an Austrian intelligence agency, had been unable to produce an accurate definition of right-wing extremism upon Lehofer's request.[164] According to Martin, this had baffled the judge. Another witness, who was a student at Klagenfurt University in Graz, claimed that a Generation Identity activist, Luca Kerbl, had deliberately punched the principle of the university in the stomach during one of their political actions.[165] In response, Luca testified that he had merely freed himself from the principal's grasp, insisting that he had lightly touched the principal at most.[166] But perhaps most notable of all was the Kurdish witness, who had discovered one of Generation Identity's stickers on the wall of his pizzeria. The sticker read, 'Islamists Not Welcome,' which refers to any advocates of Islamic militancy or fundamentalism.

"Winklhofer was hoping the Kurdish man would be an important witness for him, but it backfired," Martin told me over the phone. "Rather than testify against us, the Kurdish man told the courtroom that he not only *agreed* with the sticker's message, he was also a harsh critic of the Turkish president, Erdoğan."

Toward the middle of the trial, I noticed the stress was starting to overwhelm one of my friends, Franziska, whose boyfriend was also among the seventeen defendants. We hadn't spoken much since the trial started, but a single glance at her Instagram feed betrayed her anxiety. I clicked on her latest post, a wall of polaroid photos showcasing various Generation Identity political actions. The caption under the post read:

I'm tired of the waiting…of the wondering and the constant asking of questions like: "What if?" It's becoming difficult for me to do basic things, like focus on my job, or even to eat and sleep. I know it's pointless to dwell upon the unknowable, but I can't help it. I'm frightened for my boyfriend's future and my own.

I didn't fault Franziska for being afraid. Had the trial occurred two years ago, I probably would have completely fallen apart. I wasn't naturally stronger than her; I had simply been the target of more political repression. Perhaps, in some respects, I should've been grateful for these experiences. Each hardship was a preparation for the one that followed.

I called Franziska later that day, inviting her and another friend, Ariane, to meet up at our favorite restaurant-bar, Die Wäscherei. Located in the eighth district of Vienna, the walls of the restaurant-bar were punctuated by tall windows, flung wide open to invite in the summer breeze. There, over a round of coffees and wine spritzers, we discussed the trial and its possible outcomes.

"The hardest part is wondering," Franziska said, toying with the stem of her wine glass. "The verdict can go either way. I'm not confident in either outcome."

"Yes, but the charges are empty," Ariane reminded. "Hanging banners, spraying the streets with temporary chalk, placing stickers around the city...it's hardly serious vandalism. Plus, most of the policies they promote are similar to the ones promoted by Austrian right-wing politicians. They're not inciting hatred."

I agreed with Ariane, but I couldn't deny that Franziska also had a point. The Austrian laws were nebulous, particularly when it came to hate speech. What did 'hate speech' even mean? It was a totally subjective term. Not to mention, in the eyes of Western society, hate speech only applied to certain ethnicities and religions. For example, I couldn't recall one instance in which a person had been convicted of hate speech for criticizing Christianity. Day in and day out, people all over the world are free to openly blaspheme Jesus Christ. I've attended two pro-life marches in Vienna, and at each one, Antifa displayed a giant banner with a slogan, 'Mary should've aborted Jesus Christ.' If Martin or any other right-winger decided to display a banner calling for Allah or Mohammed to be aborted, it would make international media headlines and result in a hate speech trial. While I personally believe that hate speech falls under free speech and should never be prosecuted, the fact that criticizing certain religions warrants a criminal trial, while criticizing other religions does not, is tyrannical.

"Trials like this shouldn't be happening in Austria," Ariane insisted. "Freedom of speech is in the Constitution."

"The Austrian Constitution supports free speech, but with an exception for hate speech," Franziska pointed out.

"Hate speech trials are actually pretty common in Austria," I said. "There's never any political repression against left-wingers, but right-wingers have to deal with it all the time. The Austrian public isn't aware of it because the media doesn't report about it. But the reason this trial in particular has been spotlighted is because Generation Identity is popular, and many of their members are public personalities. The media couldn't ignore it even if they wanted to."

Ariane used her phone to Google the statistics. "A few hundred," she said. "There's been a few hundred hate speech trials in Austria this year so far."

The trials didn't stop at a few hundred. By the end of 2018, Austria would go on to host 1,328 trials for hate speech.[167]

"I'll be right back." Franziska scooted from the booth and headed for the restroom.

"I'll order you another wine spritzer," Ariane called after her.

Once the order was placed, Ariane fished through her purse for a cigarette and then asked me about the latest trial update.

"Nothing much, mostly technical stuff," I answered. "In the end, the verdict all boils down to the question of intent."

Ariane frowned, her narrowing eyes clouded by cigarette smoke. "What do you mean?"

I splashed some cream into my coffee, debating how to best explain. "Martin told me that during questioning by the judge and Winklhofer, he's being asked a lot of complex political questions. He's being asked to give step-by-step explanations of what exactly he *means* by terms like integration, inclusion, and identity. He said it often turns into an intellectual debate, whose outcome can alter the court's favor against him and possibly even lead to a conviction."

Ariane's mouth went slack. "That's crazy. So, if Martin says something that can be interpreted as hate speech during one of his explanations, then the court might decide that Generation Identity's intent all along was to commit hate speech?"

"Yes, exactly." I used my phone to pull up a photo of Generation Identity's 2016 banner action, where they had climbed on the rooftop of the Green Party Headquarters in Graz. "Do you remember the slogan 'Islamization kills' that they used in this banner action?"

"I remember." Ariane nodded.

"Basically, the judge needs to establish the intent behind this slogan," I explained. "Did Generation Identity mean that *all* of Islam is violent and that *all* of the people who practice it are murderers? In this case, the slogan would be hate speech, and Generation Identity would be convicted of being a criminal organization. But if, on the other hand, Generation Identity had intended for the slogan to refer to Islamization as a *process*—like the process of a radical, violent, and anti-democratic strain of Islam acquiring influence in the Austrian political sphere—then it could be interpreted in a different way, and it wouldn't be hate speech."

"I see." Ariane stubbed out her cigarette in the table ashtray. "But in order to truly establish Generation Identity's intent, the judge is going to have to analyze a lot more than just their banner slogans. He's going to have to analyze their entire political ideology."

"Yes, that's what he's doing, and it's probably why the trial is taking so long." I pushed away my empty coffee cup with a sigh.

Just then, Franziska returned, her dark red braids looking smooth, as if she'd redone them in the bathroom.

"I'm so sorry, but I need to get home now," she told us. "My boyfriend called and said he's on his way home from the courthouse. I want to have dinner ready by the time he arrives."

Ariane checked her wristwatch. "I actually need to get home, too."

We paid for our drinks, and then moved to the curb outside to say our goodbyes. While waiting for our taxis, I asked Franziska if she was planning on attending the final day of the trial.

"I'm not sure yet," she said. "To be honest, I don't know if I can handle it."

"But don't you think you'll end up regretting it if you don't come?"

"Maybe." She chewed her lip, looking conflicted. "Are you going?"

"Yes, Martin and I are going together. We can take you and your boyfriend with us, if you want."

"All right," she decided. "If all of us go together, I'll come."

VERDICT DAY

Martin stopped returning to Vienna near the end of the trial. The courthouse in Graz was a two-and-a-half-hour drive, much too long a trip to make daily, so he decided to remain in Graz until the evening before the verdict. While I missed him, I was grateful for his frequent calls, even if his updates weren't always a cause for celebration. Most recently, the Austrian Minister of Justice had given Winklhofer the green light to open financial investigations into fifteen Generation Identity members and three different associations affiliated with their movement. One of the goals of these financial investigations was to determine if Generation Identity was guilty of money laundering, a suspicion based on no evidence. Another goal was to determine if Martin was guilty of tax fraud, tax evasion, and misusing his donation funds.

"I think Winklhofer is starting to lose faith in a guilty verdict," Martin told me. "That's why he's casting a wider net, attacking us from all sides. He's hoping that something, anything, will stick."

I realized then at least one of the rumors about Winklhofer was correct: when he chose a target, he stuck with it, working with obsessive dedication until he saw it destroyed. Even if the judge fully acquitted Generation Identity, I doubted Winklhofer would give up his crusade. As one door closed, he would simply search for a new one to open. The risk remained that at some point, possibly years from now, he might actually succeed in his mission.

The night before the verdict, Martin and I stayed up late, sitting together on a couch in the living room of his parent's house. Nestled against him, my head resting on his chest, I reiterated the promise I had once made to him.

"No matter what happens tomorrow, I'm not going anywhere."

Martin didn't answer in words, just hugged me tighter.

I considered if I should ask him a question that, up until that point, I hadn't felt was appropriate, and decided yes. "Are you scared?"

"Yes," he answered honestly. "But not for myself. I'm scared for you and for my family...how all of these hardships have affected you. I'm scared for the future of Generation Identity and also for my country. Of all the things tomorrow's verdict will determine, the most important is whether or not Austria is free."

The next morning, on July 26, Franziska and her boyfriend rode the train to Baden, a small spa town where Martin's parents lived. From there, the four of us piled into Martin's car and drove to Graz. We tried to keep the mood light, blasting German hip-hop as we merged onto the Autobahn. Martin and Franziska's boyfriend sat in front, chatting loudly as if all were normal, while in the back seat, Franziska and I kept quieter. She offered me some fresh cake she had baked the night before, and as we ate, we steered the conversation toward mundane things like what our favorite hobbies were and how we both shared a love for Venice.

When we arrived at the courthouse, Martin and Franziska's boyfriend joined Lehofer for a final meeting. Meanwhile, Franziska and I headed straight into the courtroom in an effort to dodge the media.

Generation Identity supporters and journalists packed the seats. Animated conversation buzzed all around us—one of the journalists even broke into laughter—but somehow, the mood in the courtroom remained tense. As I took a seat next to Franziska, I searched for Winklhofer. He sat at desk, his white eyebrows furrowed, his hands steepled in a thoughtful pose. For a brief moment, I tried to put myself inside his mind, to understand the root of his hatred for Generation Identity. But since I wasn't privy to his political views, there was no true way for me to distinguish whether his motives were personal, ideological, or if he simply believed they had broken the law. All I knew was that he had spent years of his life building a case against Generation Identity and that work of that caliber took perseverance and dedication. Unless the verdict was announced in Winklhofer's favor, I was sure it wouldn't be long before we heard news that he had decided to appeal.

"Here they come." Franziska's words broke me from my thoughts.

I turned around, heartbeat quickening as the seventeen defendants filed into the courtroom. Most of the men had made an effort to dress formally, looking sharp in their pressed suits and ties, their hair freshly combed. They took their seats as the judge entered.

"Before the verdict is read, we will hear the closing statements," the judge announced.

"I'll translate for you," Franziska whispered to me.

As always, Winklhofer's statement was made with precision. He positioned himself directly before the seventeen defendants, and then repeated his accusations, insisting that, at its core, Generation Identity was a movement that carried out criminal acts. He claimed that even if the vandalism they had committed was minor, it was still vandalism and that they were also guilty of hate speech. Therefore, the judge should convict them of forming a criminal organization in accordance with Section 278 of the Austrian Criminal Code.

"You present yourselves as a front of law-abiding people, yet you are constantly breaking the law," he accused.[168] He referenced the identitarians' political action at Klagenfurt University, during which one of the activists, Luca, had been involved in an altercation with the university's principal. "One could have faced the discussion," Winklhofer argued, suggesting that the identitarians should've chosen debate over a political action. "For me, you are not a front of patriots, but a front of cowards."[169]

"He's wrong, having a debate was impossible," Franziska murmured to me. "The identitarians tried reaching out to the university several times, but the principal himself said that the identitarians weren't welcome. So, their political action was a completely legitimate form of protest."

Of course, it was. Because much of the left preferred censorship over debate. Plus, Antifa activists often went far beyond protesting, even resorting to physical violence with zero consequences. In 2019, Antifa shut down a history lecture at the University of Vienna because the lecture's professor had once given a speech at a Freedom Party event. After creating a wall with their bodies, blocking the entrance, and forcing away the attendees, not one of their members was hauled into a courtroom. On the contrary. Antifa was praised.

Winklhofer went on to cite a second identitarian political action in which the only female among the seventeen defendants had sprayed a chalk slogan onto a wall. "She is also a victim; she would never have come up with such an idea on her own. This is how your movement deals with the foot-soldiers."[170] He was critical of the fact that Generation Identity had a system of hierarchy. "You avoid acceptable forms of engagement because agitation is easier, because fact-based criticism is difficult," he accused, and then described the identitarians as "pseudo-moralists who pretend to protect the State."[171]

I frowned as Franziska translated Winklhofer's statements, thinking it was dishonest to refer to the female identitarian on trial as a victim. The girl had joined Generation Identity for the explicit purpose of engaging in activism. To allude to Martin as being some kind of puppet-master at the top was crazy. Martin himself often engaged in such activism, hanging banners, passing out campaign leaflets, and so on. But even if he didn't, maintaining hierarchy within a political movement is standard. All throughout our society we have hierarchy—in government, in education, and in the medical field. Otherwise, these systems devolve into chaos. Furthermore, if Winklhofer cared so much about vandalism, why wasn't he also dragging Antifa into court? At the moment, you can't take a casual walk through the streets of Vienna without coming across Antifa stickers and graffiti.

But perhaps most telling of all was the fact that Winklhofer had resorted to insults. *Cowards.* No, it wasn't the identitarians who were cowards. The real cowards were those who ignored the debate surrounding mass migration and the Islamization of Europe simply because they feared how it might affect their societal standing. Movements like Generation Identity, on the other hand, dealt with the price of engaging in this debate on a daily basis: censorship, vilification, and criminalization. And all for what? For daring to state controversial truths that millions of others were also thinking, but were too afraid to discuss in public.

Lehofer took the floor next. He started by addressing Winklhofer, clearly as disappointed as I was in his personal insults. "Martin Sellner had often risked his life for his political activism. He's scaled buildings to hang banners, he's chartered a ship in the Mediterranean to document NGO activity. You can say what you like about my client, but you cannot say he's a coward."

Lehofer then addressed the full courtroom, making an important point that he would later repeat in a post-trial interview with the Austrian media outlet, *Der Standard.*[172]

"I don't see a large difference between the political policies of the identitarians and those of Chancellor Kurz and Vice-Chancellor Strache. For example, the identitarians asked for the Austrian borders to be closed several years ago, and the same is now being demanded from various politicians in the Freedom Party. In my view, when a politician says Islam is not part of Europe, this goes far beyond anything that the identitarians say."

Lehofer also mentioned that even after hours of public statements from the identitarians in court, none of them had said anything that could be constituted as hate speech. Furthermore, Winklhofer had been given months to analyze the identitarians' private documents, which were seized by the Austrian Secret Police during the April house-raid, but none of the information found in these documents could be constituted as hate speech, either.

"What the identitarians say falls under freedom of speech and should, therefore, be protected by the Austrian constitution," Lehofer argued. "What has happened to my clients over the past few months is a *great* injustice…having their homes raided by police, being criminalized, being dragged in front of court…the vandalism they've committed is so minor, and yet, police were dispatched all across the country to take photos and even to lift *fingerprints* from their stickers." Lehofer gestured at the seventeen defendants, his voice growing impassioned. "Never before in my *entire* career have I witnessed a trial like this."

Lehofer ended his closing statement by reiterating the need for an acquittal, stating that a conviction would set a dangerous precedent upon which many other organizations, regardless of their political affiliation, could be prosecuted. When he was finished, the judge disappeared into a room behind his desk for a symbolic deliberation.

Franziska grabbed my hand and squeezed it tightly.

Three minutes passed.

Then five.

Franziska still hadn't let go of my hand. Maybe she hadn't noticed. Harder and harder she squeezed, until my fingers were hot and sweaty.

Martin stood in the front of the courtroom, his back facing me, his expression out of view. But somehow, I understood how he felt. We both knew that no matter how optimistic he was, no matter how well he believed the court sessions had gone, in the end, it was the judge's decision. The judge simply had to make one of two statements—guilty or not guilty—and if it was the former, their lives would be forever changed, the image of Generation Identity forever tarnished. And Martin, as the leader, would be guilty of leading hundreds of people into criminality with the tactics of showing their faces and engaging in transparent activism.

Ultimately, Martin's entire life's work as an activist was about to be judged.

After ten long minutes, the judge finally returned. He ordered the courtroom inhabitants to rise, and then addressed us in German.

I turned to Franziska, trying to determine the verdict through her expression. Eyes wide, she rocked forward on the balls of her feet, as if it would somehow help her to better hear the judge's words. And then, like a bursting dam of emotions, she broke into tears.

I searched her face, frightened. It wasn't until she turned toward me that I realized she wasn't crying tears of sadness. She was *smiling*.

"Österreich ist frei," she cried.

Austria is free.

I gripped the back of my chair, struggling to hold back tears of my own. Was it real? For a moment, my mind seemed to short-circuit, sputtering against a wave of thrilling, confusing emotions. I didn't know who to be grateful to first. *God. The judge. Lehofer.* All of them.

Most of all, I wanted to race to the front of the courtroom and hug Martin. It took all of my patience to wait to until the judge had dismissed the court session.

The judge spent several minutes clarifying his reasons for acquittal. The verdict was long, spanning twenty to thirty pages, but most importantly, he clarified that all the defendants, sixteen men and one woman, were found not guilty of forming a criminal organization— Section 278 of the Austrian Criminal Code—nor hate speech—Section 283.[173] Just one of the defendants was sentenced to pay a fine for property damage. Another defendant, Luca Kerbl, stood by his claim that he had only lightly touched the principal of Klagenfurt University, as opposed to punching him in the stomach, but the judge ruled against this claim, and Luca was sentenced to pay a fine for assault.

According to the Austrian news outlet *Tagesstimme*, 'the judge gave his reasons for acquitting the defendants by establishing, among other things, that the content of the contested claims could be interpreted in more than one way. The 'Islamization kills' banner on the rooftop of the Green Party Headquarters in Graz did not constitute a criticism of Islam, but of the policies of the Green Party and of radical Islam.

Concerning the action at Klagenfurt University, the judge argued that the defendants, too, had merely pointed out the dangers of political and radical Islam, which indeed was made clear at the time of the action. A slogan declaring integration to be a lie must therefore be understood as being directed against 'misguided policies,' and not against integration per se.'

'As the criteria for the offense of hate speech had therefore not been met, this would also be applicable in the question of forming a criminal organization: "If an organization carries out actions which are legitimate in the eyes of the law, then it is not a criminal organization, even if offenses may result from it," the judge declared. "Property damage on its own doesn't constitute Generation Identity Austria being a criminal organization." According to the law, property damage has to go beyond a certain threshold for an organization's ability to be classified as a criminal organization.'[174]

As soon as the judge dismissed the court, I joined the crowd in the entrance hall to wait for Martin. The following minutes crawled by like hours. My blood started pounding when I caught sight of his familiar black undercut near the door of the courtroom. People swarmed him; some were journalists, requesting statements, and others were loyal supporters, patting him on the back, shaking his hand, and offering their congratulations.

The moment our eyes met, Martin made a beeline for me. I smiled, then laughed as he scooped me up and swung me in the air.

We had made it. Just as he had said we would. Neither of us knew what the future held, but we were encouraged by the fact that, at least for today, Austria was free.

10

This is the true measure of love:
When we believe that we alone can love,
that no one could ever have loved so before us,
and that no one will ever love in the same way after us.
                —Johann Wolfgang von Goethe

AUSTRIA, EUROPE
AUGUST 2018

The weeks that followed were among the happiest so far of that year. In place of the stoic mood Martin had maintained during the trial, he now moved as if the weight of the world had been lifted from his shoulders. His trademark good nature, all smiles, positivity and jokes, returned. I couldn't have been happier to see him find motivation again. It was impossible to be unaffected by what happened to him, both the good and the bad. His victories, defeats and sufferings—all of them were also my own. Maybe this is a downside of love. But even if it is, I'm sure it's one that most in love are willing to accept.

On July 27, Martin and I filmed a video about the trial, sharing the details of the verdict for those who had stood by us.

Austrian politicians were already calling for a re-examination of the criminal organization law that had launched the trial in the first place. Harald Stefan, a member of the National Council for the Freedom Party, stated that Austria's liberal democracy had to endure 'criticism, such as that from the identitarians in the form of activism,' without there being any criminal judgments. He described the indictments of the public prosecutor, Winklhofer, as 'incomprehensible.' And overall, he advocated 'to take a close look at the relevant provisions of the criminal organization law on their accuracy and the extent of their restrictions on freedom of expression.'[175]

As predicted, Winklhofer had appealed the judge's verdict, meaning the case would transfer to the High Court of Austria. Since it was likely that the High Court would uphold the judge's verdict, Martin and I spared it little thought. The only setback was that Martin wasn't allowed to reclaim his possessions that had been seized by the Austrian police during the house-raid in April until the High Court had issued a final ruling.

Family and friends, who were eager to hear details of the trial, hosted parties in celebration of our victory. The most memorable of these parties was a late-night meet-up at the Das LOFT sky-bar in the second district of Vienna. The glamorous sky-bar, with its sweeping floor-to-ceiling windows, commanded a romantic view of the city by night. Bartenders dazzled patrons with tricks at the bar, which glowed in the fiery light of the electric lava ceiling. Friends from both Austria and the United Kingdom showed up, including my twin sister, Nicole. As planned, she had flown to Vienna to visit me.

The atmosphere of our group was lively and carefree, full of laughter and good humor. Deep into the night we talked, reminiscing about the past, celebrating the present and discussing projects for the future. For a fleeting moment, it felt as if we didn't have a care in the world. All that mattered was that we were together. Even after one too many close calls, we had managed not only to survive, but to overcome.

A QUESTION AND A RING

While Martin got back to work, I took a longer vacation to visit with Nicole. Thrilled at the opportunity to finally introduce her to Vienna, I showed her around the most iconic tourist spots, the coziest writing cafés, and even some of the locations where Generation Identity had performed successful political actions.

A lazy yet wonderful two weeks flew by. Sometimes, Nicole and I met up with my Austrian friends. Other times, just the two of us went exploring up steep switchback trails through forests of enchanting white trees into curious little shops tucked away in lesser-known parts of the city, and sometimes, we just lounged on the balcony of my apartment, chatting over a couple of hard ciders. We talked longer and more profoundly than we had in a while. Many of our conversations focused on the future and how it was likely that Austria would one day become my permanent home, which meant that we would eventually be separated for, perhaps, years at a time.

"Did you ever think we'd end up living on different continents?" I asked one night, as we were cooking dinner.

"Never," Nicole said.

"I think we might've taken each other for granted," I realized, "treated each other as if our time together was endless."

The mood in the kitchen grew heavy with my words. I wished I never had to let Nicole go, and it was clear to me she felt the same. All the memories we had shared together—from riding our Welsh Hackney horse in the prairies of Kansas as children, to writing in our cozy home office in California as teenagers—I wanted the chance to make more. Even if my actions hadn't always shown it, she was one of the people I loved most.

"You could always marry an Austrian," I joked.

Nicole smiled, a shadow of regret in her expression. If only life were so simple.

"My life is back in the States," she said. "Writing books, taking care of mom and dad…but that doesn't mean I'm not happy for you, Britt. I truly am."

I didn't understand what she meant by saying she was 'happy for me' until a week later, when Martin took me sailing on the Danube River.

The day was August 28, in the quiet hours before sunset. Clear and cold, the waters of the Danube were as blue as a sapphire carpet unfolding through the heart of the city. Colorful boats rocked gently on the wakes, their passengers tossing breadcrumbs to the duck families swimming by. I sat on the edge of the dock, dipping my toes into the water while Martin rented a boat. I loved the Danube. Martin and I had visited the river together once before, on July 17, to celebrate our first anniversary. It was difficult to believe that we had only known each other for a full year. In some ways, it felt like a lifetime.

"I got us a ride," Martin announced, gesturing toward a bright yellow boat with a grin. He held a red rose in one hand and his iPhone in the other, a champagne bottle peeking out from the flap of his jacket.

As he helped me into the boat, I noticed his grip was uncharacteristically slack, his palm sweaty. Why was he nervous? My suspicions heightened when, over the course of just a few minutes, he checked his phone nearly twenty times.

After a while, he broke from rowing and set the oars in the oarlocks. "I never thought I'd meet a girl like you," he said to me. "A girl who believes in the same ideals as I do, who supports my political work and who stands by me even when I'm accused of crimes and put on trial...I didn't think a girl could ever love me enough to put up with all of that."

His words were a deep echo of my own thoughts. For most of my life, I, too, had believed I might end up alone. Not because I wanted to, but because I didn't think a man like Martin existed. If I couldn't be with him, I couldn't be with anyone.

We circled the Danube River for an hour. The sun was gliding down from the sky, its last rays of light dancing on the waves before we sailed under the lamplit bridge that led back to the dock. Martin breathed deeply, seeming more nervous with each stroke of the oars. I couldn't help but smile. In the face of legal trials and life-threatening political actions, he was strong and confident, as at home as a flag on its pole. But when it came to asking me a certain question that I was becoming more and more convinced he wanted to ask, he was a castaway, plunged into new and unfamiliar waters that he had never before had to navigate.

Finally, as we drifted beneath the bridge, Martin seemed to let go. Putting the oars aside, his eyes fixed on mine, he got down on one knee.

"I've been wanting to do this for a while," he said, prying open a red velvet box.

Even though I had been expecting it, anticipating the sight of the ring and the sound of his question, I was all at once hit with a powerful flashflood of emotions that seemed to knock me outside of my own body. From afar, I watched myself give my answer as Martin pushed the ring onto my finger.

"Look behind you," Martin said.

I looked and saw a group of our friends gathered on the bridge. Some waved lighted flares above their heads; others unraveled a giant banner, handmade by Martin, that displayed the phrase: *Will you marry me?*

The sight of the banner, the ring, of Martin down on one knee—it was all that I had longed for since the day we had met. And now, a year later, it was real: a future in which, finally, we would never again have to say good-bye.

11

We make men without chests and expect of them virtue and enterprise.
We laugh at honor and are shocked to find traitors in our midst.
We castrate and bid the geldings be fruitful.
　　　—C.S. Lewis

IDAHO, UNITED STATES
SEPTEMBER 2018

Maybe I was too happy, maybe I was too high on thoughts of the future,
but the concept that I was getting married took time to fully register.
As it did, the unfamiliar shadow of change drifted over me. Years I had
spent straddling the line between childhood and adulthood, reluctant
to fully accept the latter role. I had become too attached to the idea of
youth and of having responsibility for myself alone. Martin was the first
person who made me want to alter this selfish attitude. I no longer
thought primarily of myself. I no longer considered it fair to be reckless
with my safety, either. Before all else, I embraced my duty to him.

The engagement came as a surprise to Martin's parents, but not to
my own.

"We've known since June," my dad told me over the phone. "That's
why Martin came to Idaho for a visit: he was asking us for permission."

"We didn't know exactly when he wanted to propose," my mom
added. "We've been waiting for this phone call for weeks. Have you
decided where you'll have the wedding yet?"

"Idaho," I answered with a smile. "We want to follow the tradition of getting married where the bride lives."

"You should come home soon, then," my mom urged. "There's a lot to do as far as wedding planning goes."

I followed my mom's advice. This time, leaving Martin was easier than it had been in the past because, for the first time, I saw light at the end of the tunnel. The seemingly endless flights and separations finally had an expiration date.

I dove into wedding planning shortly after arriving home. Without a doubt, my favorite part of the process was searching for a dress. I remember feeling dazed as I explored bridal shops, running my fingers across gowns with lace appliqués and pearl embroidered sleeves. Given how unconventional Martin's and my relationship was, it seemed strange to suddenly be following the normal steps that so many other relationships did.

All in all, the major parts of planning came together smoothly. With free time on my hands, I searched for a project to fill the extra slots in my day. Hesitant to write about the trial so soon, I decided to leave *Patriots Not Welcome* on the backburner, and instead, shifted my focus to working on a personal passion project. The book ended up being entitled *What Makes Us Girls* and was filled with general life advice for young women from a non-feminist perspective. The motivation came out of nowhere, striking me with enough force to see the book finished in three months.

In hindsight, I don't regard *What Makes Us Girls* as a great book, but I do regard it as genuine. The majority of its stories were born from real memories—my own personal mistakes and accomplishments.

Martin, in the meantime, was involved in a new campaign called 'UN Migrationspakt Stoppen' (Stop the Migration Pact). The campaign drew attention to the UN Global Compact for Migration, which numerous countries across the world had pledged to sign.[176] The primary red flag in the pact was that it focused on migrants rather than genuine refugees. In total, it aimed to assist 244 million migrants in their goal to migrate, meaning it wasn't some kind of humanitarian project, but rather a thinly veiled cover for an open borders policy. Each UN nation that signed was expected to open its welfare systems to migrants and, even worse, to promote positive reporting of mass migration and to penalize criticism of it. It didn't seem to matter to the UN whether or not native citizens were in support of opening their borders to millions. The goal seemed to be to shut the critics up, to make migrants a protected class, and to place the well-being of migrants over all else.

By the end of Martin's four-month campaign, the Austrian government decided *not* to follow through with their pledge of signing The UN Global Compact for Migration.[177] The decision created a domino effect, resulting in refusals to sign from several other countries such as Poland, Croatia, Czech Republic, Bulgaria, Slovenia, and more.

While I would never claim that Martin was solely responsible for the Austrian government's decision, he played an important role. It was an achievement that left me as apprehensive as I was proud. With each new success, Martin managed to make more and more enemies—the kind that never forgave or forgot. They would wait as long as it took, for months and even years, for the right moment to retaliate.

THE CALM BEFORE THE STORM

Martin flew to Idaho in early November to help with wedding preparations. During his visit, a priest performed a solemn engagement for us, a traditional ceremony in which a couple becomes officially engaged in the eyes of the Catholic Church. The ceremony took place in my parish chapel and was attended by close friends and family. Nicole stood in as one of the witnesses, signing an official certificate that declared our engagement. Afterwards, my parents hosted a beautiful, yet intimate engagement party at our home near the Spokane River. My family went above and beyond, beautifully decorating our house for the party, cooking a three-course meal from scratch, and even acting as servers during the dinner.

I couldn't have wished for a more perfect evening.

I remained in Idaho until Christmas. By that time, the final edit of *What Makes Us Girls* was finished, and the sun-filled autumn days had grown dark and snowy. For several weeks, I excitedly anticipated the book's release. Only a small percentage of my YouTube subscribers were female, so I didn't expect copies to fly off the shelves, but I hoped my advice would have some sort of positive impact. I was deeply appreciative for the hundreds of emails I received from young women over the subsequent months, telling me that the book's advice had helped them in some way like, for example, when it came to rediscovering their femininity or when it came to choosing their paths in life.

On Christmas Eve, I boarded a plane for Austria. While I was disappointed to have to spend Christmas away my family, it was the only flight I could afford at the time. The sight of Martin waiting outside the baggage claim in Vienna, smiling with a bouquet of fresh roses in hand, made the tiring hours of travel worth it.

As was tradition, we stopped for a late-night coffee at a Viennese café on our way home from the airport. Snow dusted the windowpanes, swirling outside the cafe like a million floating pearls, and twinkle lights glittered in the trees on the streets, as bright as stars shining in a clear night sky. The café atmosphere was merry with families and couples huddled together at tables glittering with cake and champagne. Martin and I, who had managed to secure a corner table, talked the night away. There was so much to celebrate: our upcoming wedding, the success of his Migration Pact campaign, and the publishing of my book. Maybe it was because it was Christmas, but for a while, the world seemed perfect, as if nothing in our lives could go wrong.

This feeling continued over the next several weeks, growing stronger and stronger, until finally, on January 23, it culminated with the Austrian High Court ruling to uphold the original verdict of Martin's trial. This meant that, once and for all, his name was cleared. Not only was he able to reclaim all of his possessions seized by the secret police in the 2018 House Raid, but he was also free to pursue new political projects without the threat of the Austrian authorities monitoring his every move.

Riding high on the good news, Martin and I decided to return to the alpine hut where we had stayed with Lauren Southern nearly a year ago. It seemed right to take a few days off, and we figured that the alpine hut was the perfect spot to celebrate.

As a general rule, I don't believe in superstition. I don't believe that certain locations are tainted with bad energy, or that they possess some sort of inextricable tie to negativity. On the other hand, this particular alpine hut has been at the center of one too many traumatic events in my life for me to regard it fondly. During my first visit in 2017, Martin and I narrowly escaped colliding with an oncoming car while sledding down a mountain. During my second visit in 2018, the Austrian Secret Police raided Martin's home, kicking off a year-long criminal trial. Finally, during my third visit in 2019, the Christchurch Shooting occurred, a terror attack that set certain events in motion which would alter the course of our lives forever.

12

Tyranny in democratic republics ignores the body and goes
straight for the soul. The master no longer says: You will think
as I do or die. He says: You are free not to think as I do. You may
keep your life, your property, and everything else. But from this
day forth you shall be as a stranger among us. You will retain your
civic privileges, but they will be of no use to you. For if you seek the
votes of your fellow citizens, they will withhold them, and if you seek
only their esteem, they will feign to refuse even that. You will remain
among men, but you will forfeit your rights to humanity. When you
approach your fellow creatures, they will shun you as one who is
impure. And even those who believe in your innocence will abandon
you, lest they, too, be shunned in turn. Go in peace, I will not take
your life, but the life I leave you with is worse than death.
   —Alexis de Tocqueville

AUSTRIA, EUROPE
MARCH 2019

Martin and I passed two peaceful days at the alpine hut. The stark
Austrian winter was in its final stages. A cool eastern wind issued across
the mountain summit, shaking wet clumps of snow from the pine-tops
in sparkling showers. Furry animals, having taken months of refuge in
their woodland shelters, were just beginning to venture out. A fox
creeping through the underbrush. A rabbit darting across the
snowbound path.

 We spent much of the daylight hours in nature. The fresh mountain
air, the sound of the snow crunching beneath our boots was calming.

At times, we didn't feel the need to talk. The closeness of walking together, of a passing smile or glance, was more than enough. We hiked until our legs grew tired, stopping only once at a traditional roadside chapel called a Marterl. There, we said a prayer, thanking God for Martin's acquittal.

"Now that the trial is over, there are a lot of projects I want to finally get started on," Martin said, when we had finished.

"But aren't there financial investigations still ongoing?" I asked, referring to the financial investigations that Winklhofer had opened during the trial.

"Yes, but they're nothing to worry about, even if they last a few more months. Right now, I want to focus on planning a charity trip to Syria."

I shook my head. "Martin, traveling to Syria isn't the same kind of dangerous as the sailing the Mediterranean. I'm not sure I'm comfortable with—"

"Don't worry." His smile was reassuring. "It's not as dangerous as you think. I'll explain the details to you, later."

We stood on a rocky outcrop of the mountain, our shadows stretching long on the trail behind us, and watched the sunset—a shining sphere splashing yellow and orange light across the clouds. There, on the quiet mountaintop, I got the distinct feeling that, once again, Martin and I were at the end of another chapter. Whatever the next chapter held, I didn't care to wonder, because in the moment, I was happy. Completely at peace.

"The next time we come back here, it'll probably be as a married couple," Martin said.

"I'll be Brittany Sellner, then." I smiled as I spoke the name. "It's going to take a while for me to get used to having a new name."

"For me, too," Martin admitted. "Have you thought about what having my name might be like?"

Under normal circumstances, I knew he would never have asked the question. However, the surname Sellner had been sullied by the media and his political opponents, so that it now came with a high cost, one that could go on to cause problems in all facets of my life: when I traveled through passport control, when I took German classes at the University of Vienna, and even when I made a reservation at a restaurant. But none of these outcomes were enough to intimidate me. I did my best to convince him how I felt.

"I'm sure there are a lot of hardships waiting for us down the road," I said. "But I'd rather have a difficult life with you than an easy life alone."

I meant what I said to Martin that day. I've never doubted it. I was simply wrong in thinking that I understood what hardship meant.

THE STORM BEGINS

I woke the following morning dehydrated. Although the mountain air was refreshing, it was uncomfortably arid. Lifting myself onto my elbow, I brushed my hand across the top of the cluttered nightstand until I located my phone. I frowned when the screen lit up; my Twitter inbox was swamped with messages, mostly from Nick. The latest message read:

Britt, write me as soon as you're awake. Shit is bad. Very, very bad. There's been a terror attack at two mosques in New Zealand.

I rolled out of bed, running my hand along the wall panels until I found the light switch. Standing barefoot in the bathroom, I navigated to the trending Twitter hashtags. The number one trend worldwide was entitled 'Christchurch Shooting' and was flooded with roughly a million tweets, many of them attached with the same photo: a man in dark clothes sitting in a vehicle. His nostrils were flared arrogantly, his lips pulled back into a savage smirk.

I searched the hashtag for verified media articles, trying to gather more information, and discovered that the man in the photo, who was the suspected shooter, was a 28-year-old Australian named Brenton Tarrant.[178] The day before, on March 15, Tarrant had driven to two New Zealand mosques and opened fire on the Muslim worshipers inside, killing a total of fifty-one people. Even more sadistic, he had made a public spectacle of his attack, livestreaming the first of his two shootings on Facebook. Although Facebook had promptly removed the livestream, people had managed to make copies and were posting clips all over Twitter.

I scrolled quickly through the clips, too disturbed to watch the footage closely. Twitter employees were trying their best to remove them, but couldn't do so fast enough. Dozens of new copies were being posted every second.

Somewhere in the midst of the chaos, people were extending the blame past Tarrant. Left-wing politicians, activists, and journalists were pointing the finger at right-wingers, saying, "*You* are to blame. Brenton Tarrant is one of yours." There were also tweets referencing the biggest YouTuber in the world, PewDiePie. There were even tweets about the popular video game, Fortnite. None of it would make much sense to me until later.

Ping.

The sound of a new Twitter message from Nick broke me from my daze. *They're going to come after Martin for this,* he wrote.

I reread the message once, twice, certain that Nick had made a typo. *What are you talking about, Nick?* I asked. *Martin has nothing to do with this.*

Doesn't matter, Nick replied. *Tarrant has a manifesto. He posted it on 8chan before the attack.*

Are you saying Martin is mentioned in the manifesto? I asked.

No, Nick responded. *Tarrant doesn't mention Martin, or Generation Identity. It's the title of the manifesto that I'm worried about.*

I asked Nick what the title was. When he didn't immediately reply, I wrote him again, not caring if I came off as frantic. *Nick, what's the title?*

The Great Replacement, he finally wrote.

I lowered my phone, a chill darting straight to my head. It didn't matter if I accepted it or not—Nick was right.

Coined by the French writer, Renaud Camus, The Great Replacement was the idea that the European population was steadily being replaced by a non-European population using methods such as mass migration. Generation Identity had frequently promoted The Great Replacement over the years, their goal being to make it acceptable for mainstream society to engage in an open debate over the topic.

"We, as Europeans, should have a say in whether or not we want open borders," Martin had often said to me. "We should have a say in whether or not our politicians should be letting millions of migrants into our countries each year."

However, in the same way that global warming is a neutral idea, so is the idea of the Great Replacement. Should a climate activist decide to commit an act of terror, murdering innocent people in the name of depopulation to save the planet, it doesn't make the idea of global warming intrinsically violent. Even the most innocuous ideas, such as equality, can inspire negative actions and be used to commit great evil.

I sat on the bed a while, digesting the horrific events of the morning, before I finally struck up the courage to enter Martin's room. He looked peaceful as he slept, his breathing calm and his face unlined by stress. It hurt my heart to think that, after only just being acquitted, he was moments away from being dragged into yet another nightmare.

Martin stirred in his bed, woken by my footsteps. "Babe, is something wrong?"

"Yes," I replied softly. "You need to check Twitter."

ACCELERATIONISM

We left the alpine hut within the hour. While we were already scheduled to check out that morning, we left in an even greater hurry than planned. We didn't speak much for the first part of the seven-hour journey. Neither of us had an appetite for breakfast, either.

Nick continued to send Twitter messages, but I couldn't stomach any more updates. Passages from Tarrant's manifesto weighed on my mind, specifically how he claimed to be an advocate of accelerationism.[179] In Tarrant's view, the Western world was headed toward a devastating collapse, with no chance of it being prevented. Instead of waiting for the collapse to gradually occur over time, he wanted to accelerate it by committing an act of terror—one he hoped would incite further violence and acts of retaliation, ultimately widening the divide between the populations of Europe and the United States along social, cultural, political, and racial lines. In other words, Tarrant rejected Martin's belief that political change could be brought about by peaceful demonstration and protest. He hoped his bloody act of terror would result in swift authoritarian repression against right-wing dissidents. He hoped it would create an atmosphere in which governments cracked down on right-wingers to the point where they overextended their hand, thus radicalizing the right-wingers and making them feel as if their only option was violent revolt.

Considering Tarrant's support for accelerationism, I wondered why he hadn't made a greater effort to publicly associate himself with popular right-wing movements. He had mentioned The Great Replacement, yes, but this reference in itself wasn't enough to destroy the right-wing. Had he compiled a list of right-wing movements that he admired in his manifesto, the damage would have been much more severe, likely resulting in the movements being investigated by the authorities and possibly even repressed by their governments. In my view, it made little sense that Tarrant had passed up such an opportunity.

"I was always afraid that, sooner or later, something like this would happen," Martin said, after we'd been driving for about thirty minutes.

"I remember you telling me that," I said.

Martin stepped on the gas pedal until he overtook the car in front of us in a rush to get home. "Generation Identity has always either barred or expelled people who are too radical," he said. "We never wanted to be in a situation where our movement was associated with someone who was a secret Nazi, or worse, who would end up resorting to violence. But on the other hand, we've always been realistic about the possibility that, eventually, someone somewhere would commit an act of violence that would negatively affect us all."

"Yes, but there have been acts of violence committed on all sides," I pointed out. "Muslims, Antifa, left and right-wing extremists... pretending that one side is completely innocent is being willfully blind to reality."

"True, but it doesn't matter. Terror attacks by Muslims and leftists are always going to be ignored or quickly forgotten. But any terror attack that can be associated with the right wing in the slightest is going to be drawn out and amplified. It'll get to the point where the average person believes that right-wing extremists are the biggest global threat."

"So, you think Tarrant is just the beginning?"

"Unfortunately, yes." Martin nodded grimly. "There will be many more like Tarrant who will decide to go on killing sprees, not only because they're evil, but because they're *weak*. Too weak to muster any sort of self-control, idealism, or discipline. And too weak to dedicate themselves to a political goal that's both effective and moral like creating a movement. The only thing they're capable of is pointing out obvious truths like the Great Replacement in the form of a self-aggrandizing manifesto, and then grabbing a gun and going off. And while they might get praise from their 8chan peers, they might get their own personal Wikipedia page, and they might even get a few fan letters in prison, at the end of the day, the only thing they truly amount to are murderers. There's no honor in killing the innocent or the defenseless." Martin hit the gas again, his fingers knotting around the steering wheel. "Men like Tarrant only make it harder, if not *impossible*, for politicians and activists like us to create change the democratic way."

I didn't know what to say. Martin was the most idealistic person I had met, so I knew he wasn't exaggerating. If he thought the entire right wing would suffer for Tarrant's crime, then it would. Whether or not his prediction would come true in a few hours or a few days did not matter. A new and unfamiliar adversity, hopeless to dodge, was barreling toward us at lightning speed. And perhaps, this time, we wouldn't be strong enough to survive it.

THE WORLD REACTS

The world's reaction to the Christchurch Shooting continued over the next several days. Half of the news cycle focused on Brenton Tarrant—what had motivated him to commit such a horrific crime, as well as how right-wing terrorists were a rising global threat—while the other half focused on New Zealand. Media photos captured the New Zealand Prime Minister, Jacinda Ardern, donning a hijab as she arrived in Christchurch to show her solidarity with the Muslim community.[180]

"I can tell you right now our gun laws will change," Jacinda Ardern told the *Associated Press*.[181]

The country's ban on assault weapons was but one of many government crackdowns enforced after the Christchurch Shooting.[182] A New Zealand citizen was sentenced to twenty-one months in prison for sharing the livestreamed video of the attack.[183] Internet service providers in New Zealand and Australia temporarily blocked websites such as 4chan, 8chan, and Kiwi Farms where copies of the video were still being shared.[184] And of course, the possession or sharing of Tarrant's manifesto was permanently banned.[185]

But since there was no way to enforce a worldwide ban of the manifesto, people in countries outside New Zealand continued to dissect its contents. As it turned out, much of the document was a shitpost. In between sincere statements such as Tarrant admitting that his hero was the notorious Norwegian terrorist, Anders Breivik,[186] Tarrant claimed that he was inspired by video games like Fortnite and Spyro.[187] He also claimed that the conservative commentator, Candace Owens, had influenced him above all,[188] which was a blatant lie. Candace Owens, a Trump supporter and an outspoken advocate of the black community, had barely so much as made a reference to Islam throughout her career. But perhaps cruelest of all, Tarrant targeted the charismatic and fun-loving Felix Kjellberg, who ran the world's largest YouTube channel, 'PewDiePie'. Moments before the Christchurch Shooting, Tarrant had referenced the popular 'Subscribe to PewDiePie' meme in his livestream.[189] The meme focused on an international campaign to keep PewDiePie as the most subscribed-to channel on YouTube. The meme had nothing to do with hatred or violence, nor did Felix Kjellberg, who has no public interest in politics. The most that can be said about him is that he rejects political correctness, that he supports the right to be offensive. Naturally, being mentioned by Tarrant took a heavy toll on Felix Kjellberg and everyone else who Tarrant had attempted to associate himself with. Like an octopus, he had unfurled his tentacles into countries across the world, dragging unsuspecting people into his crime and trying to stigmatize even the most innocuous aspects of popular culture. If anything, these actions made Tarrant's goal of accelerating the collapse of the West all the more obvious.

Numerous right-wing activists issued statements of condemnation for the Christchurch Shooting. Martin and I joined in, although it felt ridiculous having to do so. Of course, we denounced the shooting. Of course, we found the murder of innocent human beings to be immoral and horrific. We had made our support of peaceful activism clear multiple times in the past, so there should have been no mystery surrounding our stance. The problem was that blaming Brenton Tarrant wasn't sufficient for the left. They needed more targets to point the finger at—people who were publicly active in the political realm, not locked inside a prison cell.

Martin and I did our best to ignore the accusations and to return to our regular work. There wasn't much time for me to take on new projects, for I was soon due to fly to the United States to attend my younger sister's wedding. Martin, on the other hand, had to plan a trip to Syria on behalf of an identitarian charity called the Alternative Help Association (AHA). The charity's goal was to raise money for the Christian inhabitants of Maaloula, a Syrian town which had been attacked twice by jihadists in 2013. Martin planned to film a series of videos in Maaloula, asking his viewers to donate to a fundraiser in support of their town.

About a week before my flight home, I was sitting beside Martin on the balcony of his apartment, scrolling through Twitter updates on my phone. The reaction to the Christchurch Shooting was still in full swing. Most notably, the blame game was escalating. More and more left-wing activists were pointing the finger at Generation Identity, claiming it was their fault that Tarrant had gone on a killing spree due to Generation Identity's promotion of the Great Replacement. None of them cared about Generation Identity's peaceful stance. None of them cared that their false accusations could potentially have real-life ramifications, either.

"Maybe we should get married in Austria instead of Idaho," I said softly.

Martin stopped typing on his laptop, his eyebrows lowered. "Why do you say that?"

"It's just an instinct…a bad feeling I have." I shrugged, searching for the right words to voice my thoughts. "After the way the left has blamed you for the Christchurch Shooting, what if you're not allowed back into the United States? What if you fly there a few days before our wedding, and the border police decide not to let you enter?"

Martin sat back in his chair, his frown deepening. He knew I wasn't overreacting. Despite having successfully entered the United States four times in the past, the border police had briefly detailed him for questioning during his last two visits.

"It's not only that you might not be allowed into the country," I continued. "We have a lot more European friends than American ones. Plus, if we get married in Austria, I won't have to move here after our wedding. I can do it ahead of time."

Martin wrapped his arms around me, his touch reassuring. "I think it's a good idea, but we need to talk with your parents and mine before making a final decision. We can call them once I'm back from Germany."

I didn't want Martin to leave. Especially at this time, I didn't want to be alone. But since the invitation was for the birthday party of one of his best friends and biggest supporters—a party in which over a hundred guests had been invited—I knew I couldn't ask him to stay.

THE SECOND HOUSE-RAID

Martin returned from Germany two days later. He called me on the train ride home and told me he had fallen ill with the flu.

"I don't want to leave you alone while you're sick," I said. "I'll stay at your apartment tonight."

The date was Monday, March 25, around one o'clock in the morning. I waited by the window, wrapped in a blanket, until I saw a silhouette pass through the neighborhood gate. Martin's footsteps were sluggish, almost wobbly, as he traipsed up the walkway.

In the kitchen, I put a pot on the stovetop and heated some chicken broth. Unfortunately, Martin was unable to drink it. The moment he stepped inside the apartment, his hair slick with sweat, he hunched over the toilet bowl and vomited.

I watched him from the hallway, wincing at the sight of his heaving shoulders.

"Maybe you should lie down," I suggested.

"No." He wiped his mouth with the back of his hand. "Lying down will make me feel worse. I need to sit."

He positioned himself in a beanbag chair beside the open window, while I fetched a bucket from the kitchen. I also brought a glass of cool water and a few blankets.

"Danke, Schatz," he said, as he sipped the water. "I'm sure it's just the flu…nothing to worry about."

His vomiting continued throughout the night. Soon, he developed a headache and broke out into cold sweats. I considered calling his dad, who was a doctor, to ask what medicine I should give him. Thankfully, the phone call turned out to be unnecessary. Martin awoke the following morning in full health. I didn't understand how he could've recovered so quickly until Martin's German supporter informed us that the fish served at his birthday party had caused half of the guests to fall sick with food poisoning.

With Martin now feeling well enough to eat, I threw together a hash of eggs, bacon, onions, mushrooms, and parmesan cheese. I was just spooning the hash onto plates when Martin called to me from the bedroom.

"Brittany, come here."

I set down the spoon with a frown. He rarely called me Brittany. And the tone of his voice was rarely so severe. When I answered his call, I found him sitting on the bed, with his back propped stiffly against the headboard, chin tilted back, staring blankly at the ceiling. His laptop was slanted over his knees, swiveled to one side, about to fall off.

"Is everything okay?" I moved to his bedside. "Are you feeling sick again?"

Martin slowly lifted his head. "You should sit down."

Whatever he was about to tell me, whatever new nightmare was on the brink of unfolding, the only thing I knew was that I wasn't ready.

"Last night, on the train ride home, I was doing…what's the word…I was doing…" Martin's tone grew frustrated, for he often struggled to speak in English when he was stressed. "*Bookkeeping*— that's it. I was doing bookkeeping for all the donations I had received in 2018. And I noticed that one of the donations, from January 2018, was sent from a suspicious email."

"Suspicious?"

"Yes…from the email: btarrant333@hotmail.com."

"Tarrant? Martin, you don't think it's the *same* Tarrant that…?" My words trailed off.

Martin spun his laptop screen toward me, showing an open window of his Gmail account. "There's more…just now, I did a search for the email address in my Gmail account and found that back in January of 2018, I exchanged a few messages with Tarrant."

In the e-mails, Martin thanked Tarrant for his donation, a sum of 1,500 euros, explaining that it was appreciated, for he had recently had three different private bank accounts banned. Martin then directed Tarrant to his English-speaking YouTube channel, where he posted videos every few months, and added that he could meet him for a coffee or a beer if he was ever in Vienna. Tarrant replied, telling Martin that 1,500 euros was a small amount to give for the large amount of work he did, and then suggested that Martin check out Blair Cottrell and Tom Sewell, two Australian political activists whose work he followed. He also agreed to let Martin know if he decided to travel to Vienna, but the e-mail thread ended there.

My hands trembled as I scrolled through the e-mails. They were real. All of them—the messages, the names, the dates. But perhaps most startling of all was the fact that Tarrant came off as normal. No hint toward his true beliefs, no indication that he supported violent accelerationism, or that he intended to commit a terrorist attack. That the man who had written these e-mails would go on to commit such a monstrous crime seemed improbable.

"I never met Tarrant," Martin clarified. "Apart from these e-mails, we never had further contact. But still, I think I should send the e-mails to the police."

His words knocked me from my stupor. "Definitely," I agreed. "But it's probably not a good idea to send the emails to the police directly. Send them to your lawyer, Lehofer. He can forward them to the police."

"Okay, I'll send them today. But in the meantime, I don't want these messages in my inbox."

In retrospect, it was unwise of Martin to delete the e-mails. On the other hand, I wouldn't have wanted emails from a terrorist in my inbox, either.

"I'll screenshot all the messages before I delete them," Martin said. "I'll send the screenshots to Lehofer."

I left Martin alone in the bedroom, excusing myself for a glass of water. I needed a moment to process what was happening. In the kitchen, I held onto the countertop for support. My arms and legs felt loose, as if I was losing cohesion in my joints.

At first, Tarrant's donation to Martin made no sense. Why would he donate to someone who opposed his violent worldview? Why hadn't he instead donated to someone who had explicitly radicalized their base toward violence? Little by little, I began to wonder if Tarrant had deliberately fabricated a connection between himself and peaceful activists like Martin. As he had declared in his manifesto, he hoped his crime would create a spike in government repression against right-wing dissidents. He hoped the crackdown would ultimately leave those of a nonviolent mindset feeling as if they no longer had a peaceful path upon which to achieve their goals—that they had no other choice but to turn to bloodshed.

These realizations led me to question how many other people and political movements Tarrant had donated to—most likely several. Either way, information about his communications would be made public sooner or later. No doubt, the New Zealand police were analyzing his online movements. It wouldn't be long before they discovered Tarrant's donation to Martin. And when they did, I was sure they would inform the Austrian police.

Less than an hour later, my theory was realized.

Martin and I were in the kitchen. He was working on his laptop, while I washed the breakfast dishes, when we heard a loud knock at the door. We glanced up at the same time, our eyes locking, our expressions acknowledging that we knew something was wrong.

Martin put a finger to his lips. He peered through the spyhole, and his shoulders stiffened. He backed away from the door, almost soundlessly on the balls of his feet.

"Police." He mouthed the word instead of saying it.

Taking his cell phone off the table, he slipped into the bedroom and out onto the balcony, where he wedged the device between a bench and a flowerpot. Almost an entire month had passed since the Austrian

High Court had exonerated him, yet even after all that time, the police had failed to return his possessions, which had been confiscated back in 2018. For this reason, he didn't want the police to confiscate any more of his property.

The police knocked again, a loud thud that reverberated through the wood.

"I'm coming," Martin called.

He opened the door to a wall of Austrian Secret Police. There were six, maybe seven of them, all dressed in civilian attire. Five officers fanned out across the apartment and immediately began searching cupboards, rifling through drawers, and upending furniture. The remaining two officers guided Martin into the kitchen, where they instructed him to take a seat.

"Read this," they told him, unfolding a search warrant.

I lifted myself up onto the window ledge, which was the only place where I was able to stay out of the way. The police occupied every room of the modest, three-room apartment. Around me, the world seemed to dissolve into a fog of indistinct shapes. For about ten minutes, I had no idea what was going on. None of the secret police explained to me why they had come, much less spoke a word to me. I was forced to simply watch the raid unfold.

"Whose laptop is this?" one of the police asked in German, gesturing to a laptop plastered with political stickers.

"It's mine," I replied in English. While I couldn't understand most of what the police were saying—they spoke too quickly, and their Austrian accents were too thick—I had understood the question about the laptop.

"We're confiscating it."

"No, you're *not*." I dropped off the window ledge. My movements weren't aggressive, but they were firm. "I want you to tell me why you're here."

The policeman cocked his eyebrow. "We're here because of the Christchurch terror attack." He spoke as if this was self-evident.

I glanced at Martin for confirmation. He nodded.

"It's a very bad situation...very serious," the chief policeman said, rising from his seat at the table beside Martin. Tan and broad-shouldered, with a seashell necklace loose at his neck, he moved in a haze of stale cigarette smoke. "Your fiancé received a donation of 1,500 euros from a terrorist. We need to conduct a full investigation to verify there's no further connection."

"There's not."

"We'll see."

"This is happening because of Winklhofer," Martin explained, showing me the search warrant. I quickly got lost in the large blocks of German text, but at the bottom, in freshly dried ink, I saw a judge's signature. "Winklhofer still has all my financial records from the 2018 house-raid," Martin added. "He searched through them again after the Christchurch Shooting, and when he found the donation, he was able to convince a judge to approve this new house-raid."

"A house-raid because of a *donation*? But that's idiotic. It doesn't prove anything." I stepped away from the tall, close-packed bodies of the police, wishing Martin and I could speak alone. But they wouldn't let us out of their sight.

"I know, but Winklhofer doesn't care," Martin said. "In the warrant, he states that he wants to investigate me on the basis of forming a *terrorist* organization with Brenton Tarrant. If the Austrian state will allow Winklhofer to investigate me for terrorism based on such little evidence, then they'll allow him to do anything. The police chief here..." Martin motioned to the man with the seashell necklace, "he told me that if I refuse to comply with the raid, he'll arrest me."

"I'm just doing my job." The police chief crossed his large arms over his chest. "It's up to you two if you want to escalate the situation."

Martin and I saw no other option but to comply. Had the police come under any other circumstances, we would've held our ground, but this was different. Martin was being treated as guilty until proven innocent.

"So, will you hand over your laptop? Your phone, too?" the police chief asked me again.

"Am I allowed to ask questions first?"

"Make them brief." The police chief absently touched a crumpled pack of cigarettes in the front pocket of his shirt, clearly itching to go outside and smoke.

"On exactly what grounds are you confiscating my property?"

"On the grounds that you're Martin Sellner's fiancée."

Ridiculous. But I had expected as much. "If I hand over my phone and laptop, how long are you planning on keeping them? I have a flight back to the U.S. in three days."

"I'll tell you what," he extended his hand in offering. "Cooperate, and you'll have your phone and laptop back before you leave."

I stared at his hand, not wanting to shake it, not even wanting to touch it, but felt I didn't have a choice in the matter. They had threatened to arrest Martin if he refused to cooperate, meaning they would likely do the same to me. "Fine," I agreed.

Martin, cooperating to avoid arrest, retrieved the cell phone he had stashed on the balcony. He also handed over the screenshots of the e-mails he had exchanged with Tarrant. Meanwhile, the police continued their raid. They scoured every nook and cranny of the apartment. One policeman searched the bathroom, inside the cupboards, the shower, behind the toilet; one ransacked Martin's clothes; another went through our trash.

A variety of our property was seized: Martin's laptop, cell phone, secure digital cards, camera, microphone, portable hard drives, a dozen document folders, even credit cards. Similar devices were taken from me. Aside from my phone and laptop, they confiscated my camera, microphone, portable hard-drive and secure digital cards.

By the end of the two-hour raid, the tension leveled out. I told the policemen they could smoke on the balcony outside, even brewed them coffee. Most were kind enough. One told me in confidence that he thought the raid was unfounded.

"We're just doing our jobs," he pointed out.

I wondered how many injustices had been committed using those same words. "Yeah, that's what the police chief said," I replied.

The Secret Police documented our possessions with numerical labels, and stowed them away in cardboard boxes, which they hauled down to their cars.

"You and your fiancée need to accompany us to the station for questioning," the police chief told Martin when his officers had finished.

"We'll come," he agreed. "But my lawyer will also be present."

The police chief nodded and escorted Martin from the apartment first. I stayed behind in order to change my clothes since I was still wearing the sweatpants I had slept in. A policewoman supervised me while I dressed, even while I changed my underwear.

"I'm ready now," I told her.

The policewoman ushered me into a vehicle parked on the curb. I sat in the backseat, wrapped in a heavy silence as we drove to the nearest police station. It took a while for the gravity of the situation to fully register. For those first few hours, I wasn't sure how to react, or even if I should be afraid. But I certainly wasn't ashamed. Neither Martin nor I had done anything wrong—not legally, not ethically. Yes, we would comply with the Secret Police, but we weren't going to be made to feel like criminals simply because Martin had received a donation that was completely outside his control.

At the station, the police kept Martin and me separated. Martin and his lawyer, Lehofer, were escorted away for interrogation, while I signed in at the information desk. The police asked me a range of preliminary questions—like what my passport number was—before depositing me inside the station's locker room to wait my turn.

Poorly lit by overhead bulbs, the room was hemmed in by old metal lockers that had seen hard wear and tear. Police officers passed in and out, dressed to the nines in polished boots and crisp navy-blue uniforms with accenting red epaulettes. Only half wore berets, stylishly slanted off the top of the head, but all of them carried Glock pistols.

"You should take a seat," the female officer who was tasked with supervising me advised. "You're likely going to be waiting here a while."

I did and absently reached for a magazine, even though I had no intention of reading. My heart and mind were with Martin, wherever he was. I was confident in his ability to answer the Secret Police's questions, but I couldn't fathom what he must've been feeling. *Terrorism*—that was what he was being investigated for. The moment the investigation went public, there would be no going back; the accusation would *never* go away. Even when Martin was found innocent, even after the case was closed, the ramifications would go on to negatively affect him—negatively affect *both* of us—for the rest of our lives. While I had understood many of the risks of political activism, I had never anticipated consequences of this nature and magnitude, never anticipated that we could be dragged into an investigation for terrorism over someone else's crime.

An hour later, Martin's lawyer, Lehofer, stalked into the locker room. I was so relieved to see a familiar face that I leapt to my feet. Dressed in a black trench-coat, toting a leather briefcase, Lehofer looked as if he had recently come from the courtroom.

"Martin is done being questioned," he told me.

"Is he okay?"

"Yes, he's waiting for you at the information desk. But the police would like to question you, as well. They've called in a translator."

Lehofer led me up a flight of stairs, into an interrogation room that was even darker than the locker room. A desk was the main furnishing, strewn with notepads and pens and a recorder. The police chief sat in a simple office chair. Two more officers hung in the background, while a translator occupied a chair beside the police chief.

"Please, have a seat," the police chief said, taking a swig from a paper cup of coffee.

I did what he told me. Lehofer took the chair behind me, his presence reassuring. Under his watchful eye, I was confident that the interrogation would not only stay focused, but all of my responses would be accurately translated.

"Wissen Sie wer Brenton Tarrant ist?" the police chief asked.

The translator translated: "Do you know who Brenton Tarrant is?"

"The whole world knows who Brenton Tarrant is," I answered.

The translator translated my response, which the police chief scrawled onto a notepad. "Please be specific regarding your knowledge of Brenton Tarrant."

"He's the main suspect of the Christchurch Shooting," I explained. "If you really want me to go into detail, he attacked two separate mosques on March 15, killing a total of fifty-one Muslims. He livestreamed all of the killings, and he also posted a long manifesto on 8-chan sometime beforehand."

"Have you ever met Brenton Tarrant or had contact with him?"

"No. The first time I heard his name was after the shooting."

The police chief leaned forward with an inquisitive eye. "So, you've never received a donation from him? Never received any emails?"

"As I said, we've never had any contact."

I stared at the crumpled cigarette pack in his front pocket, focusing on it. In a situation as abnormal as this one, the sight of a mundane object kept me grounded.

"Are you a political activist?" the police chief asked.

"Yes, and I'm also an author. I've written two books, and I have my own YouTube channel that focuses on political commentary. Not many people here in Austria are familiar with my work because it's all in English."

The police chief transcribed my response between sips of coffee.

"Are you a member of any political movements or organizations? For example, the alt-right?"

"The alt-right isn't a movement—not in the traditional sense, anyway," I pointed out. "It's a loose coalition of right-wing groups. Some of the more radical groups embrace the name, but the others—various groups and individuals like me—feel that they've been incorrectly labeled. From the beginning, I've been an independent political activist, but I don't make a secret of my beliefs. I'm a traditional conservative and a nationalist, or in other words, I'm for putting my country first. I support peaceful policies that will put an end to mass migration, deport illegals, and secure our borders."

The police chief frowned. He seemed to be wondering where I fit into the puzzle. "So, you're not a member of Generation Identity, either?"

"No. Generation Identity is a European movement. It doesn't exist in America. But if you're asking me if I support Generation Identity, then the answer is yes."

The police chief laid his pen down on the table, content. The major portion of the interrogation was over, leaving only a few remaining questions about my political beliefs and my relationship with Martin. I kept my responses brief, but not too brief. I didn't want the police chief to think I was omitting important details. Once finished, he asked me to sign a written copy of my statements.

"I have one more thing to add before I sign," I told him.

The police chief's tone was curious. "Add what you like...*briefly*."

I wasn't even sure where to begin. Hundreds of thoughts buzzed in my mind, all that I wanted to let out, but the police chief was short on patience. "I'd simply like to go on record as saying this investigation is unjustifiable. Martin hasn't had any contact with Tarrant beyond the one-time donation, which he thanked him for in the same way that he thanks all of his donors." I acknowledged the other two policemen in the room, making sure they knew I was talking to them, too. "The moment this ridiculous investigation is made public, he's going to be crucified by the media, left-wing activists, and probably even the government. And for what? A donation that he had absolutely *no* control over? A donation that was made over a year ago, well before Tarrant became a terrorist, and at a time when Tarrant was still regarded as a law-abiding citizen who even had the right to own guns?"

"We're just doing our jobs," the police chief responded.

I had been naïve to expect a different response. I clasped my hands in frustration as I gave my statement to Lehofer, who confirmed the accurate translation.

Brittany Pettibone. I signed, and then turned the statement over to the police chief.

"You're free to go now," he said.

Free. If I wasn't so angry, I might've laughed.

Seconds later, my boots hit the stairway. I spotted Martin beside the information desk, reading through a stack of papers. He tossed them aside when he saw me and drew me into a hug.

"Are you all right?" he asked, holding my face in his hands.

"Yes…for now, at least." My breathing was labored after bolting down the stairs. "But I really don't want to go back to your apartment."

Martin felt the same. Instead, we headed for his parent's house in Baden. On the way, Martin told me that he needed to make a livestream later that evening.

"I want to be honest with my supporters upfront. Tarrant's donation will go public sooner or later. Plus, if I don't get ahead of the media storm, they'll spin it to fit their own narrative."

The media would spin the truth either way. But I understood why Martin had to try.

"I love you," was all I could say.

"I love you, too."

I felt him take my hand, felt him squeeze it firmly as I turned to stare out the window. My gaze went past the cars that roared alongside us on the Autobahn and got lost somewhere in the darkness beyond. The car was so quiet, I could hear the sound of my own breath. The fear was starting to kick in like heat slowly being turned up on a stove. I did my best to fight against it. This wasn't the time to falter, not when I needed to call my parents, not when I needed to explain the situation to my political friends, and not when I needed to support Martin. If there was ever a time he needed me to be strong, it was now. All hell was about to break loose, and we couldn't do anything to stop it, whether we liked it or not.

THE AFTERMATH

Martin wasted no time informing his supporters about the day's events: Tarrant's donation, the house-raid, the terrorism investigation, all of it. Curled up on the couch in the upstairs living room, I used his dad's cell phone to watch the livestream. The internet connection was poor, causing Martin's face to flicker and freeze onscreen, and the room's lighting washed him out, yellowing his complexion. Despite the blur of grainy pixels, his voice emerged confidently. I marveled at his composure. Calm yet somber, he looked like he had switched off all his doubts and fears. To this day, I don't know how he found the strength.

The world's reaction was immediate. Martin's supporters, who could attest to his good character—either because they had met him in person, or because they had been following his political activism for years—reacted with understanding, but the mainstream media predictably took a very different stance. All the major German-speaking media outlets condemned him. They portrayed him as being tied to a terrorist when in reality, his ties were to a man who had been an average, law-abiding citizen at the time of contact. I still remember the cover of the popular Austrian magazine, *Profil*,[190] which referred to Martin as being part of a global network of modern right-wing extremists, and published a close-up shot of his face, bearing the words: Wie gefährlich sind die Identitären? (How dangerous are the identitarians?)

And that was it. The world had found its scapegoat. From that point on, the mainstream media, the left, and even the Austrian government did everything in their power to destroy him.

Within hours, the story exploded internationally. Popular media outlets such as *BBC News* and *The New York Times* penned articles with the titles: 'Austrian far-right activist probed over links to Christchurch Attacks'[191] And 'Donation From New Zealand Attack Suspect Puts Spotlight on Europe's Far Right.'[192]

The latter *New York Times* article included quotes from Peter Neumann, director of the International Center for the Study of

Radicalization at King's College in London. In his analysis, Neumann compared the new right, and Generation Identity by extension, to *jihadis*.

"What unites jihadis and the new right is the idea that the fight has never stopped," Mr. Neumann said. "We are in a modern replay of the Crusades. This is what unites the two forms of extremism. And it mutually reinforces the narrative of Islam and the West being in an existential standoff."

Martin rejected Neumann's analogy. He countered it by comparing his link to the mosque shooting suspect to that between left-wing activists and leftist terrorists. "Someone who talks about class struggle can hardly be held responsible for leftist militants then exploding a bomb," he said.

Of course, I agreed with Martin. Granted, I was biased, but so was Neumann's argument. In *The New York Times* article, he stated, "If you relentlessly speak about an existential threat, you can't be surprised when some people take the logical next step and use violence."

If Neumann doesn't want people to relentlessly speak about existential threats, then why doesn't his concern also extend to the climate crisis? One prominent climate activist, Alexandria Ocasio-Cortez, can be quoted as saying that 'the world will end in twelve years' if we don't immediately and aggressively address climate change.[193] And another prominent climate activist, Greta Thunberg has stated, "I don't want you to be hopeful. I want you to panic. I want you to feel the fear I feel every day. And then I want you to act. I want you to act as you would in a crisis. I want you to act as if our house is on fire. Because it is."[194]

So, by Neumann's own logic, should we ban the topic of climate crisis simply because climate activists are relentlessly speaking about it as an existential threat that will logically result in violence? Should we regard *all* climate activists as extremists because some of them have been involved in violent protests?[195]

Yes, it's true that Martin regards the Great Replacement as an existential threat, but he's dedicated to protesting it peacefully. If others decide to commit violence in the name of the Great Replacement, then the perpetrators of the violence, as well as those who explicitly advocate for such violence, are solely to blame. Just as former presidential candidate, Bernie Sanders, isn't responsible for one of his campaign volunteers shooting up a Republicans' congressional baseball practice in 2017,[196] neither is Martin responsible for Brenton Tarrant's crime.

Over the next two days, I supported Martin by accompanying him to a handful of interviews in the park near his flat. I stood off in the distance, off camera, while he spoke with journalists. I was thankful that so many media outlets had requested interviews. Even if their articles were bound to portray him in a negative light, at least he had the opportunity to stand up for himself.

I saw little of Martin outside the interviews in the park. He had too many YouTube videos to film, Generation Identity meetings to attend, and television and radio interviews to give. I kept myself busy by countering the lies about us on social media and by trying to explain the situation to my political friends. Unfortunately, the situation was too detailed and too complex to explain to everyone individually. I didn't have the time or the energy to keep repeating the full story, which is one of the reasons why I decided to publish this book.

Shortly before I left Austria, the Secret Police Chief called me for a final meeting at a café in the eighteenth district of Vienna. The afternoon was sunny, too warm for drinking coffee, but I ordered one, anyway. I remember noticing the happy faces of patrons, laughing as they sipped cold beer with family and friends, and envied their normal lives. At this point, all of them had likely heard about Martin. His name and face were plastered in papers across the country. He couldn't so much as take out the trash without being recognized in the street. I wondered what these people thought about him, if they bothered to form an opinion through research, or if they automatically accepted the headlines as truth. So far, he had been met with a lot of support and encouragement, but with equal hatred and condemnation. Even the official Twitter account of the Vienna metro seemed to allude to Martin being 'a dog who should be muzzled.'[197]

I read a few chapters from a book, *Fahrenheit 451*, until the police chief and his partner arrived. He sported the same seashell necklace he had worn during the house-raid and carried the same odor of stale cigarette smoke.

"Your phone and laptop, as promised," he said, as he returned my things.

I eyed the devices with suspicion. Had they been bugged? Would the police monitor my private messages, or listen in on my private calls?

"We've also returned Martin his credit cards," the police chief added. "But the rest of your belongings, we'll keep."

"For how long?"

"A few months, maybe longer. It depends on how long the investigation takes." He passed me a document that acknowledged I had been given back my phone and laptop, and then motioned for me to sign. "How are you and Martin doing, by the way?"

I paused mid-signature, surprised he cared enough to ask. "Have you read the news?"

The police chief held up his hands, warding off the blame. "Hey, it wasn't me, but Martin who decided to make the house-raid public."

"Yes, but the house-raid would've gone public, either way," I pointed out. "Had Martin waited until the media broke the story before saying anything, people would've accused him of trying to cover up Tarrant's donation."

"You're probably right."

I watched after the police chief as he left, curious what he and his partner thought about the situation off the record. To investigate Martin was their job, yes, but on the other hand, they weren't robots. They still had their own opinions, ideas, and beliefs. Were they really so indifferent to political repression? Or were they simply indifferent so long as it wasn't their heads on the chopping block?

The next morning, a few hours before I was scheduled to fly home,

I awoke to one of the only pieces of good news I was destined to receive over the following weeks. The Austrian Interior Minister, Herbert Kickl, announced that so far, there was no evidence to suggest Brenton Tarrant had a personal relationship with Martin or anyone else in Austria's right-wing.[198]

Kickl's announcement couldn't have come at a better time, for it supported Martin's claim of innocence. The preliminary investigation had found no criminal links between him and Tarrant, and the ensuing investigation would find no such links either. But, to no one's surprise, the mainstream media chose to largely ignore Kickl's announcement in favor of continuing their attack. And right at their heels was Austrian People's Party.

Austrian Chancellor, Sebastian Kurz, who was the chairman of the Austrian People's Party, stated that he was considering a ban on Generation Identity and promised a dissolution of the group, 'if the law allows it.'[199]

I wasn't shocked by Kurz's statement. Having made his dislike of Generation Identity known in the past, I had expected him to denounce Martin, even if he did believe in Martin's innocence. But I'll admit that the response of the Freedom Party, which was in a government coalition with the Austrian People's Party at the time, did shock me. Numerous prominent Freedom Party members such as Heinz-Christian Strache and Norbert Hofer[200] distanced themselves from Martin and Generation Identity. When Norbert Hofer was asked the question, "Mit welchem Politiker wurden Sie nie auf ein Bier gehen?" (Which politician would you never go for a beer with?) Norbert Hofer replied, "Mit dem Chef der Identitären." (With the leader of the identitarians.)

"At least, Strache didn't deny the Great Replacement," Martin said, as he drove me to the airport to catch my flight back to Idaho. "At least, he still maintains it's real, which is what's most important."

I reached for Martin's hand over the console. "I wish I didn't have to leave," I said.

Martin smiled and promised he would be fine. "I've done nothing wrong, so the investigation will amount to nothing. In three months, you'll be back in Austria, and we'll get married. No one will be able to separate us again."

I returned his smile, trying to appear comforted. Since the day I met Martin, I had yet to see him overpowered, to even tread close to the borders of defeat. But I wondered if perhaps this was due to the narrow focus that he kept, concentrating only on the task at hand, steering clear of the overwhelming details. If my theory was correct, I hoped he would be able to maintain this narrow focus in the months that followed. Because if the day ever came when he allowed himself to fully acknowledge the weight of what he had to carry, I feared it might crush him.

13

Who is the happy Warrior? Who is he
That every man in arms should wish to be?
—It is the generous Spirit, who, when brought
Among the tasks of real life, hath wrought
Upon the plan that pleased his boyish thought:
Who, whether praise of him must walk the earth
For ever, and to noble deeds give birth,
Or he must fall, to sleep without his fame,
And leave a dead unprofitable name—
Finds comfort in himself and in his cause;
And, while the mortal mist is gathering, draws
His breath in confidence of Heaven's applause:
This is the happy Warrior; this is he
That every man in arms should wish to be.
                    —William Wordsworth

IDAHO, UNITED STATES
MARCH 2019

The illusion of strength I had maintained for the past two years was shattering. My energy burnt out the moment I stepped on the airplane, exposing me as I truly was—feeble, sad, depleted. In a daze, I wandered from airport to airport, from flight to flight, crumpling into my assigned seats and ticking away the hours in a blackout of sleep.

When I landed in the United States, I was met with a colder welcome than I was accustomed to. Yanking me out of the passport control line, the Seattle Airport Border Police ordered me to open my suitcases so they could perform a search.

I did as I was told. The sight of my belongings, strewn about the metal inspection table in disordered heaps, was becoming a common sight. In a way, my whole life was starting to follow the same pattern. From my property, to my digital data, to the details of my personal life, I felt as if I were slowly being stripped of every facet of my privacy.

"Can you tell me about your fiancé?" one of the border policemen asked me.

"You really don't know what's happened? You haven't read the news?"

"I'm not familiar with the situation. I'm speaking with you at the request of Homeland Security."

I took a moment to weigh the situation. The border policeman was young, only a few years older than me, with close shave and a few extra pounds packed around his middle. While he could have been telling the truth, he also could have been trying to catch me in a lie.

"It all started a few days ago…on March 25," I said. It took about twenty minutes to explain the story in full, from how Martin had discovered Brenton Tarrant's donation to how the house-raid and ensuing media storm had unfolded.

"How did the Austrian police treat you?" he asked. "Did any of them hurt you? Did you, at any point, feel threatened?"

"They treated me fine," I assured.

After the interrogation was over, I wandered out of the customs gate in a state of shock. I had never been detained at the U.S. border before. Even after the events of the past week, I hadn't expected a reaction in my own country. It was now clear that Martin's investigation was being monitored on an international level, far beyond the scope of the Austrian government alone. How, I wondered, would the U.S. authorities react long-term? Even without evidence of Martin's guilt, would they go so far as to ban him from entering the country?

Less than an hour later, I got an answer to my question. I was waiting at the departure gate for my final flight to Spokane, talking to my mom on the phone, when I received a WhatsApp message from Martin.

The U.S. Customs and Border Protection sent me an email today, he wrote. *They said my ESTA visa's been revoked, meaning I can't travel to the U.S. anymore. Canada did the same.*

"Mom, I've got to go," I said.

"Is everything alright?"

"No." I strained to keep my voice even, but a lump knotted in my throat. "I'll message you before my flight."

I headed for the restroom, waiting until I was locked inside a stall before letting out my emotions. I had feared this outcome, even before the discovery of Tarrant's donation. Not only would Martin be unable to visit my family; getting married in Idaho was no longer an option, either. Since we hadn't yet officially decided to switch our wedding to Austria, we still had a reservation at a church in Idaho and a large down-payment on a reception hall.

I wore a hooded jacket and sunglasses on the flight home. My shoulders trembled, even though I wasn't cold, but at least, I had managed to stop crying. I paid no attention to the curious stares of fellow passengers. I didn't care what they might be thinking. Given that Martin had been banned from the U.S., I had to face the daunting reality that Austria might decide to do the same to me. Two of my political friends, Martina Markota and Jack Buckby, were dealing with a similar situation. Jack, who was a citizen of the United Kingdom, had suffered through having his ESTA visa revoked over a false tip made to the FBI by Antifa four years earlier. To this day, he's still fighting to legally enter the United States to be reunited with his wife.

When I landed in Spokane, my parents were waiting for me on the sidewalk outside the airport. The sight of my dad, smiling at me from beneath his Idaho baseball cap, and my mom, holding out her arms for a hug, tugged at my heart. I hurried toward them, luggage in tow, and gave way in my mom's arms.

"It's going to be okay," she told me, as we walked to the car. "It may not seem like it now, but God isn't going to abandon you. He'll take care of you and Martin."

"This time, I don't know," I said shakily, fighting back my fear. "This situation isn't even remotely comparable to anything Martin and I have been through in the past. He's being investigated for *terrorism*. Even when he's found innocent and the investigation is closed, it'll never go away. It'll negatively affect our lives forever."

"Martin's a strong guy," my dad said. "He's not going to be brought down by this. Besides, you and Martin always knew you were going to be attacked for your political work. Now, it's just escalating."

"The next few weeks will be hard, that's certain," my mom conceded. "But it'll all die down eventually. Your dad and I and the rest of the family are here for you."

I didn't know how I deserved them. That they could be so loving, even as Martin's and my political work cast a shadow over their lives, once again highlighted my own weakness.

"You should make a YouTube video about the house-raid as soon as possible," my dad advised. "Be honest about *everything*. Martin is only able to set the lies straight on his end in the German-speaking world. You need to do it in English."

"I will," I promised, even though the last place I wanted to be was on YouTube. If anything, I wanted to leave the internet until the media storm subsided, but my dad was right. I owed my viewers an explanation, particularly those who had supported me through thick and thin over the past three years.

The quality of the video turned out poorly. Without my equipment, still in the possession of the Austrian police, I didn't have a proper microphone or camera. I used my iPhone instead. Dressed in a white shirt, my exhaustion apparent even through a fresh coat of makeup, I once again narrated the events of the past week. As soon as the video was published, I scrolled to the comment section. Gratitude overwhelmed me as I read the first few posts:

Martin handled this attack on him extremely well, from an outside perspective. Even people who don't know him told me that they stand 100% behind him.

Best of luck to both of you! We love you, Brittany and Martin! Millions of us are with you!

I also received an email from a supporter, notifying me that an immigration lawyer had made a public offer to take on Martin's case free of charge.

"You don't need to thank me for doing the case one hundred percent pro bono. It's truly an honor to get to work on your case," the immigration lawyer told me. "I should mention ahead of time, though, that it'll likely take a minimum of a year to get Martin back into the U.S."

"I expected that," I answered. "Still, Martin and I think it might be better to wait until the terrorism investigation is closed before we start the legal process. That way, the U.S. authorities won't have an excuse to deny him entry."

"Whatever you prefer," the lawyer agreed. "Just shoot me an email as soon as you two want to get started."

At home, life was more eventful than usual. With my younger sister's wedding around the corner, much of the family was busy seeing to last-minute plans. Meetings at the church and reception hall. A final dress-fitting. Helping guests with hotel bookings. My mom even took it upon herself to bake the wedding cake.

In the evenings, when the commotion had wound down, I took our family dog on walks with Nicole. On one night in particular, the local playground was empty as we passed, the swings rattling in an unseasonal wind, cold enough to eat through our coats.

"You've been quiet today," Nicole said. She wrapped the leash handle around her fist, trying to control our dog's excited tugs. "How are you doing?"

"I don't really feel like myself," I confessed.

"It's understandable that you feel isolated and alone right now, Britt. Most people have no idea what you're going through." She paused a moment. "Please don't take what I'm about to say the wrong way: I don't think you should show how you're feeling so publicly. For one, people might think you're defeated by what's happening to Martin. But you're *not*. Plus, our sister's getting married, and I know it'll mean a lot to her if you're involved in the planning if you look a little happier for her."

I acknowledged her point, even though I didn't want to. Celebrating was the last thing I wanted to do right then. But my younger sister was getting married, and since I had been home, I hadn't had the energy to show interest in her wedding. "Worried is a better word for how I feel," I said. "Worried I might be banned from Austria or that Martin might be targeted."

"Targeted by whom?"

"Well, there are a lot of radical Muslims who want revenge for Christchurch. And given that the media's portrayed Martin as being connected to the crime, it's not a stretch to think—"

"Britt, don't," Nicole broke in. "You'll only make yourself sick with worry. The only way to stay sane right now is to stay positive."

"I don't know how not to worry."

"What about a distraction? You still have your own wedding plans to finish."

"I guess I could try that," I said, as my phone buzzed in my pocket. My dad was calling.

"Hey, where are you?" he asked.

"Out for a walk with Nicole. Do you need me to come home?"

"No, I just wanted to tell you some good news. The Kootenai County Republicans are holding their monthly meeting in a few weeks. One of the committee members is a supporter of yours and invited you to speak about Martin's ban from the U.S. He said there's a chance the Kootenai County Republicans might be able to help him out. Do you want to go?"

"Absolutely."

I didn't have to think it over. Of all the places I had imagined receiving help, the Idaho Republican Party was last on the list. But I welcomed the invitation, and I couldn't wait to meet the committee supporter who had contacted my dad. He was among the few who had offered me a concrete way of helping Martin.

THE FIRST ILLEGAL LEAK

In the days that followed, I focused on preparing a speech for the Kootenai County Republicans and discussing wedding plans with Martin's mom. Since it was difficult for me to see to all the plans from overseas, her help was invaluable. She worked day and night, securing a priest, a church, and a location for the reception. She even mailed out invitations, half of which were in German, the other half in English.

I knew she was suffering. Martin's whole family was. Despite how deeply the attacks against him hurt her, somehow, she managed to keep her spirits up. Her messages were accented with smiley faces, family photos, and thoughtful words of encouragement. Like my own mom, she said we needed to put the future in God's hands.

"I found a great deal on a flight to Croatia for you in early May," Martin told me one night over the phone. "It's only a few hours from Austria, so I can drive there to meet you. We can use the time to finish planning our wedding."

I stared at the screenshot of the flight info, noting that the trip was for an entire week. I could hardly believe it. Even in the chaos of the investigation, he had thought to plan it.

"The only thing I want is to see you again," he said.

It was all I wanted as well. For me, our meet-up in Croatia was the light at the end of the tunnel, the hope that kept me going. I even downloaded an iPhone app to count down the days. In any other situation, I could've waited the full three months to see him again, but the terrorism investigation had changed everything.

"I think I'm being followed," Martin mentioned near the end of our call.

"By the police?"

"Yes." I heard the sound of a shade being lifted, as if he was looking out the window. "There's a suspicious van that's been parked outside my apartment for the last few days. I'm pretty sure they're surveilling me."

"And they're allowed to do that?"

"They're allowed to do whatever they want. Since I'm under investigation for terrorism, I don't really have any rights."

I didn't think Martin was being paranoid. I was sure he was being followed. But I was shocked to later learn the full extent of the Secret Police's surveillance. A surveillance van was indeed parked outside his apartment complex, remaining there for somewhere between one to two months. The Austrian secret police had used an IMSI-catcher, a device that gave them the ability to monitor all of his communications, from his phone calls, to his text messages, to his internet traffic. The police had also used geo-location to track his movements twenty-four hours a day. They had even reached out to Big Tech companies like Google for Gmail messages and Facebook for WhatsApp messages, requesting access to all the messages Martin had ever written, including those that had been deleted.

"Do you really think the Secret Police believe you're guilty?" I asked.

"No, but there are plenty of powerful leftists with motives of their own behind this investigation. In the end, they don't care so much about me or Generation Identity. Their real target is the Freedom Party, and we're just stuck in the crosshairs. For example, if the Secret Police were to discover communications between me and the Freedom Party during their investigation, the information would be used by the media and various politicians to attack the Freedom Party. Of course, no such communications exist, but since the Freedom Party advocates for a lot of the same policies we do, any negative information that comes out about me will likely be used to attack them."

A chilling thought suddenly occurred to me. "Do you think they'd go so far as to illegally leak your data?"

"At this rate, I wouldn't put it past them," Martin said. "Maybe the Secret Police wouldn't leak anything, but someone else who has access to my data might."

I wished Martin had been wrong. I wished the corruption of the Austrian state hadn't been so predictable. Unfortunately, though, Martin was on the brink of not just one, but multiple illegal leaks.

The first occurred a day or so later, when I was sitting by the fire in my living room, reading the news over a cup of coffee. It was morning, too early for anyone else to be awake. Even the family dog was still asleep. He snored beside me, his head on my lap, his furry tail warming my feet. I opened the Twitter app on my phone and scrolled through the timeline, pausing when I spotted a *BBC News* article that read, 'Austrian far-right activist condemned over swastika.'[201]

Austria's *Kleine Zeitung* reported that 'Mr. Sellner had admitted to police in 2006 that he and a companion stuck a swastika poster on a synagogue in the town of Baden bei Wien, to the south-west of the capitol Vienna.'

'Responding to the report on Twitter, Mr. Sellner said it was no secret that he had been active in the Neo-Nazi scene when he was younger but had 'left that behind a long time ago.' He had never taken part in acts of violence, he added.'

Immediately, I dialed Martin's number. The phone rang—twice, three times with no answer. I tried calling again, pulling on my boots as I did so. Why, thirteen years later, was a 2006 police report suddenly popping up? And why was the media presenting it as if it had any sort of relevance to the present? I didn't know. The only thing I knew was that I needed to talk to Martin. The phone continued to ring. Five, then six times. Still no answer.

Grabbing my coat, I headed outside for some fresh air. As I crossed the street and turned down the sloping path that led to the Spokane River, I felt a whole new level of disgust for the media. The revelation that Martin had been involved in the right-wing extremist scene in his youth wasn't a revelation at all. For years, Martin had spoken publicly about it; not to mention, it had been a focal point of the 2018 trial in Graz. He had even told me about the swastika sticker when we first started dating. He said he had placed the sticker on a gate outside the synagogue in his former hometown for two reasons. Firstly, to protest the arrest of a 68-year-old British man, David Irving, who had been imprisoned in Austria in 2006 for denying the Holocaust over a decade earlier in 1989,[202] and secondly, to protest the Austrian law which forbade publicly displaying the swastika under penalty of a ten-year prison sentence.

Of course, I believed what Martin had done was wrong. Of course, I believed his actions were indefensible and worthy of condemnation. But on the other hand, I found it dishonest for the mainstream media to act as if Austrian political figures having radical pasts was a unique occurrence. For example, in 2007, in was revealed that former Austrian Vice-Chancellor Heinz-Christian Strache had participated in parliamentary games with an alleged Neo-Nazi group during his youth.[203] Several leftwing politicians also had extremist pasts. But most of these political figures weren't the same people they had been ten, fifteen, or twenty years earlier. And neither was Martin. His family knew it, and so did his friends and supporters. The mainstream media was simply searching for any information, no matter how irrelevant to the present, to paint him as a dangerous extremist. Then, pointing a finger at the Freedom Party, the media would condemn them for daring to promote the same political policies as the 'dangerous extremist' Martin Sellner.

Martin returned my call an hour later.

"Sorry I didn't pick up," he apologized. "I was filming a video."

"It's okay, I just called because I saw the news. Martin, why is this story only coming out now? Why wasn't it made public years ago?"

"The police report shouldn't exist," he explained. "The police should've deleted it back in 2006 when the case was dropped. I was never charged with a crime; I was too young. I did one hundred hours of community service."

"So, the police in Baden saved the report?"

"I guess someone at the Baden Police Station could've saved it and decided to leak it now, or maybe it was the owner of the synagogue...I don't know. But either way, the report was illegally leaked."

He moved the phone from his ear, talking abruptly in German. It sounded like he had been stopped by a passerby in the street. The woman used the phrase, "Sie haben bei Ihrer letzten Pressekonferenz großartige Arbeit geleistet," which signaled that she was a supporter. But I was certain that, in the wake of the leaked police report, not all of his encounters would be as friendly.

"Sweetheart, maybe you should take a break," I suggested, when he returned to the call. "Stay with your family for a few days. I think this new media storm is going to last a while."

"I can't ignore this," he said. "I have to make a statement. I've already filmed a video that I'll publish in a few hours, and after that, I have to plan a political demonstration."

"How do you think your supporters are going to react?"

"I think my viewers will support me because they know who I am today, but the media, the left, and the Austrian Government are going to double-down on attacking Generation Identity in an effort to get our movement banned. At this point, even the Freedom Party has denounced us. Most of their members have turned a blind eye to the repression. They're too concerned with their own reputations to speak out, even though they know it's unjust. I understand now that they're never going to allow me to be defined by anything other than my past. But there's no use in being angry over it. What's done is done, and I just have to live with it."

I disagreed. Even if I wasn't angry over the leaked police report, I felt there was no justification for Martin's political opponents, and particularly the Freedom Party, to hold him to his decade-old mistakes, to engage in eternal condemnation. This sort of behavior often led former extremists to believe that rehabilitation was useless. Without hope of escaping their negative pasts, they saw no point in trying to be better. Ultimately, many ended up choosing the only option they believed was available to them: retreating back into their echo chambers, spiraling deeper and deeper into radicalization as they went.

"I'm afraid there's more bad news," Martin said. "Syria rejected my visa because of the terrorism investigation, so I can't travel there with the Alternative Help Association to help the villagers of Maaloula. And also, the priest who agreed to marry us just contacted my mom and told her he doesn't want to marry us in Austria. He thinks the Austrian media will attack him, so the only way he'll agree to marry us is if we have the wedding in Italy with just our families as guests."

I came to a sudden halt on the footpath. "Are you serious?"

"Unfortunately, yes." Voices echoed on the opposite end of the line, as if Martin had just entered a group of ten to twenty people. "I've just arrived at the Generation Identity Office," he explained. "I have to talk with a few of our members now, but I'll call you again right after, and we can talk about what to do about the priest. I love you."

He hung up the phone.

I sat on the riverbank, on a rocky patch scattered with driftwood. Shouts of excitement echoed from a pair of water-skiers as their boat roared by, the sounds of people who were as full as I was empty. Piece by piece, I felt like I was being hollowed out. It wasn't the first time that people were afraid to politically associate with us, but I couldn't believe these fears were now extending into the religious sphere. Why should the media care which priest married us? It wasn't as if by performing the marriage the priest would be taking a political stance; he would simply be administering a sacrament. I'll admit that, for a time, I was angry at the priest. I was even angry at God. But my anger only lasted until I reminded myself that, as holy as many of them were, priests weren't perfect. Expecting every single priest to be courageous one hundred percent of the time was unrealistic. Plus, I hadn't always been perfectly courageous either, so I had no right to judge.

We'll find another priest, I told myself. Somewhere out in the world, I was sure the right one existed. The only thing I had to do was keep faith in God, and if I could do that, then God would send him to us.

Martin remained in the spotlight for the next several weeks. Whether it was articles about his U.S. ban, his terrorism investigation or the swastika sticker, the media didn't let up. News of his U.S. ban in particular ignited celebration amongst leftists. The amount of misinformation they promoted across social media was far too large to respond to, much less to read. But the foundation of their accusations was always the same: Martin was a Nazi. Ironically enough, many of the leftists who made this claim were self-professed supporters of communism, an ideology that has so far been responsible for nearly one-hundred million deaths worldwide.[204]

I called Martin every night. His video statement about the leaked police report had been well-received, giving him the time and the energy to plan a political demonstration about the Great Replacement. Had I not called him on the day of the leak, I might have never even known he had been concerned.

"The media articles haven't slowed, but there's no use in trying to respond to all of them," he told me. "I'm just focusing on the work I have ahead."

"I think that's best," I told him. "It's hard to read all the lies about you, though."

"I don't care so much anymore about what they write," Martin said. "Like the politicians, they lie and have a clear agenda, but the real perpetrator, the *real* person to blame is Brenton Tarrant. He's the one who murdered over fifty innocent people. He's the one who linked himself to me, despite knowing I was against violence, and dragged me into his crime. He's turned out to be the perfect tool of the mainstream media and the left. They are willfully fulfilling his agenda and using him to attack patriotic structures."

I recalled Tarrant's dead-eyed face, still being printed alongside Martin's in dozens of articles. Scowling. Ugly. It was the face of a man who had created a ripple effect, one that started with his victims and pooled across the world to cause hundreds of others, including Martin and me, unimaginable adversity.

Martin was right that Tarrant was the real perpetrator. On the other hand, I couldn't be as indifferent as Martin was toward the media.

Their slander wasn't simply cruel; it was destroying lives. It was causing people to lose their reputations, jobs, and livelihoods. To add even more harm, most journalists liked to cherry-pick stories to suit their own narratives, sensationalizing certain events while twisting the facts of others, and this had real-world consequences.

An example of this occurred on April 21, not long after Martin's and my phone conversation. The day was Easter Sunday, sometime in the early morning. Hundreds of Christians were attending Mass on the island country of Sri Lanka when a group of Islamic terrorists entered three churches and three five-star hotels, detonating bombs that resulted in the deaths of 290 innocent people. Over 500 others were injured.[205] Within hours, pictures of the church attacks popped up on social media; the trending page displayed reels of horrific carnage. Bodies of young and old were crushed beneath chunks of exploded rock, their mutilated limbs red and blistered in the heat. More bodies were slumped over the pews or strewn across the floor with their loved ones grieving over their mutilated remains.

Most of the mainstream media reported on the Sri Lanka Easter Bombings. Some outlets published the facts—how the bombings were a calculated attack on Christianity[206]—while others admitted that the bombings had been carried out as revenge for the Christchurch Shooting.[207] But, contrary to how they had reported on the Christchurch Shooting, articles featuring the names and faces of the terrorists were missing. Also missing were articles about how Islamic terrorism was a rising global threat that needed to be combatted. "Not all Muslims are to blame," they said, while publishing articles such as the following: 'Sri Lanka's Muslims fear retaliation after Easter attacks on Christians'[208] and 'Not your enemies: Sri Lanka Muslims fear backlash after blasts.'[209]

With a death toll that was five times higher than the Christchurch Shooting, where was the public outcry? Where was the global mourning with the Christian community, the calls to de-platform radical Muslims from social media, and the house-raids against anyone who might've once sent the terrorists an email? The truth was that, after a few days, the Sri Lanka Easter Bombings were largely forgotten. When you get to a certain point, you come to understand the power of the mainstream media: it is able to make the world remember what it wants them to remember and to forget what it wants them to forget.

THE KOOTENAI COUNTY REPUBLICAN MEETING

New people were arriving at my house every day. With my younger sister's wedding due to take place in a few days, friends and relatives were traveling to Idaho, transforming the atmosphere into one of anticipation and excitement. My mom hosted a bachelorette lunch, meetups with the groom's family, and game nights. Sitting around the game table, eating chips, and drinking chocolate martinis, we played a favorite board game Settlers of Catan late into the evenings.

Three days before the wedding, I attended the Kootenai County Republican Central Committee meeting with my parents. The boats in the Coeur d'Alene harbor rocked in the cool evening wind, and the sunset looked like a bright orange oil lamp that was slowly being snuffed out. It brought to mind the sunset I had watched with Martin in the Austrian Alps. How different our lives had been only a few weeks earlier!

When we arrived at the meeting, my dad introduced me to the committee member who had invited me to speak a few weeks prior. The man was middle-aged with a carefully trimmed goatee and russet hair that was done over in a slick backcomb. A husband and father, he was a Christian who also worked a regular job outside of politics.

I smiled as I shook his hand, thinking that he fit the stereotype of wholesomeness that was common amongst Idahoans. But meeting him also made me feel guilty. Given how notorious the Christchurch Shooting had become, I knew that he and the rest of the Kootenai County Republicans would face an onslaught of media attacks if they stood up for us. Maybe, I told him, it would be better if I didn't go through with giving my speech.

"No, you should definitely speak," he answered. "Don't worry about the media—we're used to their attacks. If the committee votes to pass a resolution to help your fiancé, we'll stand by it."

"I don't know how to thank you."

"No thanks needed. Even if I don't agree with everything you say, I know political persecution when I see it."

Roughly a hundred people had gathered inside the meeting hall. Most were spectators, come to observe, since the committee meetings were open to the public. The remaining attendees were committee members. Their tables formed a large ring around the room with an open spot in the center reserved for speakers.

The meeting began with a series of announcements, and then shifted into a period of resolution proposals. I looked over my speech notes as half a dozen other people took turns proposing resolutions, most of which concerned issues in the local community.

"Brittany Pettibone."

"I'm here." I rose at the sound of my name.

"Please propose your resolution."

Nervous butterflies stirred in my stomach as I walked to the center of the room. I hadn't delivered a speech in a while, plus I figured most people had no idea who I was. I did my best to acknowledge each of the committee members before speaking. I told myself that, in the end, it didn't matter if I was able to convince them to help me. What mattered most was that I was trying to help Martin.

"Firstly, thank you so much for the opportunity to speak," I began. "For those who don't know me, my name is Brittany Pettibone, and I'm a Catholic American Nationalist. I've been politically active since 2016, when I started campaigning for President Trump. But today, I'm not here to talk about that. I'm here to talk about the recent political persecution that my fiancé and I have faced in the wake of the Christchurch Shooting."

With each word, my confidence grew. I told the committee as much of Martin's story as possible, about how he was the leader of Generation

Identity Austria, which opposed mass migration and the Islamization of Europe, but which was dedicated to peaceful protest. I told them about Martin's achievements, including the Defend Europe Mission and his campaign against the Global Compact for Migration. I told them about his 2018 trial, about the hate speech charges and about how he had been fully acquitted. Then I addressed our present predicament, explaining the house-raid and the terrorism investigation that had resulted from Brenton Tarrant's donation. "Several other political people and groups received donations from the Christchurch shooter,"[210] I stated, "but none of them had to endure raids, investigations, nothing. A few of them were simply called in for interviews." I also mentioned that Martin wasn't trying to move to the United States—we simply wanted to get married— and that he had traveled to the United States four times in the past without causing any trouble.

"I want to thank you for drafting a resolution today to possibly help my fiancé get back into the U.S.," I said at the end of my speech. "It's a case of political persecution where, since we don't have a platform the size of the media, we really can't do much on our own. Thank you very much for listening."

The room erupted into applause. I nodded in thanks, taken aback, for I hadn't expected such a response.

"Excuse me," one of the committee members cut in, "but are you the girl who makes videos with Lauren Southern?"

"Yes, we were banned from the UK together," I replied.

"This girl is the real deal," the man said to the rest of the room. "Thanks for showing up tonight."

I returned to the back of the hall and took a seat next to my parents.

"You did great," my mom whispered.

"Thanks, mom." I squeezed her hand.

The committee members discussed the resolution before casting their votes. As predicted, they brought up the possibility of media attacks if they chose to get involved.

"Yes, but we shouldn't be making decisions based on how we think the media will react," one of the committee members pointed out.

"If we're only capable of standing up for political freedom when it's easy, then our principles aren't very solid," said another.

The panel continued making comments until a committee member to whom I hadn't yet been introduced cut in.

"I know a bit about Martin and Brittany," he said. "I've been following the news surrounding them for a while. While I don't agree with all of Martin's beliefs, I do know that he's not an extremist. He's simply concerned with mass migration and Islam, which, as we all know, are two of the most controversial political issues these days." He looked around the room, gesturing at specific members of the committee. "Those of you who mentioned that the media will attack us if we pass Miss Pettibone's resolution are right. And let me be clear— the negative coverage will be unlike anything we've received before. All of you need to understand this before casting your votes. But I personally *am* going to vote in support of this resolution. To me, free speech and political freedom aren't just empty buzzwords. What do they mean to you?"

It was now time to vote. Hands rose into the air, slowly at first, and then continuing until every hand on the panel pointed skyward.

Unanimous.

As I looked around the room, witnessing all the hands raised in Martin's and my defense, my impression of the Republican Party radically changed. Much of the overall party was cowardly and self-serving, yes. But not in Idaho. In Idaho, it was clear that at least some of the party still valued acting on principle.

Later that night, I expected to already see news reports about the resolution. To my surprise, the media kept silent. It wasn't until later, a few days after my sister's wedding, that the articles started to trickle out. *Vice News* wrote, 'The Idaho GOP is helping an alt-right YouTube star marry her Austrian white nationalist boyfriend.'[211] And *The Hill* wrote, 'Idaho Republicans urging government to allow Austrian nationalist into the U.S. to marry alt-right YouTuber.'[212]

I had to laugh. Their slander was never very creative. Alt-right. White nationalist. And every so often there was a conspiracy theorist label thrown in.

Despite having never been a member of the alt-right, the media had no qualms about falsely attaching me to the label. The only thing that set this particular attack apart from the others was that a local reporter showed up at my family's home unannounced. Since our address wasn't public, I had no idea how he had gotten it. The only thing I knew was that his actions were invasive, closer to that of a stalker than a professional journalist. I didn't interview with him.

Thankfully, the Kootenai Country Republicans, who had anticipated backlash from the media, refused to back down. In an e-mail, Kootenai County GOP chairman Brent Regan said 'the party took up the resolution to help Pettibone because she is a constituent. He said the resolution had nothing to do with her ideology. Rather, he said, the party was concerned about freedom of political speech.'[213]

'Duane Rasmussen, a former vice chairman who remains active in the Kootenai County GOP, defended the resolution, contending federal authorities have no good reason to prevent Sellner from entering the United States. "It's not a resolution in support of his cause," Rasmussen said. "It's a resolution in support of him getting married."'[214]

In the end, even if the Kootenai County Republicans' resolution didn't lead to Martin's U.S. travel privileges being reinstated, I remained thankful. For me, the proof of their moral character had never been about defending my beliefs, it had been about defending my rights.

REUNITED IN EXILE

Once the dust from the Kootenai County Republican media storm had settled, life slowed down. The quiet days allowed me to return to my regular schedule of filming YouTube videos and writing *Patriots Not Welcome*. I even found time to gather the necessary paperwork to apply for an Austrian visa. As soon as Martin and I were legally married, I would be eligible to live in Austria on a family visa. The application process turned out to be more complicated than anticipated. More than a dozen documents were required, including a series of background checks—local, state, and even a background check from the FBI. All the documents needed official German translations, as well as seals from the Secretary of State called Apostilles, which verified the documents' authenticity.

Finally, in early May, I boarded a flight to Croatia. Unlike in the U.S., the border police at the Zagreb Airport gave me no trouble. They simply stamped my passport, waving me through the customs gate as I hurried back into Martin's arms. He looked healthier. Eyes bright, his skin lightly tanned, he wore a pair of black New Balance sneakers and a clean blue polo shirt. The way the material fit to his body suggested that he had maintained his strict workout regimen. Had I not known better, I might have guessed he had been on vacation during the past two months.

"I can't believe you're really here." I laughed, touching his face again to make sure.

He gave me a kiss. "I missed you, too."

We drove to the city of Zadar. Rich in cultural heritage and situated on the Adriatic Sea, Zadar was one of the Croatia's oldest cities. It offered an array of Roman ruins, medieval churches, and historical monuments. Apart from the many tourist sites, its white sandy beaches and wild shepherd trails made it the perfect location for a quiet getaway.

We rented two rooms in a charming blue-and-white hotel near the seaside. There, we dove into wedding plans. We couldn't help but laugh at how complex the process was. First, we arranged a legal marriage in Vienna on July 5, just a few days after I was scheduled to return to Austria. The reason we needed to get legally married so early was so that I could apply for an Austrian visa, which could take as long as three months to be approved. Then, on August 13, we arranged to have a secret church marriage in the Austrian countryside with only our families and closest friends in attendance. Lastly, on August 17, we planned a larger reception at a castle ruin outside of Vienna, inviting our friends from around the world. As unorthodox as having three separate wedding celebrations was, it felt fitting given the circumstances.

After a few days of wedding-related work, we allowed ourselves to relax. We took a long bike ride, racing each other across the famous City Bridge and getting lost amidst the tourist shops on the other side. We visited prominent historical sites in the old town, including the Church of Saint Donatus, and ate traditional Croatian food at tasty, hole-in-the-wall restaurants. The prices were wonderfully cheap in comparison to Vienna.

During our exploration, we discovered a scenic beach café with a long white deck that stretched over the open sea. Waves splintered against the wooden pilings as we leaned over the railing, bright blue and capped with foam.

"Do you think we'll ever have a normal life?" I asked Martin, stretching out under a sun umbrella to escape the heat.

"No," he said. "I'm sure we'll have a few peaceful months here and there, but it won't last…not unless we manage to defeat the leftist power structure in Austria. I think it's good that we've been able to acknowledge the risks of our political work and use them to decide if getting married and having a family is the right thing to do."

"It's definitely right," I repeated, for we had already agreed that it was. All throughout history, even in situations a thousand times more dangerous than ours, young men and women had continued to choose family. Plus, many of our fellow political activists had spouses and children of their own.

I pulled off my sunglasses, squinting through the slanting sunlight as I gazed westward. Somewhere in the distance lay the Austrian border, the final barrier between Martin's and my new life. Either the Austrian police would let me pass, allowing us to wed as planned, or we would once again have to start from scratch and plan our wedding elsewhere.

"Oh, I almost forgot to tell you," Martin said. "My mom found a priest in Austria who agreed to marry us."

"She did?"

"Yes, and he couldn't be more perfect. He understands our situation better than most people. You wouldn't believe some of the things he's had to go through."

Martin explained that he was a young British-Australian priest named Father J, who had been stationed in Austria a few months prior. But before joining the priesthood, he had been a political activist who had repeatedly traveled to Burma to protest the regime's genocidal persecution of Burma's border people—many of which were Father J's close friends. As punishment for his protest, Father J had been arrested and deported from Burma three times. He had also suffered through a brutal interrogation that included physical torture and two long imprisonments, one of which lasted over a year and was spent in solitary confinement. Locked in a cell, Father J was forced to sleep on the dirt with little food and water. But, somehow, in a show of heroic courage, he had continued his protest by going on a twenty-day hunger strike.

The longer Martin spoke, the more I felt like he was describing a fictional character. That someone had been able to persevere through such adversity seemed impossible. I realized then that, as difficult as things were, my hardships were nothing in comparison with what many others had to suffer. In some ways, Father J's story left me with a bad conscience. Oftentimes in the past, when God had handed me trials, I had failed to accept them, at least not as happily as I could've. Instead, I had wished them away, hoping for peace.

Regardless, I was happy I hadn't been wrong about one thing: that the right priest to marry us existed. The only thing I had to do was keep faith in God, and if I could do that, then God would send him to us.

On our final day in Croatia, Martin knocked on the door of my hotel room sometime before dawn. I checked the clock on the nightstand, my eyes winking from fatigue: it was only six. I assumed he had been awake for a while, for he was already showered, shaved, and dressed.

"Sorry for waking you up so early," he said, when I opened the door.

"There's been another illegal data leak."

Somehow, even before Martin said another word, I guessed the content of the leak. Brenton Tarrant's emails. Yes, the Secret Police had promised to secure Martin's data, but I had realized long ago that their promises were empty. The Austrian state was utterly incapable of preventing illegal leaks. Certain people with privileged access were too self-interested, too corrupt. The content of these emails was of interest to too many third parties, including the Austrian media.

"Do you know who leaked them?" I asked.

"No," Martin said. "Aside from Winklhofer and the Austrian Secret Police, multiple people in the Austrian government have access to my data, so there's no real way of figuring out who's responsible."

Reports about the illegal leak started in Austria, but quickly made their way to the United States. Within hours, I spotted a headline from *The Guardian* that read: 'Christchurch shooter's links to Austrian far right more extensive than thought.'[215]

Most of the articles accused Martin of having been dishonest about his e-mail exchange with Tarrant. They reported that Martin had claimed to have only ever sent a single thank you e-mail to Tarrant. They also reported that the Austrian Secret Police had discovered the e-mail exchange as a result of their own investigative skills.

The truth was that Martin had personally given the e-mails to the Austrian Secret Police on the day of the house-raid. Moreover, just two days after the house-raid went public, Martin had revealed to the *New York Times* that he and Tarrant had exchanged more than one e-mail.

'A quote from the article read: 'He gave me a generous donation and I thanked him, that's all,' Mr. Sellner said in a telephone interview Wednesday, condemning the attack but acknowledging that the two men had written back and forth a few times over email.'[216]

Of all the statements that President Trump has made, he was perhaps never more accurate than when he labeled the media the enemy of the people.[217]

For the most part, Martin and I remained undeterred. The

mainstream media had sullied our reputations to such an extent that it hardly mattered anymore. Martin went on to address the illegal leak in a YouTube video, while I was asked to address it by the U.S. authorities—Homeland Security, in particular. On my way home to Idaho, the U.S. Border Police stopped me at the border, asking me to explain why the mainstream media was reporting about Martin having 'newly uncovered links' to Brenton Tarrant. I told them the truth, just as I had last time, the only difference being that I was in much better spirits.

In the end, it took much longer than a single day to regain my full strength. Along the way, I experienced several bad momenta. But after comparing my own struggles with those of people like Martin and Father J, I was able to be much stronger overall. Soon, even the most shocking experiences began to feel normal, as mundane as brushing my teeth before bed. For example, in mid-May, two FBI agents showed up at my house for questioning. Perhaps, I could've succeeded in reaching this mindset much earlier on had I simply accepted my life for what it was. The moment I finally did, I realized that the burdens I was carrying weren't burdens at all. They were opportunities.

THE FALL OF THE FREEDOM PARTY

I kept a close watch on Austrian politics over the following days. Martin was convinced that the tension in the Austrian government, which had been escalating since his house-raid on March 25, was reaching a point of implosion. And implode it did. But contrary to what many had predicated, the cause of the implosion had nothing to do with Martin or Generation Identity.

I was in the garage, jogging on the treadmill, when Martin told me about the news.

Strache is probably going to have to resign, Martin wrote over WhatsApp.

I hopped off the treadmill, toweled sweat from my face, and

searched Twitter for news about Strache. English articles weren't published for a few days, but they eventually reported that Heinz-Christian Strache, who was the Vice-Chancellor of Austria and the leader of the Freedom Party, had been the target of a sting operation, during which one of his private meetings was secretly filmed. Although the footage was originally taken in July 2017, for some reason, it wasn't leaked to the media until May 2019.

On May 17, two popular German media outlets, *Der Spiegel* and *Süddeutsche Zeitung*, published a video showing Strache and his parliamentary leader, Johann Gudenus, holding a private meeting at a lavish resort in Ibiza with a woman who claimed to be the niece of a Russian oligarch.

'The most damaging part in the video was the discussion of how [the woman] might take control of the *Kronen Zeitung*, Austria's largest-circulation tabloid, and use it to help the Freedom Party's (FPÖ) campaign. In return, Strache said he would arrange for public construction tenders currently awarded to Austrian giant Strabag to be given to her instead.'[218]

'Strache and Gudenus, who had initiated the meeting, resigned on May 18th, saying their behavior was 'stupid, irresponsible, and a mistake.' Shortly after their resignations, the Chancellor of Austria, Sebastian Kurz, of the centre-right Austrian People's party (ÖVP), called snap elections, likely to be held in September.'[219]

To this day, it remains unclear who planned the sting operation. In his resignation statement, Strache called the video 'a honey trap stage-managed by intelligence agencies.'[220]

Naturally, the scandal fractured the government coalition between the Freedom Party and the Austrian People's Party. The Freedom Party also shed support among its own fanbase. New elections were held in September 2019, which saw Sebastian Kurz of the Austrian People's Party take the victory.[221] This time, though, he didn't form a government coalition with the Freedom Party. He formed a government coalition with the left-wing socialist Green Party.[222] For an example of the Green Party's anti-Austrian rhetoric, the Green Party's youth party posted a picture of dog feces on Facebook on Austria's National Holiday in 2020 with the caption: Love of Homeland—stop celebrating Austria![223]

The Austrian media and left-wing politicians had gotten their wish. The Freedom Party, while not completely destroyed, was severely crippled. Many claimed it would never be able to regain the status it had lost. As a result, the media's focus on Martin and Generation Identity loosened. Articles popped up here and there, but with the Freedom Party ousted from the government, their attacks became less frequent. So, when Martin was the target of a second Christchurch-related house-raid on June 18, it wasn't talked about nearly as much as the first. Despite having no new evidence upon which to perform a raid, the Secret Police raided Generation Identity's office in Vienna, as well as Martin's private studio where he filmed his YouTube videos.

"In my opinion, I think they know they're abusing the legal system," Martin told me on the phone afterwards, "but they also know they can't get access to my data any other way. Lehofer is convinced that the High Court of Austria will rule the house-raids illegal—the problem is that it could take months to reach a verdict. In the meantime, they have full access to my data. And yours, too."

"We have nothing to do with Tarrant, so as long as they don't continue leaking our private information to the media, I don't really care," I said.

"The illegal leaks will definitely continue," Martin assured. "Also, when the police interrogated me today, they told me that they're now formally investigating you along with me. They said it's because you once interviewed the Australian guy, Blair Cottrell. Tarrant was a follower of his work."

"I've interviewed dozens of right-wingers over the past two years," I pointed out. "Do the police know that my YouTube channel used to strictly be for political interviews?"

"I'm not sure. The police basically just told me they want to question you once you're back in Austria. They want to know why you deleted your interview with Blair Cottrell from YouTube."

"So, they plan to let me back into the country?"

"Yes. Lehofer said there's little chance they'll ban you. But if for some reason they do try, Lehofer can represent you."

I didn't mind meeting with the Secret Police again. I had deleted my interview with Blair Cottrell from YouTube several months before the Christchurch Shooting occurred, which they could verify with YouTube itself if they wanted. Along with the Cottrell interview, I had deleted a handful of others, either because they weren't of interest to my audience, or because they had poor video and sound quality. But many of them, including the Cottrell interview, were still available on my BitChute channel. The police could easily have watched it if they wanted to. On the other hand, I didn't understand why Cottrell was such a point of concern. He wasn't under investigation in his own country. Furthermore, like Martin and me, he strongly condemned Tarrant's crime.

I kept close to my family through June, especially to Nicole. Once I was married, I wasn't sure when I would see her again. Or my parents. There was a chance it could be years. But even if our paths were on the brink of fully diverging, I took comfort in the fact that we would always be a part of each other's lives. We passed the days doing everything together, from playing board games to having barbecues in the backyard. Sometimes, we also went on outings, such as lunch at the Coeur d'Alene resort or a boat ride down the winding Spokane River.

At the end of June, I finally made the long-awaited trip back to Austria. I was standing in line at the Seattle Airport, waiting to board my flight, when a policewoman tapped me on the shoulder.

"Where are you going, Miss Pettibone?" she asked.

"I'm returning to Austria."

"Do you have any political events planned?"

I smiled. "No. I'm getting married."

"And how long do you plan on staying in Austria?"

"Permanently."

The policewoman returned my smile, allowing me to step back in line. "Good luck, Miss Pettibone."

"Thank you."

My airplane traveled from Seattle to Frankfurt. From there, I caught a connecting flight to Croatia. When I landed, Martin was waiting for me at the Zagreb Airport, his trusty car ready to make the four-hour trip to Austria. I cranked up the stereo as we drove, keeping a lively mood despite the wild beating of my heart. This was it.

At the Austrian border, Martin handed our passports to a policeman sitting inside a roadside booth. The policeman stamped Martin's passport first. Then he moved onto mine. When he opened it, I closed my eyes, far too anxious to watch. But watching didn't prove necessary in the end because I felt the car start to move. Slowly at first. Then faster and faster until we were flying along the Autobahn. Around me, there were familiar spruce trees. Familiar wild bellflowers. Familiar rolling hills, packed with grazing cattle. And then, somewhere amidst it all, there was Martin's voice, barely perceptible above the blaring music on the stereo.

"Welcome home, baby."

14

It is not the critic who counts; not the man who points out how
the strong man stumbles, or where the doer of deeds could have
done them better. The credit belongs to the man who is actually
in the arena, whose face is marred by dust and sweat and blood;
who strives valiantly; who errs, who comes short again and again,
because there is no effort without error and shortcoming; but who
does actually strive to do the deeds; who knows great enthusiasms,
the great devotions; who spends himself in a worthy cause; who at the
best knows in the end the triumph of high achievement, and who at the
worst, if he fails, at least fails while daring greatly, so that his place shall
never be with those cold and timid souls who neither know victory or defeat.
                    —Theodore Roosevelt

AUSTRIA, EUROPE
JUNE 2019

A flock of birds soared over Westbahnhof Station. Travelers rushed to
catch trains; others leisurely browsed the bank of souvenir shops. I
watched people go about their business, enjoying a latte on a shaded
patio across from the station. Although my reasons for being there
were less than pleasant, I was in a smiling mood, happy to be back in
Austria.

"Miss Pettibone," Lehofer said by way of greeting. He had emerged
from the police station adjacent to the patio, where he had supervised
Martin's latest interrogation by the Secret Police.

"It's already my turn?" I asked, setting down my coffee.

"No, it seems not. The police decided they don't need to question you, after all. That you once interviewed Blair Cottrell isn't sufficient to warrant a second interrogation."

"You're sure? It's really not a problem, speaking to them."

"I'm sure. The police would simply repeat questions they've already asked you, and there's no need. Better if you go home now. Martin will be another few hours."

I did what Lehofer suggested, boarding the next available train home. The Austrian Secret Police later informed me to be on standby. They said they might need to contact me sometime in the following weeks, but in the end, they didn't. I never heard from them again. And I would not receive an update regarding the investigation until months later, when the High Court of Austria made a ruling on the legality of the two house-raids.

In the meantime, I focused on Martin's and my legal marriage. The ceremony took place on July 5, at the Standesamt (registry office) in the twentieth district of Vienna. The morning sky was blue and cloudless, a balmy breeze rustling the colorful awnings of street shops. Martin and I drove to the Standesamt together, the windows rolled down and the stereo volume turned up. I smiled as he gradually accelerated, as if arriving early would somehow result in us being able to get married sooner.

"Are you nervous?" Martin asked, straightening his tie in the car mirror.

I reached over the console to help him. "I thought I would be, but no."

"I realize this isn't the real wedding," Martin said. "But still, once I say yes, it'll be forever."

"Me, too," I told him. And I knew we both meant it.

The ceremony resembled a traditional wedding. I walked down a long stone aisle, between two rows of velvet chairs where Martin's family and our closest friends sat. At the end of the aisle, Martin and I joined hands to recite our vows—his in German and mine in English. My heart felt full, hardly able to contain its happiness as we promised ourselves to one another. Then we signed the marriage license, sealing our union in the eyes of the state.

"You're halfway to being Brittany Sellner now," Martin said, when I had finished signing.

"Even if it's only halfway, it's progress," I replied with a laugh.

While being legally married was of course important to us, as Catholics, the true validity of our marriage resided in the sacrament and in making our vows before God. We decided to remove our rings until the day of our real marriage on August 13.

After the ceremony, Martin's parents surprised us by renting a carriage drawn by a pair of regal Lipizzaner stallions. For nearly an hour, we rode along the Hauptallee, a romantic avenue shaded by chestnut trees in the Vienna Prater. The ride ended at the historic Lusthaus Building, once a hunting lodge and now an upscale restaurant. There, Martin's family and a few of our friends were waiting for us. We celebrated through the afternoon, dining on minced veal butter schnitzel and Apfelstrudel with creamy vanilla sauce. Martin's mom, Gabi, gifted me a turquoise necklace that had been passed down generationally—an official welcome into the family.

"I couldn't be happier that you and Martin found each other," she said, as she fastened the necklace claps at the nape of my neck. "And I want to be there to help both of you with whatever you need, including applying for your visa. Before we can get started, though, you need to order a passport with your new last name."

"I'll apply for the passport tomorrow," I promised.

Even now, I still feel indebted to Gabi. Without her help, both the visa application and the wedding wouldn't have worked out so smoothly. On top of helping plan both of our reception parties, she planned the rehearsal dinner. She also spent months searching for the right church and the right priest to officiate our wedding, Father J.

When I finally met him in person, he made a lasting impression. He was powerfully tall, with broad shoulders and a bearded chin, and he wore a sweeping black cassock that didn't detract from his masculine appearance, but somehow enhanced it. By all accounts, he was a widely loved priest, yet the shadow in his eyes suggested a past filled with hardship. There wasn't a bitter note in him, however, only contagious joy and classic good humor. The wisdom in his advice not only prepared Martin and I for our upcoming marriage, but for any and all political trials that might come our way. He told us that God's love was soon to become our own bond. That as long as we offered all the natural goods of our marriage to Him, our marriage would be indestructible.

In early August, wedding guests began arriving—some from the United States, some from the United Kingdom, and others from around Europe. I was happiest to see my parents, who had come early to spend time with me. When I met them at the airport in Vienna, it felt like a collision of two worlds. I couldn't wait to introduce them to my new home, to the city where I had experienced many of the events, both good and bad, that had played a role in shaping who I had become. From a stroll along the Danube River to enjoying a coffee at our favorite Viennese café, Martin and I showed them as much of the city as we could. However, there was a limit to our sight-seeing, for my mom had promised to help Martin's mom with the rehearsal dinner.

It took place in the early evening of August 9, at the family home of Martin's parents in Baden. About twenty guests attended, all seated at a long table garnished with summer flowers and white linen. Flickering candlelight cast soft shadows on the smiling faces of family and friends, who got along as if they had known one another all their lives. There were polished champagne flutes and elegant porcelain plates topped with ornately folded napkins; each place setting came with a unique name-card that had been handmade by Martin's father.

Gabi had spent two full days in the kitchen, preparing a four-course meal from scratch: an appetizer of spinach-salmon wraps topped with seasoned tomatoes, a fresh fruit salad, roasted pork with buttered parsley potatoes, and for dessert, sweet hazelnut cake and foam-topped cappuccinos. All through the evening, she and my mom darted from kitchen to table, piling plates and refilling glasses, happily catering to every guest.

The table conversation mostly touched on the wedding: where

everyone would stay the night before and how the schedule of the church marriage would unfold. Father J even went so far as to arrange a backup plan if the location of our church was leaked. Overall, I wasn't worried. I had the reassuring feeling that, from the beginning, God had always intended for our wedding to happen this way.

THE SECRET WEDDING

On August 12, our wedding party made the three-hour drive to the market town of Tamsweg. Situated in the Central Eastern Alps, the town was couched between lush highland meadows and windy fields of grass. Idyllic white houses with gilded window frames bordered the market square, where an Austrian flag danced proudly on a pole.

Our wedding party split into two groups upon arrival. Martin's group traveled to a hostel on the edge of town, and my group stayed overnight in a charming yellow-stone hotel in the market square. The rooms were modern yet quaint, with waxed wood floors that reflected the lamplight, softly textured beds sheets of red-and-white linen, and paintings of the alpine wintertime mounted on its wood-paneled walls. I was particularly fascinated by the bathroom; it had its own sound system and set of pulsing disco lights, which I immediately put to use.

Throughout the hotel, wedding guests scurried about, seeing to last-minute preparations. Apart from my parents and grandparents, who were lodging in Salzburg overnight, most of my guests had arrived. We met in the hotel restaurant for a meal of chicken schnitzel and fries, laughing and joking as we exchanged memorable, sometimes embarrassing, stories from the past. I was happiest to see my French friend, Juliette, whom I had known since high school. After about an hour, we managed to steal away to the balcony of my hotel room for a private conversation. Gently misting rain softened the deep nighttime shadows.

"I'm so grateful you're here, Julie," I told her.

"I wouldn't have missed it for the world, Britt. I knew you and

Martin would get married since the first time I saw you two together in 2017."

"I knew it, too," I admitted. "A lot of people think the idea of love at first sight is stupid, and to be honest, so did I before meeting Martin, but it's what happened to me. I don't think I could ever put into words how much I love him."

"You don't have to. You've shown it with all you've been through together." Juliette nudged my arm with a wink. "Are you nervous yet?"

I was actually more relaxed than I thought I would be. On top of having had a healthy appetite for dinner, I was also able to fall asleep quickly that night. But the reality did kick in eventually, starting the next morning, when I woke up to a text message from Martin's mom.

Brittany, I just got the news! Your visa has been APPROVED! No more worrying or waiting. You can finally stay here with Martin in Austria!

I leapt out of bed with an excited scream, accidentally waking up Juliette, who had slept in a bed beside mine. I couldn't believe it—not only that the visa had been approved, but that I had happened to receive the news on the day of our wedding. The weight on my shoulders seemed to dissolve and scatter like sparks in the wind. All throughout the morning, I moved as lightly as if I had wings, first to the local flower shop, and then to the hair salon. Juliette and I tried not to laugh when the stylist speared my hair with a hundred bobby-pins to hold my updo intact. She then sprayed half a bottle of hairspray onto the updo, freezing it in place.

"My head feels like a bowling ball," I joked to Juliette as we made our way back to the hotel.

"Yes, but it looks beautiful," she promised. "The stylist did a great job."

We found my mom and Franziska in the hotel lobby, waiting with hot coffee and buttered scones. They already wore their wedding outfits—my mom in a beautiful plum gown that complimented the light-catching silver in her hair and Franziska in a pale-pink sleeveless gown, holding out her arms for a hug.

"Hurry up and put on your wedding dress," she urged, as we rode the elevator to my hotel room. "I can't wait to see you in it."

Juliette switched on the radio in the bathroom, setting the mood, and I removed the dress from its wrapping. Ivory and glittering, the Oleg Cassini gown rested slightly off my shoulders, its lace design inspired by the ornate motifs found in royal palaces. Crafted with three types of lace motifs and two thousand beads and sequins, the gown was topped off with a long lace veil that extended behind me for nearly fifteen feet.

"Can we go to the church now?" I asked as soon as Juliette finished attaching my veil.

My mom laughed sweetly. "Not just yet. The ceremony still doesn't start for a while. Plus, as the bride, it's tradition to arrive fashionably late."

The four of us visited for another hour. We took photos and videos to mark the occasion while drinking the coffee and eating the scones.

Sometime around eleven, my dad knocked on the door. "You ladies ready?" he asked. "The car is waiting outside."

My heart beat wildly as I headed out to the parking lot, my veil draped heavily over one arm. It didn't stop as my dad pulled away from the hotel and drove down a narrow road that led out of Tamsweg and wound deep into the forested mountains. My mom, Juliette, and Franziska chatted in the back seat, but I was too nervous to join in. I craned my neck as we rounded each bend, hoping to spot the church in the distance. Five, six, seven turns—and then there it was. Tall and stately, with a white-stone bellower, the church loomed like a holy fortress through the misting rain. The interior, devoid of electricity, was illuminated by yellow candlelight. A red carpet ran between the dark wood pews, leading up to a gold-leafed altar that housed hand-painted statues of various saints. Bouquets of fresh yellow, white, and pink flowers adorned the foot of the main altar crucifix, while more bouquets were fastened with ribbons to each chair.

I assumed Martin was already waiting at the altar. If he hadn't been nervous the night before, I was sure that, like me, he was now.

My dad held an umbrella over my head and guided me out of the car. In the church vestibule, Juliette adjusted my train, straightening the folds until it reached full length.

"Are you ready?" my dad asked me.

I nodded. I had been ready for a long, long time. "I love you, dad."

He took my arm in his. "I love you, too."

The low hum of music rumbled through the church. Deep and haunting, a professional quartet from Salzburg played the traditional Canon D on cellos and violins.

"It's time," Martin's brother said with a wink. "You can go in now."

I took a deep breath, reminding myself to walk slowly. My grip tightened on my dad's arm as he ushered me through the open doors of the vestibule, into the softly lit church. And that's when I saw him— standing at the altar in a tailored black suit and yellow-rose lapel, smiling at me as he awaited my return to him for the last time. I squeezed the bouquet, using all my effort not to cry. I was so happy, my heart too overwhelmed by the thought that all we had fought for, all that we had desired and imagined and promised to each other for so long was finally in front of us, brought closer and closer with each step.

At the end of the aisle, my dad gave me away. Gently, Martin accepted me into his care, taking my hand and leading me to our private pew before the altar. There, we knelt side-by-side, our smiles radiant, our eyes a reflection of the love that only the two of us knew.

The ceremony began with a sermon from Father J. Dressed in opulent gold vestments embroidered with pink roses, he climbed the stairs to a gilded pulpit on the side of the church. "Today, you receive the sacrament of matrimony," he told Martin and me. "That means Christ offers grace in abundance to make your marriage invincible. His own love becomes your bond. Treasure this, thank Him for it, plead with Him daily to renew it, and you will achieve in time and eternity everything He wants of you." Father J smiled assuredly, and then addressed the full church. "Love is known in Christ, in sacrifice. A strong union can bear sacrifice. Martin and Brittany have both already made sacrifices for the common good, and who can doubt that much more will be demanded of them? How will their marriage bear the strain? Brittany has already left her country and made sacrifices of her work for the sake of Martin's work. How can a marriage bear when the husband must often be absent; when the husband risks his safety; when the mission of husband and wife brings the authorities into the family home? Well, there is no predetermined, theoretical limit: it depends upon two people. One, how much will the wife sacrifice herself for this; and second, how much the husband will show his gratitude for her so doing? Martin, so long as you thank Brittany, because you love her; so long as you listen to Brittany, because you love her; so long as you weigh her advice and consider her requests, because you love her, then who can set a limit?"

At the end of Father J's sermon, the altar servers brought out our marriage crucifix. In the eyes of the Catholic Church, marriage is indissolubly linked with the Cross of Christ, so if one of the spouses abandons the other, they are in turn abandoning Christ on the Cross. Martin and I knelt before the crucifix as Father J blessed it. Then, placing our right hands over one another's on the crucifix, we took our vows.

"Repeat after me," Father J told us.

Martin's tone was certain, steadfast as he repeated, "I, Martin Michael Sellner, do take thee, Brittany Alicia Merced Pettibone, for my lawful wife…"

"I, Brittany Alicia Merced Pettibone, do take thee, Martin Michael Sellner, for my lawful husband; to have and to hold, from this day forward, for better, for worse, for richer, for poorer, in sickness and in health, to love and to cherish till death do us part; and thereto I plight thee my troth."

"The rings." Father J signaled the altar servers to bring out the gold wedding bands. Inscribed on both was the date of our marriage and a secret Latin phrase. Father J took a moment to bless the rings before we completed our vows. "With this ring, I thee wed, and I plight unto thee my troth." We pushed the rings onto each other's fingers, sealing our marriage in the eyes of God.

"You're married now." Father J smiled. "Congratulations, Mr. and Mrs. Sellner."

Martin and I returned to our private pew. In the midst of our gratitude, of our insuppressible bliss, we both felt prepared. Not just for today, but for all the years to come. Even in the face of the most trying hardship, all we had ever needed was each other. And now that we had been joined, not simply by a manmade law, but by God, there wasn't a force on earth that could ever truly separate us.

The ceremony continued with a Tridentine Catholic Mass in Latin, during which Martin and I received Holy Communion. At the closing of the Mass, we approached a statue of the Blessed Virgin Mary at one of the side altars, where we offered a prayer and placed a vase of flowers at her feet. Then, leading me back in front of the altar railing, Martin dipped me backwards, and we kissed for the first time as man and wife. A flurry of camera clicks sounded from the church pews, their lenses tracking us as we walked hand in hand out of the church.

Outside, the skies had cleared. Martin and I greeted each guest as they emerged, thanking them for attending and for their well wishes. From there, we gathered for group photos: the bridal party, individual photos of our families, and then one in which we were all together. Martin's brother, Thomas, thoughtful as ever, surprised Martin and me with a ride in his old classic car, which had an intricate bouquet of yellow flowers mounted on the hood. The photographer followed us as we climbed inside, capturing photos that would become some of our most cherished memories.

On the way to the reception, we stopped for more photos in a grassy field carpeted with purple flowers. Mountains reared sky-high around the field, their blue-green colors muted through the shimmering veil of fog. We had only been taking photos for fifteen minutes before it started raining again. But Martin and I didn't mind. We stayed there in the field, posing, kissing, and laughing as rain pelted down around us until the photographer finished his shots.

The reception was held at the house of a close friend of the Sellner family. It was kept private, with a limited guest list of forty people and a strict no-cell phone policy. The only photos permitted were those taken by the photographer. The party, which was almost entirely planned by the family friend, was complete with a caterer, a three-tier wedding cake covered in red frosting roses, live music, and even an opera singer.

Martin and I sat at the head of a room filled with elegant tables that sparkled with silver dinnerware. Each chair had its own place card and personalized menu. Throughout a series of toasts and speeches, the caterers served a five-course meal. While all of the speeches were heartfelt, my dad's touched me the most. Due to all the excitement, it hadn't occurred to me how much I would miss him and my mom and how grateful I was for their endless love and support. In starting my new life, I had to say good-bye to my old one. But in that old life, the example of how to have a fruitful marriage had been set down for me by them.

The reception continued late into the night. Martin and I left before it ended around nine because our hotel was about an hour drive in Salzburg. Since he couldn't yet enact the tradition of carrying me over the threshold of our house, Martin instead carried me into his car. I laughed as he spooled my long wedding veil around my waist and then hoisted me into his arms, running quickly toward the parking lot to escape the rain.

Infinitely happy. That was how we felt. From the legal marriage to the church marriage, we couldn't have asked for a more perfect wedding.

Yet a final celebration remained.

It took place four days later on August 17 at a castle ruin outside of Vienna with over a hundred and fifty guests. Among them were friends from around the world.

Baldwin and Nick had flown in from the United States, which made me happier than I could express. It was the first time I had met Baldwin in person, but considering how much we had been through during the 2016 presidential election—and the fact that we had maintained a friendship since then—the meeting felt natural, as if we had been neighbors for years. Likewise, I couldn't wipe the grin off my face when I first spotted Nick. Having been short on funds, he had worked extra hard during the months leading up to the wedding just to afford a ticket. Even to this day, it amazes me how a few chance online meetings could've evolved into such genuine and lasting friendships.

My childhood friends, Juliette and Melissa, and two of my political friends, Rebecca and Robyn, also attended. Of the hundreds of women I knew, these four were among the most special. My Irish friend, Seán, and my UK friends, Lucy and Michael, also showed up, evoking the adventures we had shared during my visits to London, my UK ban, and the unforgettable events at Speaker's Corner. Even the Defend Europe crew made an appearance. Seeing the whole crew again gave us the feeling that everything had come full circle. We had been together when Martin and I had met, and for the first time since then, all of us were reunited.

The castle ruin retained the enigmatic ambiance of an era long past. In German, it was called Burgruine Senftenberg, and it had been a refuge for the Austrian people during the first Turkish siege of Vienna. Inside its crumbling but proud walls, there was a large stone patio, where we erected a billowing white tent and multiple rows of wooden tables. An entire roasted pig was served, with warm bacon sauerkraut and enough beer to send everyone stumbling home. Alongside the tent stretched a lush green lawn, which we used for dancing, wedding games, and delivering speeches. The speeches lasted almost two hours, for the floor was open to anyone who wished to say a word. Most of our friends did, speaking about how we had met, the adventures we had shared, and how happy they were to celebrate such a significant day with us. Father J also performed a special marriage blessing, after which he offered words of advice regarding our spiritual and political futures.

Toward the end of the party, Martin and I shared our first dance as Mr. and Mrs. Sellner. Since Martin had proposed to me on the Danube River, we chose the Blue Danube Waltz as our song. I'll never forget how lovingly he smiled at me, how tenderly he held my waist. His eyes showed the same look he had often given me in the past when, even during the hardest moments, he had promised we were going to make it. And now, we had.

THE AUSTRIAN HIGH COURT RULING

Martin and I settled quickly into our new life. Given that I now had an Austrian visa, we finally felt that we were in a position to plan for our long-term future: where we wanted to live, what we wanted to accomplish politically, and most importantly, starting a family.

We split the summer days between vacation and work. Martin, who wanted to launch a new political movement, forged ahead with even more dedication than before. The movement was called 'Die Österreicher' (The Austrians). Unlike Generation Identity, it wasn't a youth movement, but a movement for patriots of all ages. One of its primary goals was to host the largest patriotic demonstration in Vienna in which a crowd of five-thousand Austrian citizens showed their faces, marching peacefully in protest of the Great Replacement.

I, on the other hand, no longer made politics a top priority. While I contributed whenever I could, I felt it was more important to be a supportive wife to Martin, and to work on assimilating into the Austrian culture. This included learning what I could about the people, the country and its history, getting a new driver's license, and, of course, taking German language courses.

The months flew by like days. Summer turned to autumn, and autumn turned to winter. During this wonderful period, a single dark storm cloud loomed over our otherwise happy marriage: the terrorism investigation. Nearly a year had passed with no word regarding when it would reach a conclusion. The Austrian high court hadn't made a ruling on the legality of the house-raids, either. It wasn't until December 12, 2019, that this finally changed.

I was sitting in home in my office, writing a chapter of this book, when I received a call from Martin.

"Babe, I'm on my way home. You'll never guess what's happened," he said. His voice hitched with excitement, and he sounded winded, as if he had broken into a run. "I just got a call from Lehofer and he told me that the Austrian High Court has finally made their ruling—*both* of the house-raids have been declared illegal."

Immediately, I hung up the phone. This wasn't the sort of news I wanted to celebrate over the phone. Pulling on my boots, I raced outside to meet him. He was entering through the front gate, his face bright, grinning happily. I ran toward him, crying out with joy as I jumped into his arms. While both of us had suspected that the Austrian High Court would rule the house-raids illegal, neither of us could have predicted how liberating the moment would feel.

The Austrian High Court's ruling stated that from the beginning, there was never a sufficient basis upon which to carry out the house-raids. Their ruling also extended to the multiple investigations that were currently being conducted into Martin's and Generation Identity's finances, which Winklhofer had launched back in 2018 during the criminal organization trial.

Winklhofer had never presented clear evidence of why he suspected Martin of being a member of an international terrorist organization, but still, he had been permitted to instrumentalize the legal system to achieve his goals. All of his tactics were listed in the internal documents that Lehofer provided to Martin. Apart from having invaded Martin's private life using twenty-four-hour surveillance of his location and communications, Winklhofer's investigation had also caused irreparable damage to Martin's reputation and police-state-style repression toward Generation Identity. But now, nearly a year later, the Austrian High Court had granted Lehofer's appeals, which meant that

Winklhofer and the Austrian secret police had to return our personal property. To no one's surprise, they took their time doing so.

Three months later, on March 2, 2020, Martin and I drove to the police station for a final rendezvous with the Secret Police. The tables in our meeting room were piled with boxes of equipment: computers, laptops, phones, cameras, microphones, binders of personal documents, and more. The collection included property that had been seized during three house-raids: one in 2018 and two in 2019.

The Secret Police asked Martin to sign a document, acknowledging that our possessions had been returned, before handing over the boxes.

Martin smiled at he signed on the dotted line.

"Don't be too happy," one of the policemen said. "The terrorism investigation isn't over yet."

"Yes, but with the house-raids being ruled illegal, it soon will be," Martin replied.

And he was right.

Two months later, on May 12, Martin and I received news that both the financial investigations and the terrorism investigation had been closed. A forty-two-page document, provided by the Austrian High Court, listed all of the reasons for our exoneration. We exchanged triumphant smiles as we read through it. We had done it. Two long years of repression later, and here we were, still happy, still politically committed, and still as in love as ever. As expected, Winklhofer appealed the verdict, but ultimately, the Austrian High Court again ruled us innocent on December 28 of 2020. Around the same time, the New Zealand Royal Commission of Inquiry published a more than 750-page report on the Christchurch shooting,[224] in which they revealed that during an interview with Brenton Tarrant, Tarrant himself had verified Martin's claim that the two of them had never met. The report also revealed that Tarrant had donated to several other well-known right-wingers, none of whom had their houses raided or were investigated for terrorism—nor should they have been. Like Martin, all of these people condemned not only the Christchurch shooting, but violence in general. The reason I mentioned their donations was to highlight the fact that, despite being among a large group who received donations from Tarrant, Martin was the only person targeted in his home country and internationally by the media, left-wing activists, political parties, the judicial system, and law enforcement.

I'm aware that, apart from the people who directly follow our work, most of the world will never know the truth about Martin's and my story. When it came to news of our exoneration, the same mainstream media that had reported on the accusations against us with such ardent zeal either published a few lazy headlines about the verdict or remained silent altogether. And our political opponents, with their vehement hatred for our cause, remain to this day at our throats. Martin has never once committed a crime; he advocates for peaceful political activism, and he has been exonerated from a trial and multiple investigations; however, these facts don't matter to his opponents, who are as determined as ever to shut him down. Just a few days after Martin and I received news of our final exoneration from the terror investigation in December of 2020, the Austrian government announced a ban on the names and logos of Martin's political movements Identitäre Bewegung Österreich (Identitarian Movement Austria) and Die Österreicher (The Austrians). The Austrian government also banned Martin from engaging in political activism on all federal buildings. And perhaps most sickeningly, a prominent counter extremism organization that advises numerous politicians and lawmakers placed Martin on their 2021 list of the twenty most dangerous people in the world.[225] The list primarily featured terrorists—extremists who have *murdered* innocent human beings—and yet Martin was likened to these murderers due to the fact that he doesn't want the Austrian identity, language, and culture to be transformed by mass immigration.

But we are not afraid.

We've come to realize that in a world as totalitarian as ours, the fight isn't so much about keeping ourselves safe from vilification and repression; it's not even about victory and defeat; it's about living our lives, albeit imperfectly, in service of God, our families, and our countries. Perhaps, in this way, we might succeed in being remembered as having taken part in this war, even if we are ultimately unable to witness its outcome. But for now, the road that Martin and I are walking has not ended. Our fight is not over, and neither is our story. It's simply the end of this particular story.

ACKNOWLEDGEMENTS

First and foremost, I am especially grateful to my twin sister, Nicole, for editing five separate drafts of this book, dedicating countless hours of her time to ensuring its readiness for publication. Thank you to Justin Reamer for his diligent copy-editing, and his fastidious eye. Thank you to Lucy Brown for photographing my author and book cover photos. Thank you to Nick Monroe for meticulously double-checking my sources. Thank you also to Nick Monroe and Seán H. for being swift and reliable beta readers. Special thanks to my parents for their constant love, advice, and encouragement. And last but certainly not least, I am grateful to my beloved husband, Martin Sellner, for assisting me with designing and fact-checking this book.

NOTES

CHAPTER 2

[1] 'Transcript: Donald Trump's Taped Comments About Women', *The New York Times*, 8 October 2016, article found at https://www.nytimes.com/2016/10/08/us/donald-trump-tape-transcript.html

[2] Eliza Relman, 'These are the sexual-assault allegations against Bill Clinton', *Business Insider*, 4 June 2018, article found at https://www.businessinsider.com/these-are-the-sexual-assault-allegations-against-bill-clinton-2017-11?r=DE&IR=T

[3] Marie Solis, 'Did Hillary Clinton Help Bill Clinton Intimidate and Discredit His Rape and Sexual Misconduct Accusers?', *Newsweek*, 17 November 2017, article found at https://www.newsweek.com/did-hillary-clinton-help-bill-clinton-intimidate-and-discredit-his-accusers-714636

[4] 'Highlights from the second presidential debate: Trump fights dirty against Clinton', *Guardian News*, 10 October 2016, video found on YouTube at https://www.youtube.com/watch?v=Irw956jPLOA

[5] 'Highlights from the second presidential debate: Trump fights dirty against Clinton', *Guardian News*, 10 October 2016, video found on YouTube at https://www.youtube.com/watch?v=Irw956jPLOA

[6] Patrick Howley, 'Hillary Clinton Email Scandal Explained', *Breitbart*, 31 October 2016, article found at https://www.breitbart.com/politics/2016/10/31/hillary-clinton-email-scandal-explained/

[7] Anthony Zurcher, 'Hillary Clinton emails – what's it all about?', *BBC News*, 6 November 2016, article found at https://www.bbc.com/news/world-us-canada-31806907

[8] 'Highlights from the second presidential debate: Trump fights dirty against Clinton', *Guardian News,* 10 October 2016, video found on YouTube at https://www.youtube.com/watch?v=Irw956jPLOA

[9] Rudy Takala, 'CNN anchor warns: 'Illegal' for you to look at WikiLeaks, *Washington Examiner*, 16 October 2016, article found at https://www.washingtonexaminer.com/cnn-anchor-warns-illegal-for-you-to-look-at-wikileaks

[10] 'Trump Questions for CNN', Email ID 25846 published by *WikiLeaks*, email found at https://wikileaks.org/dnc-emails/emailid/25846

[11] 'HRC Paid Speeches', Email ID 927 published by *WikiLeaks*, email found at https://wikileaks.org/podesta-emails/emailid/927

[12] 'Re: From time to time I get the questions in advance', Email ID 5205 published by *WikiLeaks*, email found at https://wikileaks.org/podesta-emails/emailid/5205

[13] 'Megyn Kelly is a bimbo', Email ID 6087 published by *WikiLeaks*, email found at https://wikileaks.org/dnc-emails/emailid/6087

[14] 'Julian Assange: A timeline of Wikileaks founder's case', *BBC News*, 19 November 2019, article found at https://www.bbc.com/news/world-europe-11949341

[15] 'Fwd: Dinner', Email ID 15893 published by *WikiLeaks*, email found at https://wikileaks.org/podesta-emails/emailid/15893

[16] 'Marina Abramovic Spirit Cooking', *RAM radioartemobile and Zerynthia*, 10 March 2009, video found on YouTube at https://www.youtube.com/watch?v=3EsJLNGVJ7E&feature=emb_title

[17] Andrew Russeth, 'Marina Abramovic on Right-Wing Attacks: 'It's Absolutely Outrageous and Ridiculous'', *ARTnews*, 4 November 2016, article found at https://www.artnews.com/art-news/news/marina-abramovic-on-right-wing-attacks-its-absolutely-outrageous-and-ridiculous-7255/

[18] Megan Brenan, 'Americans' Trust in Mass Media Edges Down to 41%', *Gallup*, 26 September 2019, article found at https://news.gallup.com/poll/267047/americans-trust-mass-media-edges-down.aspx

[19] 'Re: Did you leave a handkerchief', Email ID 55433 published by *WikiLeaks*, email found at https://wikileaks.org/podesta-emails/emailid/55433

[20] Andrew Breitbart tweet from 4 February 2011, tweet found at https://twitter.com/AndrewBreitbart/status/33636278100561920

[21] Kurt Zindulka, 'Report: Paedophiles on Twitter and Instagram Using Cheese and Pizza Emojis to Share Images', *Breitbart*, 29 August 2020, article found at https://www.breitbart.com/europe/2020/08/29/peadophiles-on-twitter-and-instagram-using-cheese-and-pizza-emojis-to-share-child-porn-report/

[22] 'Comet Ping Pong and OBAMA...and Podesta?', Email ID 19742 published by *WikiLeaks*, email found at https://wikileaks.org/podesta-emails/emailid/19742

[23] Reid Cherlin, Rob Fischer, Jason Zengerle, and Jason Horowitz, 'The 50 Most Powerful People in Washington' *GQ*, 18 January 2012, article found at https://www.gq.com/gallery/50-most-powerful-people-in-washington-dc

[24] Archive of Instagram photo found at https://archive.fo/YJJnJ

[25] Archive of Instagram photo found at https://archive.is/5UecO

[26] Archive of Instagram photo found at https://archive.is/1ZbjH

[27] Bruce Rodgers, 'Gay Talk: A (Sometimes Outrageous) Dictionary of Gay Slang (formerly entitled The Queens Vernacular)', book found on Amazon at https://www.amazon.com/Gay-Talk-Outrageous-Dictionary-Vernacular/dp/0399503927

[28] Archive of Instagram photo found at https://archive.vn/C2Vgn

[29] Laura Wainman, 'Inside Homes: Private Viewing', *Washington Life Magazine*, 5 June 2015, archived version of article found at https://web.archive.org/web/20161127044053/http://washingtonlife.com/2015/06/05/inside-homes-private-viewing/

[30] 'Biljana Djurdjević', 10 January 2017, photos mentioned at timestamps 1:20 and 6:44, video found on YouTube at https://www.youtube.com/watch?v=DedTupHJvpg

[31] Laura Wainman, 'Inside Homes: Private Viewing', *Washington Life Magazine*, 5 June 2015, archived version of article found at https://web.archive.org/web/20161127044053/http://washingtonlife.com/2015/06/05/inside-homes-private-viewing/

[32] 'Re: Hellow!', Email ID 48488 published by *WikiLeaks*, email found at https://wikileaks.org/podesta-emails/emailid/48488

[33] Ciara McCarthy, 'Dennis Hastert sentenced for crimes connected to molestation allegations', *The Guardian*, 27 April 2016, article found at https://www.theguardian.com/us-news/2016/apr/27/dennis-hastert-sentenced-prison-child-molestation

[34] Jessica Dawson, 'Married, With Art', *The Washington Post*, 23 September 2004, article found at https://www.washingtonpost.com/archive/lifestyle/2004/09/23/married-with-art/dee9a0d0-0f0d-4505-b0ef-2f0e1bd1e0e0/

[35] 'Pizzagate: CBS Ben Swann', *Personal Growth Courses*, video found at https://www.personalgrowthcourses.net/video/s/pizzagate-cbs-ben-swann

[36] Ben Collins, 'Meet Ben Swann, the Republican Pizzagate Truther Hosting Atlanta's CBS Nightly News', *The Daily Beast,* 18 January 2017, article found at https://www.thedailybeast.com/meet-ben-swann-the-republican-pizzagate-truther-hosting-atlantas-cbs-nightly-news

[37] Caroline Kenny, 'Political Prediction Market: Clinton's odds rise again', *CNN*, 8 November 2016, article found at https://edition.cnn.com/2016/11/07/politics/political-prediction-market-hillary-clinton-donald-trump/index.html

[38] Anna North, 'Alan Dershowitz helped sex offender Jeffrey Epstein get a plea deal. Now he's tweeting about age of consent laws', *Vox*, 31 July 2019, article found at https://www.vox.com/identities/2019/7/30/20746983/alan-dershowitz-jeffrey-epstein-sarah-ransome-giuffre

[39] John R. Schindler, 'It Sure Looks Like Jeffrey Epstein Was a Spy—But Whose?', *Observer*, 10 October 2019, article found at https://observer.com/2019/07/jeffrey-epstein-spy-intelligence-work/

[40] Malia Zimmerman, 'Flight logs show Bill Clinton flew on sex offender's jet much more than previously known', *Fox News*, 13 May 2016, article found at https://www.foxnews.com/us/flight-logs-show-bill-clinton-flew-on-sex-offenders-jet-much-more-than-previously-known

[41] Danielle Zoellner, 'Bill Clinton again denies visiting Jeffrey Epstein's island as Netflix documentary reveals new claims', *The Independent*, 27 May 2020, article found at https://www.independent.co.uk/news/world/americas/bill-clinton-jeffrey-epstein-filthy-rich-island-netflix-documentary-a9535486.html

[42] Nicole Einbinder, 'From Bill Clinton to Naomi Campbell: Here are some of the famous people who have flown on Jeffrey Epstein's private plane, which has been dubbed the 'Lolita Express'', *Insider*, 9 July 2019, article found at https://www.insider.com/famous-people-flown-jeffrey-epsteins-private-plane-lolita-express-2019-7

[43] Maria Puente, 'Kevin Spacey scandal: A complete list of the 15 accusers', *USA Today*, article found at https://eu.usatoday.com/story/life/2017/11/07/kevin-spacey-scandal-complete-list-13-accusers/835739001/

[44] Jacqueline Gualtieri, 'Kevin Spacey Says "Kill Them With Kindness" and Another One of His Accusers Dies', *Distractify*, 15 April 2020, article found at https://www.distractify.com/p/kevin-spacey-accusers-now

[45] Jon Swaine, 'Jeffrey Epstein accuser: video exists of underage sex with powerful men', *The Guardian*, 7 February 2015, article found at https://www.theguardian.com/uk-news/2015/feb/07/jeffrey-epstein-accuser-video-footage-sex-powerful-men

[46] Jason Slotkin, "Pizzagate' Gunman Pleads Guilty To Charges', *NPR*, 24 March 2017, article found at https://www.npr.org/sections/thetwo-way/2017/03/24/521377765/pizzagate-gunman-pleads-guilty-to-charges

[47] Merrit Kennedy, "Pizzagate' Gunman Sentenced To 4 Years In Prison', *NPR*, 22 June 2017, article found at https://www.npr.org/sections/thetwo-way/2017/06/22/533941689/pizzagate-gunman-sentenced-to-4-years-in-prison?t=1589298523834

[48] Tom Winter, 'Who is Jeffrey Epstein, and why has he been arrested again?', *NBC News*, 11 July 2019, article found at https://www.nbcnews.com/news/crime-courts/who-jeffrey-epstein-why-has-he-been-arrested-again-n1027241

[49] '60 Minutes Investigates The Death Of Jeffrey Epstein', *CBS News*, 5 January 2020, article found at https://www.cbsnews.com/news/did-jeffrey-epstein-kill-himself-60-minutes-investigates-2020-01-05/

[50] Mark Hosenball, 'FBI studies two broken cameras outside of cell where Epstein died: source', *Reuters*, 28 August 2019, article found at https://www.reuters.com/article/us-people-jeffrey-epstein-cameras/fbi-

studies-two-broken-cameras-outside-cell-where-epstein-died-source-idUSKCN1VI2LC

[51] Josh Halliday, 'Jimmy Savile: timeline of his sexual abuse and its uncovering', *The Guardian*, 26 June 2014, article found at https://www.theguardian.com/media/2014/jun/26/jimmy-savile-sexual-abuse-timeline

[52] Mark Sweney, 'BBC bosses still trying to cover tracks over Savile in 2012, says Andy Kershaw', *The Guardian*, 26 February 2016, article found at https://www.theguardian.com/media/2016/feb/26/bbc-bosses-cover-tracks-savile-2012-andy-kershaw

[53] 'Video: Leaked ABC News Insider Recording Exposes #EpsteinCoverup "We had Clinton, We had Everything"', *Project Veritas*, 5 November 2019, video found on YouTube at https://www.youtube.com/watch?v=3lfwkTsJGYA

[54] Ben Quinn, 'Sweden drops Julian Assange rape investigation,' *The Guardian*, 19 November 2019, article found at https://www.theguardian.com/media/2019/nov/19/sweden-drops-julian-assange-investigation

[55] 'Julian Assange: Wikileaks co-founder arrested in London', *BBC News*, 12 April 2019, article found at https://www.bbc.com/news/uk-47891737

[56] Siladitya Ray, 'Trump Didn't Pardon Wikileaks Founder Julian Assange And His Supporters Aren't Happy', *Forbes*, 20 January 2021, article found at https://www.forbes.com/sites/siladityaray/2021/01/20/trump-didnt-pardon-wikileaks-founder-julian-assange-and-his-supporters-arent-happy/

[57] Corky Siemaszko, Phil McCausland, Alexandra Jaffe and Emmanuelle Saliba, Euronews, 'Dozens Arrested in Anti-Trump Protests Around Inauguration', *NBC News*, 20 January 2017, article found at https://www.nbcnews.com/storyline/inauguration-2017/anti-trump-protesters-pepper-sprayed-eve-inauguration-outside-deploraball-d-n709321

58 Chris Tomlinson, 'Tomlinson: Europe's Antifa History Should Serve As A Warning To America', *Breitbart*, 4 June 2020, article found at https://www.breitbart.com/europe/2020/06/04/tomlinson-europe-antifa-history-should-serve-warning-america/

59 Politico Staff, 'Full text: 2017 Donald Trump inauguration speech transcript', *Politico*, 20 January 2017, article found at https://www.politico.com/story/2017/01/full-text-donald-trump-inauguration-speech-transcript-233907

60 Ben Jacobs, 'Hillary Clinton calls half of Trump supporters bigoted 'deplorables'', *The Guardian*, 10 September 2016, article found at https://www.theguardian.com/us-news/2016/sep/10/hillary-clinton-trump-supporters—bigoted-deplorables

61 Chad Sokol, 'WSU College Republicans leader says he was attacked amid D.C. inauguration protests', *The Spokesman-Review*, 20 January 2017, article found at https://www.spokesman.com/stories/2017/jan/20/wsu-college-republicans-leader-says-he-was-attacke/

62 Peter Hermann, 'Protestor pleads guilty to conspiring to disrupt DeploraBall for Trump supporters', *The Washington Post*, 7 March 2017, article found at https://www.washingtonpost.com/local/public-safety/protester-pleads-guilty-to-conspiring-to-disrupt-deploraball-for-trump-supporters/2017/03/07/3f55f3da-0347-11e7-b1e9-a05d3c21f7cf_story.html

CHAPTER 3

63 Paige St. John, '21 arrested as hundreds of Trump supporters and counter-protesters clash at Berkeley rally', *Los Angeles Times*, 14 April 2017, article found at https://www.latimes.com/local/lanow/la-me-ln-berkeley-trump-rally-20170415-story.html

64 Oath Keepers website found at https://oathkeepers.org

[65] 'Brittany Pettibone speaking clips at Battle of Berkeley 3', 16 April 2017, video found on YouTube at https://www.youtube.com/watch?v=dXP1H1h5uII

[66] Tom Ciccotta, 'Berkeley Police Arrest Local Professor For Allegedly Beating Trump Supporters With Bike Lock', *Breitbart*, 25 May 2017, article found at https://www.breitbart.com/tech/2017/05/25/berkeley-police-arrest-local-professor-for-allegedly-beating-trump-supporters-with-bike-lock/

[67] 'Berkeley: Footage shows U-lock beating at rally for Donald Trump', *Mercury News*, 26 May 2017, video found on YouTube at https://www.youtube.com/watch?v=ZGaIFfH7bT0

[68] Emilie Raguso, 'Eric Clanton takes 3-year probation deal in Berkeley bike lock assault case', *Berkeleyside*, 8 August 2018, article found at https://www.berkeleyside.com/2018/08/08/eric-clanton-takes-3-year-probation-deal-in-berkeley-rally-bike-lock-assault-case

[69] Jeremy W. Peters and Thomas Fuller, 'Ann Coulter Says She Will Pull Out of Speech at Berkeley', *The New York Times*, 26 April 2017, article found at https://www.nytimes.com/2017/04/26/us/ann-coulter-berkeley-speech.html?_r=0

[70] 'Nightcrawling After A Small Riot In Paris', *Tim Pool*, 8 May 2017, video found on YouTube at https://www.youtube.com/watch?v=jcRWN073ekw 'Story Time: No-Go Zones', *Lauren Southern*, 25 May 2017, video found on YouTube at https://www.youtube.com/watch?v=758_eiHzZqE

[71] Caitlin Dickson, 'As neo-Nazis grow bolder, the 'antifa' has emerged to fight them', *Yahoo! News*, 14 August 2017, article found at https://news.yahoo.com/neo-nazis-grow-bolder-antifa-emerged-fight-195800993.html

[72] 'Operational Portal Refugee Situations', a service provided by *The UN Refugee Agency*, data found at

https://data2.unhcr.org/en/situations/mediterranean?page=1&view=grid&T
ype%255B%255D=3&Search=%2523monthly%2523

CHAPTER 4

73 Saphora Smith, 'Europe grapples with distinction between refugees and economic migrants', *NBC News*, 2 February 2019, article found at https://www.nbcnews.com/news/world/europe-grapples-distinction-between-refugees-economic-migrants-n965161

74 'Immigration to Italy: a look at the numbers', *The Local Italy*, 12 June 2018, article found at https://www.thelocal.it/20180612/immigration-to-italy-numbers

75 'Number of immigrants who arrived by sea in Italy from 2014 to 2021', *Statista*, data found at https://www.statista.com/statistics/623514/migrant-arrivals-to-italy/

76 Sarah Wildman, 'A European alt-right group wants to take to the sea to stop rescuers from saving migrants', *Vox*, 17 July 2017, article found at https://www.vox.com/world/2017/7/6/15804196/generation-identity-identitarians-alt-right-migration-islam-refugees-europe

77 Barbie Latza Nadeau, 'Alt-Right Group Plans to Hunt Migrants at Sea', *The Daily Beast*, 5 June 2017, article found at https://www.thedailybeast.com/europes-alt-right-goes-to-sea-to-sink-migrants-and-scuttle-rescuers-2

78 Angela Giuffrida, 'Sicilian mayor moves to block far-right plan to disrupt migrant rescues', *The Guardian*, 21 July 2017, article found at https://www.theguardian.com/world/2017/jul/21/sicilian-mayor-port-block-ship-c-star-trying-disrupt-migrant-rescues-far-right

79 Angela Giuffrida, 'Sicilian mayor moves to block far-right plan to disrupt migrant rescues', *The Guardian*, 21 July 2017, article found at

https://www.theguardian.com/world/2017/jul/21/sicilian-mayor-port-block-ship-c-star-trying-disrupt-migrant-rescues-far-right

80 Rachel Lewis, 'Stranded Anti-Immigration Ship Gets Help From Refugee Rescue Boat', *Time*, 11 August 2017, article found at https://time.com/4896962/anti-immigration-ship-rescue-ngo-boat/

81 Michael R. Gordon, Helene Cooper and Michael D. Shear, 'Dozens of U.S. Missiles Hit Air Base in Syria', *The New York Times*, 6 April 2017, article found at https://www.nytimes.com/2017/04/06/world/middleeast/us-said-to-weigh-military-responses-to-syrian-chemical-attack.html

82 'Libyan coastguard chases Golfo Azzurro out of their waters', *Defend Europe*, 22 August 2017, video found on YouTube at https://www.youtube.com/watch?v=Py8cbLqvvlY

83 Patrick Wintour, 'Number of migrants arriving in Italy from Libya falls by half in July', *The Guardian*, 11 August 2017, article found at https://www.theguardian.com/world/2017/aug/11/number-of-migrants-arriving-in-italy-from-libya-falls-by-half-in-july

84 'Migrant crisis: Italy approves Libya naval mission', *BBC News*, 2 August 2017, article found at https://www.bbc.com/news/world-europe-40802179

85 Silvia Sciorilli Borrelli, 'Matteo Salvini: Italy's ports are closed to migrant vessels', *Politico*, 16 June 2018, article found at https://www.politico.eu/article/matteo-salvini-migration-italy-ports-closed-to-migrant-vessels/

86 Claire Farrugia, 'PN backs government decision to ban 'ship of hate'', *Times of Malta*, 21 August 2017, article found at https://timesofmalta.com/articles/view/patrijotti-maltin-collecting-food-and-water-for-ship-of-hate.656124

87 Tim Diacono, 'Malta's Far-Right 'Patriots' Help Refuel 'Ship Of Hate'', *Lovin Malta*, 22 August 2017, article found at

https://lovinmalta.com/news/maltas-far-right-patriots-help-refuel-ship-of-hate/

[88] Claire Caruana, 'Malta closes ports to migrant NGO ships – government confirms', *Times of Malta*, 29 June 2018, article found at https://timesofmalta.com/articles/view/malta-closes-ports-to-migrant-ngos-ships-government-confirms.683102

CHAPTER 5

[89] Kelly McLaughlin, 'Austria tells Italy to stop bringing migrants to mainland Europe and offering 'a ticket to the continent' as Sicilian mayor vows to block far-right activist ship looking to disrupt rescues', *Daily Mail Online*, 21 July 2017, article found at https://www.dailymail.co.uk/news/article-4718520/Austria-tells-Italy-stop-bringing-migrants-mainland.html

[90] 'A message to UC Berkeley from MILO and the Berkeley Patriots', *Milo*, 18 September 2017, video found on YouTube at https://www.youtube.com/watch?v=rn5Xgak1zzA

[91] Jack Montgomery, 'Hungary Builds A Wall, Cuts Illegal Immigration By Over 99 Per Cent', *Breitbart*, 16 September 2017, article found at https://www.breitbart.com/europe/2017/09/16/hungary-builds-a-wall-cuts-illegal-immigration-by-over-99-per-cent/

[92] 'How Hungary Cut Illegal Immigration By Over 99%', *Brittany Sellner*, 5 November 2017, video found on YouTube at https://www.youtube.com/watch?v=LjWD4V-l4tA

[93] Matt Pearce, 'As Trump seeks reelection, immigrant voters stand in his path', *Los Angeles Times*, 23 October 2019, article found at https://www.latimes.com/politics/story/2019-10-23/trump-attacks-immigrants-new-naturalized-citizen-voter-registration
Jason Richwine, 'More Immigration Would Mean More Democrats',

National Review, 3 October 2017, article found at
https://www.nationalreview.com/2017/10/immigration-democratic-party-
republican-party-dream-act-party-affiliation-conservatives-limited-
government-traditional-values/

[94] 'H-1B Visas: Harming American Workers', *Federation For American
Immigration Reform*, April 2018, article found at
https://www.fairus.org/issue/workforce-economy/h-1b-visas-harming-
american-workers
Matthew Sussis, 'Untold Stories: The American Workers Replaced by the
H-1B Visa Program', *Center for Immigration Studies*, 4 May 2019, article
found at https://cis.org/Report/Untold-Stories-American-Workers-
Replaced-H1B-Visa-Program

[95] Karina Chabour, Audrey Racine, and Valérie Dekimpe, 'France: After the
Nice terror attack, dealing with trauma and trying to move on', *France 24*,
21 November 2019, article found at
https://www.france24.com/en/20191120-france-how-to-move-on-with-life-
after-nice-terror-attack

[96] Sara Kamouni, 'Night Of Terror Bataclan massacre – what happened
during the Paris terror attacks, where is the theatre and how many died?',
The Sun, 6 February 2018, article found at
https://www.thesun.co.uk/news/2163925/bataclan-massacre-paris-attacks-
2015-anniversary-latest/

[97] Merrit Kennedy and Camila Domonoske, 'The Victims Of The Brussels
Attacks: What We Know', *NPR*, 31 March 2016, article found at
https://www.npr.org/sections/thetwo-way/2016/03/26/471982262/what-
we-know-about-the-victims-of-the-brussels-attack

[98] 'Berlin lorry attack: What we know', *BBC News*, 24 December 2016,
https://www.bbc.com/news/world-europe-38377428

[99] 'A Chat With Tommy Robinson', *Brittany Sellner*, 27 October 2017, video found on YouTube at https://www.youtube.com/watch?v=6GAi4jiZQB4

[100] Oliver JJ Lane, 'Identitarian Activists Unfurl Giant 'Defend London, Stop Islamisation' Banner On Westminster Bridge', *Breitbart*, 23 October 2017, article found at https://www.breitbart.com/europe/2017/10/23/identitarian-activists-unfurl-giant-defend-london-banner-westminster-bridge/

[101] 'The Historic Results of President Donald J. Trump's First Two Years in Office', 20 January 2019, archived version of White House briefing found at https://archive.is/H6Zwc

[102] Full details about how Martin Sellner has been censored found on his website at https://martin-sellner.at/meine-loeschungen/

[103] Cassandra Fairbanks, 'Instagram Forces Right-Wing Author Brittany Pettibone to Delete All Photos With Her Political Activist Husband – Including From Their Wedding', *The Gateway Pundit*, 5 April 2020, article found at https://www.thegatewaypundit.com/2020/04/instagram-forces-right-wing-author-brittany-pettibone-delete-photos-political-activist-husband-including-wedding/

[104] Paul Bois, 'Disney Producer Apologizes For Wishing Covington Boys 'Into The Woodchipper'', *The Daily Wire*, 22 January 2019, article found at https://www.dailywire.com/news/disney-producer-apologizes-wishing-covington-boys-paul-bois

[105] Nina Mast, 'Far-right activists and "alt-right" trolls are using the #MeToo movement to bolster their xenophobia', *Salon*, 11 February 2018, article found at https://www.salon.com/2018/02/11/far-right-activists-and-alt-right-trolls-are-using-the-metoo-movement-to-bolster-their-xenophobia_partner/

[106] Daniel Greenfield, 'Muslim Migration and Rape Statistics in Europe', *DC Dirty Laundry*, 16 December 2018, article found at https://dcdirtylaundry.com/muslim-migration-and-rape-statistics-in-europe/

[107] Brendan O'Neill, 'We have to talk about these Pakistani gangs', *Spiked*, 15 January 2020, article found at https://www.spiked-online.com/2020/01/15/we-have-to-talk-about-these-pakistani-gangs/

[108] Lara Keay, 'Whistleblowing detective says police chiefs should face charges over Asian grooming gang scandal that saw 97 men left free to rape or abuse 57 young girls because officers feared arrests would 'stoke racial tensions'', *Daily Mail Online*, 14 January 2020, article found at https://www.dailymail.co.uk/news/article-7885313/Child-victims-grooming-gangs-failed-Manchester-police-report-finds.html

[109] Sara M. Moniuszko and Cara Kelly, 'Harvey Weinstein scandal: A complete list of the 87 accusers', *USA Today*, article found at https://eu.usatoday.com/story/life/people/2017/10/27/weinstein-scandal-complete-list-accusers/804663001/

[110] Amelia Mason, 'How Weinstein's Sexual Misdeeds Remained An Open Secret For So Long', *WBUR*, 13 October 2017, article found at https://www.wbur.org/artery/2017/10/13/weinstein-sexual-misdeeds-open-secret

[111] David Harsanyi, 'Opinion: The smearing of Kavanaugh is an attack on the Supreme Court', *The Detroit News*, article found at https://eu.detroitnews.com/story/opinion/2019/09/26/opinion-smearing-kavanaugh-attack-supreme-court/2431773001/

[112] 'A Kavanaugh Accuser Recants', *The Wall Street Journal*, 4 November 2018, article found at https://www.wsj.com/articles/a-kavanaugh-accuser-recants-1541371466
Jack Crowe, 'Fifth Kavanaugh Accuser Recants' *National Review*, 26 September 2018, article found at https://www.nationalreview.com/news/fifth-brett-kavanaugh-accuser-

recants/
John Nolte, 'Brett Kavanaugh's Accuser's Classmate Retracts Claim
'Incident Did Happen'', *Breitbart*, 20 September 2018, article found at
https://www.breitbart.com/politics/2018/09/20/brett-kavanaugh-accusers-
classmate-retracts-claim-incident-did-happen/

[113] Eliza Relman and Sonam Sheth, 'Here are all the times Joe Biden has
been accused of acting inappropriately toward women and girls', *Business
Insider*, 4 May 2020, article found at https://www.businessinsider.com/joe-
biden-allegations-women-2020-campaign-2019-6?r=DE&IR=T

[114] John Nolte, 'Nolte: Alyssa Milano Still 'Admires' Biden After Credible
Sex Assault Allegation', *Breitbart*, 30 April 2020, article found at
https://www.breitbart.com/entertainment/2020/04/30/nolte-alyssa-milano-
still-admires-biden-after-credible-sex-assault-allegation/

[115] Susan Faludi, ''Believe All Women' Is a Right-Wing Trap', *The New York
Times*, 18 May 2020, article found at
https://www.nytimes.com/2020/05/18/opinion/tara-reade-believe-all-
women.html

[116] Linda Hirshman, 'I Believe Tara Reade. I'm Voting for Joe Biden
Anyway', *The New York Times*, 6 May 2020, article found at
https://www.nytimes.com/2020/05/06/opinion/tara-reade-joe-biden-
vote.html

[117] Samuel Osborne, 'Organisers cancel Ukip youth conference, blaming
threats from 'hard left'', *The Independent*, 3 September 2017, article found
at https://www.independent.co.uk/news/uk/politics/ukip-young-
independence-conference-sheffield-stand-up-to-racism-martin-sellner-anne-
marie-waters-a7926791.html

[118] 'YI Conference Banned After Leftist Security Threats Amid "Orwellian"
Political Correctness', *Independence Daily*, 6 March 2018, article found at
https://independencedaily.co.uk/yi-conference-banned-leftist-security-
threats-amid-orwellian-political-correctness/

CHAPTER 6

[119] HM Chief Inspector of Prisons, 'Report on an unannounced full follow-up inspection of Colnbrook Immigration Removal Centre', 18–22 June 2007, PDF found at
https://www.justiceinspectorates.gov.uk/hmiprisons/wp-content/uploads/sites/4/2014/05/2007-Colnbrook_IRC.pdf

[120] Diane Taylor, 'Murder inquiry after immigration centre detainee dies in fight', *The Guardian*, 2 December 2016, article found at
https://www.theguardian.com/uk-news/2016/dec/02/murder-inquiry-colnbrook-immigration-centre-detainee-dies-fight

[121] HM Chief Inspector of Prisons, 'Report on an unannounced full follow-up inspection of Colnbrook Immigration Removal Centre', 18–22 June 2007, PDF found at
https://www.justiceinspectorates.gov.uk/hmiprisons/wp-content/uploads/sites/4/2014/05/2007-Colnbrook_IRC.pdf

[122] Chris Tomlinson, 'Identitarian Activists Martin Sellner And Brittany Pettibone Detained At Heathrow Ahead Of Planned Speech', *Breitbart*, 11 March 2018, article found at
https://www.breitbart.com/europe/2018/03/11/hold-austrian-identitarian-leader-martin-sellner-arrested-at-heathrow-airport-ahead-of-planned-speech/

[123] 'Brittany Pettibone & Martin Sellner Arrive in Vienna after UK Detention', *Tommy Robinson*, 11 March 2018, video found on YouTube at
https://www.youtube.com/watch?v=taIgxSDmgaY&bpctr=1580495286

[124] 'Meet the Couple Detained for Free Speech in the UK', *Tommy Robinson*, 12 March 2018, video found on YouTube at
https://www.youtube.com/watch?v=dPzzr0LpeuU&bpctr=1580495520

[125] 'The Tommy Robinson Interview That Got Me Banned From The U.K.', *Brittany Sellner*, 14 March 2018, video found on YouTube at
https://www.youtube.com/watch?v=WnQ3pmDjfkc

126 ''Allah Is Gay' – Here's What Happened In Luton', *Lauren Southern*, 22 March 2018, video found on BitChute at https://www.bitchute.com/video/AxjH5hZYTbQ/

127 Jules Suzdaltsev, 'Was Jesus Gay?', *Vice*, 6 July 2015, article found at https://www.vice.com/en_us/aus/8gkgj4/was-jesus-gay-702

128 Jack Montgomery, '22-Year-Old Conservative Lauren Southern Claims 'Lifetime Ban' From UK For 'Allah Is Gay' Social Experiment', *Breitbart*, 27 March 2018, article found at https://www.breitbart.com/europe/2018/03/27/lauren-southern-given-lifetime-ban-uk-allah-gay-social-experiment/

129 'Why The UK is "Banning" Right Wing Youtubers & Activists, Child Marriage in the US, and More', *Philip DeFranco*, 12 March 2018, video found on YouTube at https://www.youtube.com/watch?v=48hVnPw4gjo

130 'European Parliament on Right-Wingers Banned From UK', *Lauren Southern*, 14 March 2018, video found on YouTube at https://www.youtube.com/watch?v=odGiYJdFtE0

131 'The Full Story: Why We Were Banned From The U.K.', *Brittany Sellner*, 12 March 2018, video found on BitChute at https://www.bitchute.com/video/4glysfmgOC0/

132 'Hear the Speech the UK wanted Banned (from Speaker's Corner)', *Tommy Robinson*, 25 March 2018, video found on YouTube at https://www.youtube.com/watch?v=xH4Uy3LfyZ4&bpctr=1580504219

CHAPTER 7

133 Sam Dorman, 'An estimated 62 million abortions have occurred since Roe v. Wade', *Fox News*, 22 January 2021, article found at https://www.foxnews.com/politics/abortions-since-roe-v-wade

[134] 'Critical Race Theory', *New Discourses*, article found at https://newdiscourses.com/tftw-critical-race-theory/

[135] Tommy Curry, 'Critical race theory', *Britannica*, article found at https://www.britannica.com/topic/critical-race-theory

[136] Damon Young, 'Whiteness is a Pandemic', *The Root*, 17 March 2021, article found at https://verysmartbrothas.theroot.com/whiteness-is-a-pandemic-1846494770

[137] Mark LeVine, 'Abolishing whiteness has never been more urgent', *Al Jazeera*, 17 November 2019, article found at https://www.aljazeera.com/opinions/2019/11/17/abolishing-whiteness-has-never-been-more-urgent

[138] Selim Algar and Kate Sheehy, 'NYC public school asks parents to 'reflect' on their 'whiteness'', *New York Post*, 16 February 2021, article found at https://nypost.com/2021/02/16/nyc-public-school-asks-parents-to-reflect-on-their-whiteness/

[139] Luke Rosiak, 'Teachers Compile List Of Parents Who Question Racial Curriculum, Plot War On Them', *The Daily Wire*, 16 March 2021, article found at https://www.dailywire.com/news/loudoun-teachers-target-parents-critical-race-theory-hacking

[140] 'Migrants vs European Youth In French Alps', *Lauren Southern*, 25 April 2018, video found on BitChute at https://www.bitchute.com/video/3LpEd1sowdQ/

[141] Marine Le Pen tweet from 22 April 2018, tweet found at https://twitter.com/MLP_officiel/status/987924496186200064

[142] Chris Tomlinson, 'France To Increase Border Security After Identitarians Use Helicopters, Trucks In Alps 'Defend Europe' Action', *Breitbart*, 24 April 2018, article found at https://www.breitbart.com/europe/2018/04/24/french-interior-minister-increase-border-security-identitarian-defend-europe-action/

[143] Chris Tomlinson, 'French Identitarian Activists Arrested Following 'Defend Europe' Mission In The Alps', *Breitbart*, 30 January 2019, article found at https://www.breitbart.com/europe/2019/01/30/french-identitarian-activists-arrested-defend-europe-mission-alps/

[144] David Chazan, 'Far-Right activists who blocked migrants from crossing French border handed six-month sentence', *The Telegraph*, 29 August 2019, article found at https://www.telegraph.co.uk/news/2019/08/29/far-right-activists-blocked-migrants-crossing-french-border/

[145] Chris Tomlinson, 'French 'Crimes Against Humanity, Genocide, War Crimes' Body to Investigate Anti-Migration Protest', *Breitbart*, 16 February 2021, article found at https://www.breitbart.com/europe/2021/02/16/french-crimes-against-humanity-genocide-war-crimes-body-investigate-anti-mass-migration-protest/

[146] 'France bans far-right anti-migrant group Generation Identity', *France 24*, 3 March 2021, article found at https://www.france24.com/en/france/20210303-france-bans-far-right-anti-migrant-group-generation-identity

[147] Chris Tomlinson, 'Austrian Police Raid Multiple Identitarian Activists' Homes, Including Martin Sellner's', *Breitbart*, 28 April 2018, article found at https://www.breitbart.com/europe/2018/04/28/austrian-police-raid-multiple-identitarian-members-homes-including-martin-sellner/#

[148] 'What happened at the Bataclan?', *BBC News*, 9 December 2015, article found at https://www.bbc.com/news/world-europe-34827497

[149] Chris Tomlinson, 'Austrian Police Raid Multiple Identitarian Activists' Homes, Including Martin Sellner's', *Breitbart*, 28 April 2018, article found at https://www.breitbart.com/europe/2018/04/28/austrian-police-raid-multiple-identitarian-members-homes-including-martin-sellner/#

CHAPTER 8

[150] 'White Noise', *The Atlantic*, documentary found at https://www.theatlantic.com/white-noise-movie/

[151] 'Aleksandr Dugin on Millennials, Modernity and Religion', *Lauren Southern*, 20 June 2018, video found on YouTube at https://www.youtube.com/watch?v=sl2—OHvxK4

CHAPTER 9

[152] Victoria Friedman, 'Tommy Robinson: Trials, Protests, A Media Blackout, And Global Attention', *Breitbart*, 31 May 2018, article found at https://www.breitbart.com/europe/2018/05/31/tommy-robinson-trials-protests-media-backout-global-attention/

[153] Chris Tomlinson, 'Austria's New Vice-Chancellor Shares Video Slamming Prosecution Of Generation Identity', *Breitbart*, 20 May 2018, article found at https://www.breitbart.com/europe/2018/05/20/populist-austrian-vice-chancellor-slammed-prosecution-identitarian-movement/

[154] 'Prozess gegen Identitäre: "Ihre Motivation ist auf Hass ausgerichtet"', *Die Presse*, 4 July 2018, article found at https://www.diepresse.com/5458245/prozess-gegen-identitare-ihre-motivation-ist-auf-hass-ausgerichtet

[155] 'Prozess gegen Identitäre: "Ihre Motivation ist auf Hass ausgerichtet"', *Die Presse*, 4 July 2018, article found at https://www.diepresse.com/5458245/prozess-gegen-identitare-ihre-motivation-ist-auf-hass-ausgerichtet

[156] 'Prozess gegen Identitäre: "Ihre Motivation ist auf Hass ausgerichtet"', *Die Presse*, 4 July 2018, article found at https://www.diepresse.com/5458245/prozess-gegen-identitare-ihre-motivation-ist-auf-hass-ausgerichtet

157 'Auftakt im Identitären-Prozess: 'Der Vorwurf der Hetze ist völlig daneben'', *Tagesstimme*, 4 July 2018, article found at https://www.tagesstimme.com/2018/07/04/identitaeren-prozess-gestartet-vorwurf-hetze-daneben/

158 Chris Tomlinson, 'Austrian Identitarians Fully Acquitted Of 'Mafia' And Hate Crime Charges', *Breitbart*, 27 July 2018, article found at https://www.breitbart.com/europe/2018/07/27/austrian-identitarians-fully-acquitted-mafia-hate-crime-charges/

159 'Prozess gegen Identitäre: "Ihre Motivation ist auf Hass ausgerichtet"', *Die Presse*, 4 July 2018, article found at https://www.diepresse.com/5458245/prozess-gegen-identitare-ihre-motivation-ist-auf-hass-ausgerichtet

160 'Trial of Identitarian Movement begins: 'The accusation of hate speech is completely unhinged'', *Tagesstimme*, 4 July 2018, article found at https://www.tagesstimme.com/2018/07/04/trial-of-identitarian-movement-austria-begins-the-accusation-of-hate-speech-is-completely-unhinged/

161 'Trial of Identitarian Movement begins: 'The accusation of hate speech is completely unhinged'', *Tagesstimme*, 4 July 2018, article found at https://www.tagesstimme.com/2018/07/04/trial-of-identitarian-movement-austria-begins-the-accusation-of-hate-speech-is-completely-unhinged/

162 'Trial of Identitarian Movement begins: 'The accusation of hate speech is completely unhinged'', *Tagesstimme*, 4 July 2018, article found at https://www.tagesstimme.com/2018/07/04/trial-of-identitarian-movement-austria-begins-the-accusation-of-hate-speech-is-completely-unhinged/

163 'Trial of Identitarian Movement begins: 'The accusation of hate speech is completely unhinged'', *Tagesstimme*, 4 July 2018, article found at https://www.tagesstimme.com/2018/07/04/trial-of-identitarian-movement-austria-begins-the-accusation-of-hate-speech-is-completely-unhinged/

164 'Identitarians on trial: witness clears activists of property damage charge', *Tagesstimme*, 19 July 2018, article found at https://www.tagesstimme.com/2018/07/19/identitarians-on-trial-witness-clears-activists-of-property-damage-charge/

165 'Identitarians on trial: disruption of university lecture in the spotlight', *Tagesstimme*, 11 July 2018, article found at https://www.tagesstimme.com/2018/07/11/identitarians-on-trial-disruption-of-university-lecture-in-the-spotlight/

166 'Identitarians on trial: disruption of university lecture in the spotlight', *Tagesstimme*, 11 July 2018, article found at https://www.tagesstimme.com/2018/07/11/identitarians-on-trial-disruption-of-university-lecture-in-the-spotlight/

167 Günther Oswald, 'Mehr als 2.300 Verfahren wegen Verhetzung und Wiederbetätigung', *Der Standard*, 11 March 2019, article found at https://www.derstandard.at/story/2000099343608/bereits-mehr-als-2-300-verfahren-wegen-verhetzung-und-wiederbetaetigung

168 'Freisprüche in Grazer Identitären-Prozess', *Der Standard*, 26 July 2018, article found at https://www.derstandard.at/story/2000084171603/identitaeren-prozess-letzte-runde-im-verfahren-in-graz

169 'Freisprüche in Grazer Identitären-Prozess', *Der Standard*, 26 July 2018, article found at https://www.derstandard.at/story/2000084171603/identitaeren-prozess-letzte-runde-im-verfahren-in-graz

170 'Freisprüche in Grazer Identitären-Prozess', *Der Standard*, 26 July 2018, article found at https://www.derstandard.at/story/2000084171603/identitaeren-prozess-letzte-runde-im-verfahren-in-graz

[171] 'Freisprüche in Grazer Identitären-Prozess', *Der Standard*, 26 July 2018, article found at https://www.derstandard.at/story/2000084171603/identitaeren-prozess-letzte-runde-im-verfahren-in-graz

[172] 'Freisprüche in Grazer Identitären-Prozess', *Der Standard*, 26 July 2018, article found at https://www.derstandard.at/story/2000084171603/identitaeren-prozess-letzte-runde-im-verfahren-in-graz

[173] 'The Identitarian Movement on trial: The reasons they were acquitted', *Tagesstimme*, 27 July 2018, article found at https://www.tagesstimme.com/2018/07/27/the-identitarian-movement-on-trial-the-reasons-they-were-acquitted/

[174] 'The Identitarian Movement on trial: The reasons they were acquitted', *Tagesstimme*, 27 July 2018, article found at https://www.tagesstimme.com/2018/07/27/the-identitarian-movement-on-trial-the-reasons-they-were-acquitted/

CHAPTER 10

[175] Julian Schernthaner, 'Nach Identitären-Freispruch: FPÖ Justizsprecher will Strafrechtsänderung', *Tagesstimme*, 28 July 2018, article found at https://www.tagesstimme.com/2018/07/28/nach-identitaeren-freispruch-fpoe-justizsprecher-will-strafrechtsaenderung/

CHAPTER 11

[176] 'Global Compact For Migration', PDF document found at https://refugeesmigrants.un.org/sites/default/files/180713_agreed_outcome_global_compact_for_migration.pdf

[177] Francois Murphy, 'Austria to shun global migration pact, fearing creep in human rights', *Reuters*, 31 October 2018, article found at https://www.reuters.com/article/us-un-migrants-austria/austria-to-shun-global-migration-pact-fearing-creep-in-human-rights-idUSKCN1N50JZ

CHAPTER 12

[178] 'Christchurch shootings: How the attacks unfolded', *BBC News*, 18 March 2019, article found at https://www.bbc.com/news/world-asia-47582183

[179] Rob Waugh, 'What is 'Accelerationism', the belief followed by New Zealand terror attacker?' *Metro*, 18 March 2019, article found at https://metro.co.uk/2019/03/18/accelerationism-belief-followed-new-zealand-terror-attacker-8930673/

[180] Collette Devlin, 'Prime Minister Jacinda Ardern shares the grief of New Zealanders after the Christchurch mosque shootings', *Stuff*, 16 March 2019, article found at https://www.stuff.co.nz/national/politics/111339737/prime-minister-jacinda-ardern-shares-the-grief-of-new-zealanders-after-the-christchurch-mosque-shootings

[181] Steve McMorran and Nick Perry, 'After massacre, New Zealand leader shows resolve, empathy', *Associated Press*, 17 March 2019, article found at https://apnews.com/f80e79bb61ba460695b308c5552f83ef

[182] 'New Zealand approves new gun laws just weeks after mosque attack', *NBC News*, 10 April 2019, article found at https://www.nbcnews.com/news/world/new-zealand-approves-new-gun-laws-just-weeks-after-mosque-n992881

[183] 'New Zealand man jailed for 21 months for sharing Christchurch shooting video', *BBC News*, 18 June 2019, article found at https://www.bbc.com/news/world-asia-48671837

[184] Alexandra Ma, '4chan, 8chan, and LiveLeak blocked by Australian internet providers for hosting the livestream of New Zealand mosque shootings,' *Business Insider*, 20 March 2019, article found at https://www.businessinsider.com/new-zealand-shootings-isps-block-4chan-8chan-liveleak-over-stream-2019-3?r=DE&IR=T

[185] Tripti Lahiri, 'Why it's a crime to download or print the mosque shooter's manifesto in New Zealand', *Quartz*, 25 March 2019, article found at https://qz.com/1579660/new-zealands-manifesto-ban-explained-by-its-chief-censor/

[186] Jonathan Pearlman, 'New Zealand mosque suspect Brenton Tarrant 'an ordinary white man' inspired by Anders Breivik', *The Telegraph*, 15 March 2019, article found at https://www.telegraph.co.uk/news/2019/03/15/new-zealand-mosque-shooterbrenton-tarrant-says-attack-inspired/

[187] Jim Edwards, 'The chilling number of misunderstood 'jokes' in the Christchurch killer's manifesto show how few people understand the disinformation ecosystem of the alt right', *Business Insider*, 30 December 2019, article found at https://www.insider.com/memes-in-christchurch-brandon-tarrant-manifesto-2019-12

[188] Lia Eustachewich, 'Conservative Candace Owens 'influenced me above all': New Zealand gunman', New York Post, 15 March 2019, article found at https://nypost.com/2019/03/15/conservative-candace-owens-influenced-me-above-all-new-zealand-gunman/

[189] Anthony Cuthbertson, ''Subscribe To Pewdiepie': What Did Christchurch Mosque Gunman Mean In Final Words Before Shooting?', *The Independent*, 15 March 2019, article found at https://www.independent.co.uk/life-style/gadgets-and-tech/news/new-zealand-shooting-attack-pewdiepie-subscribe-youtube-mosque-a8825326.html

[190] Christa Zöchling, 'Wie gefährlich sind die Identitären?', *Profil*, 30 March 2019, article found at https://www.profil.at/oesterreich/identitaeren-sellner-aufloesung-10708785

[191] 'Austrian far-right activist probed over links to Christchurch attacks', *BBC News*, 27 March 2019, article found at https://www.bbc.com/news/world-europe-47715696

[192] Katrin Bennhold, 'Donation From New Zealand Attack Suspect Puts Spotlight on Europe's Far Right', *The New York Times*, 27 March 2019, article found at https://www.nytimes.com/2019/03/27/world/europe/new-zealand-attack-europe-far-right.html

[193] Tom Toles, 'Opinion: Ocasio-Cortez says the world will end in 12 years. She is absolutely right', *The Washington Post*, 24 January 2019, article found at https://www.washingtonpost.com/opinions/2019/01/24/ocasio-cortez-says-world-will-end-years-she-is-absolutely-right/

[194] "Our house is on fire': Greta Thunberg, 16, urges leaders to act on climate', *The Guardian*, 25 January 2019, article found at https://www.theguardian.com/environment/2019/jan/25/our-house-is-on-fire-greta-thunberg16-urges-leaders-to-act-on-climate

[195] 'Violence and arrests as climate activists protest in UK and France', *SBS News*, 22 September 2019, article found at https://www.sbs.com.au/news/violence-and-arrests-as-climate-activists-protest-in-uk-and-france

[196] Nicole Gaudiano, 'Alleged gunman James Hodgkinson volunteered on Bernie Sanders' campaign', *USA Today*, article found at https://eu.usatoday.com/story/news/politics/onpolitics/2017/06/14/alleged-gunman-james-hodgkinson-worked-bernie-sanders-campaign/102847514/

[197] Chris Tomlinson tweet from 14 April 2019, tweet found at https://twitter.com/TomlinsonCJ/status/1117423389549969410

[198] Chris Tomlinson, 'Austrian Interior Minister: No Personal Relationship Between Christchurch Suspect And Martin Sellner', *Breitbart*, 31 March 2019, article found at https://www.breitbart.com/europe/2019/03/31/austrian-interior-minister-no-personal-relationship-between-christchurch-suspect-and-martin-sellner/

[199] Chris Tomlinson, 'Austria Considers Ban On Identitarian Movement After Christchurch Killer Donation', *Breitbart*, 27 March 2019, article found at https://www.breitbart.com/europe/2019/03/27/austria-considers-ban-identitarian-movement-christchurch-killer-donation/

[200] '"Mit Identitären-Chef würde ich nie Bier trinken"', *Heute*, 9 April 2019, article found at https://www.heute.at/s/norbert-hofer-fpoe-interview-11-fragen-mit-identitaren-chef-wurde-ich-nie-bier-trinken-42340293#story_comments

CHAPTER 13

[201] 'Austria far-right activist condemned over swastika', *BBC News*, 4 April 2019, article found at https://www.bbc.com/news/world-europe-47822454

[202] 'David Irving jailed for Holocaust denial', *The Guardian*, 20 February 2006, article found at https://www.theguardian.com/world/2006/feb/20/austria.thefarright#maincontent

[203] Leila Al-Serori and Oliver Das Gupta, 'The Strache files', *Süddeutsche Zeitung*, article found at https://projekte.sueddeutsche.de/artikel/politik/artikel-e207627/

[204] 'America honors 100 million victims of communism', *Share America*, 29 November 2017, article found at https://share.america.gov/america-honors-100-million-victims-of-communism/

[205] Dharisha Bastians and Kai Schultz, 'Blasts Targeting Christians Kill Hundreds in Sri Lanka', *The New York Times*, 21 April 2019, article found at https://www.nytimes.com/2019/04/21/world/asia/sri-lanka-bombings.html

[206] Doug Bandow, 'A Calculated Attack on Christianity', *National Review*, 23 April 2019, article found on https://www.nationalreview.com/2019/04/sri-lanka-bombings-were-calculated-attack-on-christianity/

[207] Sanjeev Laxman and Ben Kesslen, 'Sri Lanka bombings were retaliation for Christchurch shooting, defense minister says', *NBC News*, 23 April 2019, article found at https://www.nbcnews.com/news/world/sri-lanka-bombing-was-retaliation-christchurch-shooting-defense-minister-says-n997391

[208] Pamela Constable, 'Sri Lanka's Muslims fear retaliation after Easter attacks on Christians', *The Washington Post*, 24 April 2019, article found at https://www.washingtonpost.com/world/asia_pacific/sri-lankas-muslims-fear-retaliation-after-easter-attacks-on-christians/2019/04/24/9fffdfc8-6611-11e9-a698-2a8f808c9cfb_story.html

[209] "Not your enemies': Sri Lanka Muslims fear backlash after blasts', *Al Jazeera*, 24 April 2019, article found at https://www.aljazeera.com/news/2019/04/enemies-sri-lanka-muslims-fear-backlash-blasts-190424081042798.html

[210] Byron Kaye and Tom Allard, 'New clues emerge of accused New Zealand gunman Tarrant's ties to far right groups', *Reuters*, 4 April 2019, article found at https://www.reuters.com/article/us-newzealand-shooting-australia-extremi/new-clues-emerge-of-accused-new-zealand-gunman-tarrants-ties-to-far-right-groups-idUSKCN1RG095

[211] Tess Owen, 'The Idaho GOP is helping an alt-right YouTube star marry her Austrian white nationalist boyfriend', *Vice*, 30 April 2019, article found

at https://www.vice.com/en_us/aus/neanqm/the-idaho-gop-is-helping-an-alt-right-youtube-star-marry-her-austrian-white-nationalist-boyfriend

[212] Zack Budryk, 'Idaho Republicans urging government to allow Austrian nationalist into US to marry alt-right YouTuber', *The Hill*, 30 April 2019, article found at https://thehill.com/homenews/state-watch/441447-idaho-county-gop-urging-federal-government-to-allow-austrian-nationalist

[213] Chad Sokol, 'Kootenai County GOP urges feds to let Austrian nationalist into U.S. to marry alt-right YouTube pundit', *The Spokesman-Review*, 27 April 2019, article found at https://www.spokesman.com/stories/2019/apr/27/kootenai-county-gop-urges-feds-to-let-austrian-nat/

[214] Chad Sokol, 'Kootenai County GOP urges feds to let Austrian nationalist into U.S. to marry alt-right YouTube pundit', *The Spokesman-Review*, 27 April 2019, article found at https://www.spokesman.com/stories/2019/apr/27/kootenai-county-gop-urges-feds-to-let-austrian-nat/

[215] Jason Wilson, 'Christchurch shooter's links to Austrian far right 'more extensive than thought', *The Guardian*, 16 May 2019, article found at https://www.theguardian.com/world/2019/may/16/christchurch-shooters-links-to-austrian-far-right-more-extensive-than-thought

[216] Katrin Bennhold, 'Donation From New Zealand Attack Suspect Puts Spotlight on Europe's Far Right', *The New York Times*, 27 March 2019, article found at https://www.nytimes.com/2019/03/27/world/europe/new-zealand-attack-europe-far-right.html

[217] Brett Samuels, 'Trump ramps up rhetoric on media, calls press 'the enemy of the people'', *The Hill*, 5 April 2019, article found at https://thehill.com/homenews/administration/437610-trump-calls-press-the-enemy-of-the-people

[218] 'What you need to know about Austria's 'Ibiza-gate' video', *The Local Austria*, 26 May 2019, article found at https://www.thelocal.at/20190526/what-you-need-to-know-about-austrias-ibiza-gate-video

[219] Philip Oltermann, 'Austria's 'Ibiza scandal': what happened and why does it matter?', *The Guardian*, 20 May 2019, article found at https://www.theguardian.com/world/2019/may/20/austria-ibiza-scandal-sting-operation-what-happened-why-does-it-matter

[220] Philip Oltermann, 'Austria's 'Ibiza scandal': what happened and why does it matter?', *The Guardian*, 20 May 2019, article found at https://www.theguardian.com/world/2019/may/20/austria-ibiza-scandal-sting-operation-what-happened-why-does-it-matter

[221] 'Conservative leader Sebastian Kurz wins Austria election but far right takes a beating', *CNBC*, 29 September 2019, article found at https://www.cnbc.com/2019/09/29/austria-election-conservative-leader-kurz-wins-but-far-right-takes-a-beating.html

[222] 'Austria: Greens enter government for first time, join Kurz's conservatives', *Deutsche Welle*, 1 January 2020, article found at https://www.dw.com/en/austria-greens-enter-government-for-first-time-join-kurzs-conservatives/a-51853261

[223] 'Grünes Kacke-Posting bringt Kanzler Kurz in Erklärungsnot', *Info Direkt*, 27 October 2020, article found at https://www.info-direkt.eu/2020/10/27/gruenes-kacke-posting-bringt-kanzler-kurz-in-erklaerungsnot/

CHAPTER 14

[224] 'Report of the Royal Commission of Inquiry into the terrorist attack on Christchurch Mosques on 15 March 2019', 26 November 2020, report found at https://christchurchattack.royalcommission.nz/the-report/

[225] Oliver Harvey, 'The Extreme Team: World's most dangerous men and women revealed – from neo-Nazis to Islamic terrorists', *The Sun*, 4 January 2021, article found at https://www.thesun.co.uk/news/13647848/worlds-most-dangerous-men-and-women/